SPIRIT, SPACE & SURVIVAL
African American Women in (White) Academe

SPIRIT, SPACE & SURVIVAL

African American Women in (White) Academe

edited by Joy James & Ruth Farmer
foreword by Angela Y. Davis

ROUTLEDGE · NEW YORK & LONDON

Published in 1993 by

Routledge
29 West 35 Street
New York, NY 10001

Published in Great Britain by

Routledge
11 New Fetter Lane
London EC4P 4EE

Library of Congress Cataloging-in-Publication Data
Spirit, space and survival : African American women in (white)
    academe / edited by Joy James and Ruth Farmer.
        p.   cm.
    Includes bibliographical references (p.   ) and index.
    ISBN 0-415-90636-9—ISBN 0-415-90637-7 (pbk.)
    1. Afro-American women—Education (Higher) 2. Afro-American
college teachers. 3. Afro-American college administrators.
4. Discrimination in higher education—United States. I. James,
Joy, 1958–   . II. Farmer, Ruth, 1953–   .
LC2781.S69   1993
378'.0089'96073—dc20   92-41374
                                                                      CIP

British Library Cataloguing-in-Publication Data also available.

We learn much from our mothers: how to think, why we think and to care for the people about whom we think. Their lessons guide us through and help us to go beyond survival.

This book is dedicated to Virginia Elam, Beatrice Adderley, Lunia Farmer, Portia Lunia Andrews, Sylvan Williams, Minnie James, Mattie Bailey, to all our mothers.

Contents

Appendix

Foreword

Throughout the history of African American women, education has been a site of ever-evolving, complex, and frequently frustrating battles. *Spirit, Space and Survival: African American Women in (White) Academe* maps some of the contemporary battlefields in higher education on which Black women teachers and administrators are reevaluating, clashing with, and challenging old practices, while simultaneously articulating new ones.

This invaluable collection raises difficult questions about prospects for community and solidarity among young "African American women working as untenured assistant professors, lower-echelon administrators, and artist-in-residence instructors" (as the editors describe the contributors) within institutions that are still riddled with racism, sexism, homophobia, and class-based elitism. At the same time, the anthology itself is a determined and passionate act of solidarity. In sharing experiences, theoretical insights, and educational practices, it crosses the diverse divides separating disciplines, cultures, spiritual practices, and theoretical paradigms, as well as those that separate the "academy" from the "community" and Black women academics from one another.

While *Spirit, Space and Survival* specifically reflects the experiences, theorizing, and practices of young African American women academics in the 1990s, it traverses many boundaries. It speaks, for example, to women of my generation, and particularly to those of us who, as women of color, have sought for decades to formulate relationships with the university that resist the routine construction of academic environments as isolated from and unrelated to the communities, cultures, and spiritual traditions that have shaped our lives.

By giving voice to new ways of thinking about and organizing around academic issues, this anthology has inspired me to rethink my first encounter with the academic hierarchy. Had I been in possession of a work collectively authored by African American women in academe,

I might have combatted far more effectively the isolation and disorientation I initially experienced upon being fired from UCLA by the University of California Regents. With such a work in hand, how much more deeply I could have interrogated the complex intersections of racism, sexism, and the politics of conservatism!

This work reminds me of what had yet to be articulated twenty-five years ago about Black women's roles in predominantly white institutions of higher education. In doing so, it makes abundantly clear—even in the face of hauntingly familiar structures of oppression and marginalization—how radically the terms and terrain of struggle have been transformed by the interventions of women like Joy James, Ruth Farmer and all who have contributed to *Spirit, Space and Survival*.

Angela Y. Davis
University of California, Santa Cruz
December, 1992

Acknowledgments

We thank Ernest Allen Jr., and the Banneker Center, University of Massachusetts, Amherst, for invaluable support for this anthology. Also thank you to: John Stansfield for his suggestions; and Sekani Ifetayo (Heidi Brooks) and Andrea Thembi James for their technical assistance. Finally, we appreciate our editor Cecelia Cancellaro's encouragement and commitment to this project, and her assistant Maura Burnett's diligence throughout production and our final changes.

Introduction

Where We Stand

Spirit, Space and Survival: African American Women in (White) Academe is an anthology by the least institutionally empowered in academe: African American women working as untenured assistant professors, lower-echelon administrators, and artist-in-residence instructors. *Spirit, Space and Survival* began several years ago in conversations among African American women after a women's studies conference in the Midwest. Its objective is to incorporate voices of African American women often ignored or muted in academe. This book examines the dilemmas and contributions of African American women struggling with Eurocentric disciplines, students, faculty, and administrators in predominantly White institutions. It also shares the pedagogies and strategies we use to manipulate, reform and transform disciplines for the development of education and our communities within and outside of academe. Raising questions about our work, roles, and identities, this writing presents both critiques of academia and autobiographical stories. We write to critically examine various oppressions reflected in and reinforced by academe. We also write to retain our voices, to name and identify ourselves as independent women thinkers and actors inside the uniformity of institutions.

The work of Delores Saunders and Yolanda Moses makes important contributions to the limited published research on African American women faculty and administrators. Saunders writes in "Tenure for Black Faculty an Illusion in the White Academy" that:

> Black faculty in traditionally white institutions (TWIs) are dramatically underrepresented. In 1973, for example, Black faculty represented 4.1 percent of all faculty in institutions of higher education. The proportion of Black faculty in TWIs in 1983 represented a

1

decline from 4.4 percent in 1977. In 1987, Black faculty constituted
somewhere between a high of 2.9 percent to a low of 1.3 percent.[1]

In 1987, African American women earned 2 percent of the professional
degrees (1,585), 2 percent of the doctoral degrees (572), and 3 percent
of the master's degrees (8,716).[2] African American women received 46
percent of the professional degrees, 54 percent of the doctoral degrees,
and 63 percent of the master's degrees awarded to African Americans.[3]
Yolanda T. Moses' study, *Black Women in Academe,*[4] explores the
status of these African Americans. Moses reports that over 70 percent
of all African Americans with doctorates are employed in colleges and
universities. There, African American women are concentrated in the
lower ranks. In 1985, African American women faculty comprised 1.9
percent of full-time faculty: 0.6 percent of full professors, 1.4 percent
of associate professors, 2.7 percent of assistant professors, and 3 percent of instructors, lecturers, and others. In that same year, 3.4 percent
of administrators in higher education were African American women,
the majority of whom were employed on Black campuses and concentrated at levels below dean. In academe, where scholarship and professional input are often denigrated because of race and gender biases, we
are underrepresented and overly concentrated in positions without
institutional power. To challenge the discriminatory hiring, promotion,
and tenure practices diminishing the space of African American women
academics, we took up this writing project.

Writing does not come easy. African American women junior faculty
and lower-level administrators are hindered from writing and publishing by enormous pressures and responsibilities that our White peers
are rarely required to shoulder. Many of these pressures result from
the subtle and overt racism of our work sites. Most African American
women need to restructure programs in order to effectively work within
them. The work environments of the editors, as example, were tense
and unsupportive throughout much of this project. Joy James was
confronted with assertions by some senior faculty that developing
"Black Women's Studies" and antiracist organizing with graduate and
undergraduate students were "local turf battles" destabilizing the
Women's Studies program. Later when serving as acting co-director of
the program, the time consumed by administrative and committee
work for an antiracist, multicultural women's studies program made
writing a luxury. The research time for program service eventually
provided to James is a rarity for most junior African American faculty.
However, the nature of structural change in the program was problem-

atic as WoSt faculty made choices that mirrored rather than confronted institutional bias.[5]

Ruth Farmer's work environment was more discouraging and revealing of institutional gross indifference to African American women academics and multicultural and antiracist women's studies. Stating budget constraints as the reason, Barnard College's administration first threatened and then fired all staff of Barnard's Center for Research on Women (BCROW) in "restructuring": Farmer, as Associate Director, as well as an African American administrative assistant, and an European American director were all fired. As a result of this restructuring, BCROW acquired a new, all-White staff with little experience with women's studies or multicultural studies, and little demonstrative commitment to continuing BCROW as a space recognizing the significant contributions of women of color.

African American women in universities work within environments which are often not only nonsupportive but at times outright hostile. They (we) are expected to perform mightily—with little reward—and to be grateful that we are allowed in the halls of learning. Overworked and underrecognized, we are forced to cope with office and university policies as well as the racism, sexism, and homophobia inherent in these environments and the larger society.

Throughout the process of editing this anthology, we were alternately saddened and frustrated, or amazed at how we managed, in work environments where our "Blackness" is considered problematic, to squeeze in an hour or a half hour of writing or editing time. Missed deadlines were constant reminders of how hard African American women work—for others—leaving little creative energy for our own lives. Being able to write anything at all under these circumstances is difficult. Yet we continued and continue to write. We write because unless we as African American women shape a reality, and make a space for ourselves to creatively share our stories, education remains an elitist, White and/or male domain. Writing by, and not simply about, African American women is part of taking our space to challenge a stultifying hegemony and work to develop academe. This book, *Spirit, Space and Survival,* is part of that process.

Overview

The following chapters are organized into three sections and reflect a weaving of the themes "Spirit," "Space" and "Survival." The first section, *Spirit* centers on spiritual and intellectual sources and inspirations. It begins with "Mixed Blood, New Voices" by Kaylynn Sullivan TwoTrees. As an African American-Lakota ritualist and teacher of ceremony and religion, TwoTrees confronts the issues of antispiritualism in academe, and the need to restore ritual to academe's repetitive routine. With her guidance in making power objects, students explore their identities, fears, and relationships to African and Native American spiritual traditions. Following traditional paths, TwoTrees describes both personal and professional growth teaching in the Western Liberal Arts Program at Miami University, Oxford, Ohio. This growth does not stem from a nurturing or supportive environment, which is perhaps an anomaly for African American women academics. TwoTrees' decision to place the spiritual teachings and rituals of African American and Lakota ancestors in the center of her learning and teaching comes from her understanding of the ancestors as actively influencing our lives.

The demand to include our cultures within academe has been a driving force in making a space for artist-teachers like Kaylynn Sullivan TwoTrees and Joyce Scott. Maintaining and expanding a tradition of African American women artists is integral to the work of Joyce Scott. In "Carrying On" Scott presents her work, which is a "disruptive" model due to its satire and its creative challenges to mainstream education. Through her creativity and irreverence she risks having her pedagogy labeled "interesting" but "unscholarly." Scott, like TwoTrees, uses art to educate and push the confines of mainstream academe. Like TwoTrees' dance and drumming, Joyce Scott's quilting, beading and fiberwork provide messages that expand the narrow definitions of education and learning.

The recovery of the dignity and power of our traditions and expanding educational definitions is also a concern of Joy James, who focuses on theory. In "African Philosophy, Theory, and 'Living Thinkers'," James explores the relationships between African-centered philosophy, critical thinking, and women's political activism. James, who teaches theory in Women's Studies, University of Massachusetts-Amherst, examines "living thinkers" (defined in Kongo philosophy as those who theorize and act on behalf of the community) and the praxis of revolutionary African American women. She describes these forms of thought as valuable political theory or theorizing often neglected in academe.

Space, Section II, critiques and hopefully disturbs the rigidity of certain academic disciplines. Elizabeth Hadley Freydberg's "American

Studies: Melting Pot or Pressure Cooker?" explores American Studies in the context of the mythology of seamless assimilation. Freydberg, like James, challenges the erasure or misuse of African American women's words. For Freydberg, the North American "melting pot" is more accurately defined as a "pressure cooker." An assistant professor of African American Studies at Northeastern University in Boston, Freydberg examines the perpetuation of American mythology and mystification in academia. The inclusion of studies of African American women will dispel the cultural amnesia of American Studies, according to Freydberg, while providing the basis for a realistic encounter and comparative appraisal of American, African, and European cultures.

Inclusivity and comparative studies are central to the work of Helán Page, an assistant professor of Anthropology at the University of Massachusetts-Amherst. Page compares people of African descent in the Caribbean and in the United States in the chapter "Teaching Comparative Social Order and Caribbean Social Change." Each student's ability to see the connectedness of African people in the diaspora is, according to Page, a method for "opening up the narrow straits of mainstream awareness," personalizing global politics for both students and instructor. The womanist perspective which she uses pushes students to conceptualize reality and relationships outside of the strictures of academic thinking.

In "Making Room for Emancipatory Research in Psychology: A MultiCultural Feminist Perspective," Kim Vaz, a psychologist at the University of South Florida, examines the "emancipatory" agenda by which psychology can serve in African liberation. Vaz writes of "survival stories" passed on from her grandmother and mother. These stories are connected to Vaz's own mental and emotional survival in academia as an African American woman. They provide the context for rethinking a discipline where patriarchy and racism have narrowly defined mental health and have designated the survival and coping methods of oppressed peoples as "pathological."

Setting the standards or norms for ourselves as healthy and balanced rather than pathological means redefining the images of ourselves as they appear in society and literature. In "Deconstructing, Reconstructing, and Focusing Our Literary Image," Nagueyalti Warren, an assistant dean at Emory University and assistant professor of Literature, explores the misrepresentation of African American women in U.S. literature and the need to reclaim and redefine ourselves, our images, and our identities. Warren provides new images through her poetry shared in this chapter.

Echoing Warren's concerns for standards, Joy James' "Teaching Theory, Talking Community" examines academia's canonization of White European thinkers and its neglect of African "living" thinkers. She argues that academe's racial-sexual politics mandate European or Eurocentric reflections on life as universal, while depicting African or Afracentric reflections as personal and particular. James maintains that decentering Eurocentrism breaks with the irrationality of Eurocentric-academic theory, and the double standards and biases created by White supremacy within it. She also examines the use of social justice activism as part of a progressive pedagogy connected to theorizing.

Our final section, *Survival* considers past and present conditions and future needs for African American women in academe. We begin with "The Revolution Within: Transforming Ourselves," in which Patricia Coleman-Burns challenges African Americans to confront the crisis in ethics and leadership within the United States. Her political views are rooted within the African American community, which taught her to work against racism, sexism, and internalized oppression and bigotry. Using a "study-in" by radical students demanding an Africana Studies department when she taught at Wayne State University in Detroit, Coleman-Burns examines the basis of struggle within the African American community. Coleman-Burns believes that African Americans have been the one persistent group challenging the hypocrisy of the "American dream," and for this reason are uniquely positioned to provide leadership for the rest of society. According to Coleman-Burns, leadership requires that we deal with misogyny, homophobia, anti-intellectualism among ourselves, and our complicity with oppression. Patricia Coleman-Burns taught predominantly African American students while at Wayne State. Her chapter raises issues easily overlooked in critiques of White universities: How do African American academics meet the needs of African American students in predominantly White institutions? How do we work with African American students to recognize our complicity in oppression?

Dianne Smith's chapter, "African American Women Teachers Speak about Child Abuse," also focuses on meeting the needs of students; however, these are children survivors. Smith discusses African American women teachers and their reluctance to report child sexual abuse. As an assistant professor of Education and Pedagogy at the University of Missouri at Kansas City, Smith writes of a body of research and knowledge which is accepted with great difficulty within academia and society. Smith conducted a series of interviews with African American teachers of primary and secondary schools. Bringing to her research the need to transform silence into assertive speaking, Dianne Smith makes the issues of "inclusivity" and "responsibility" concrete in ways uncommon in academe. A significant number of male and female students struggle with the emotional and mental scars of being survivors of sexual abuse. Academia must willingly and competently address the pervasive reality of incest and sexual abuse to create classroom environments which promote learning.

Adrienne Andrews, assistant professor of anthropology at Smith College, conducted a series of interviews with African American women academics focusing on the women's perceptions of academic survival and success. "Balancing the Personal and the Professional" examines the attitudes of African American women in academe, and in the process raises issues around our assimilation in White universities. In these interviews, and through our own self-interrogation, we see how we may mirror classist and heterosexist assumptions and at times align ourselves with dominance. For example, the suggestion that an interviewee seek support for her many responsibilities as educator-mother-wife by obtaining "live-in help" is an ironic one that requires reflection. The luxury of hiring domestic workers is a rare privilege for many of us and a contradiction for all of us. Historically, African American women were segregated into domestic work; using it to advance our academic careers calls for an analysis. Buying into roles and stereotypes which we have tried so hard to escape, the joke turns on us, the "live-in help" of universities: those expected to—at bargain wage—counsel, mentor and mother students, faculty, staff, and programs.

In "Place But Not Importance: The Race for Inclusion in Academe," Ruth Farmer also examines the position of African American women in academe, but this time as administrators. Given our miserably low numbers in decision-making positions, power dynamics consistently work against African American women trying to do viable work. According to Farmer, racism and sexism block the recognition of the contributions African American women make to academe, and hinder upward mobility to decision-making ranks. The absence of administrators of color creates a void in resources for institutions, and robs all students of the opportunity of having people of diverse backgrounds serve as mentors and role models. Farmer, who views curriculum integration projects as palliatives supplanting transformation, presents structural change as a prerequisite to permanent, institutional inclusivity. However, most administrations are not creating a place for these necessary changes to take root. Although students and faculty are demanding to be better educated about the people with whom they share this world, administrators state that their institutions "cannot afford" to hire or expand. If the decision-makers are academic traditionalists, according to Farmer, there is little likelihood in these current economic-political times of cutbacks and race-baiting of a real break from patriarchal, White supremacy as the norm.

Concerns

As academics, we represent some of the diversity of African American womanist thought and politics. Confronting over a decade of conservative, reactionary national policies that undermined economic decency, reproductive rights, and quality public education, this book is a testimony to the spirit of African American women who work for humanizing education and society. This anthology reflects our different perceptions and responses to political-educational crises. Whatever our political perspectives, we are all encouraged to choose "apolitical" careerism or corporate politics over community-centered activism. The political experiences of some African American academics, such as antiKlan organizing on campus and supporting African American student demonstrations for Africana Studies, contribute to making the larger community more central to academia and this book. However, they remain an anomaly and problematic.

In working on this project we have faced more directly various problems, including the fact that often African American women in White universities and colleges are isolated from African American communities. Academics may reject the lessons of activists whose political struggles forced White academe to open its doors to us. Neglecting that knowledge, we lose the opportunity for learning responsibilities greater than those of assimilation into academic castes. We lose the chance to be in community with ourselves as a people. That is too much to lose.

We miss opportunities to form community within academia by not adequately affirming each other and ourselves in ways that are viable for our future as African Americans. We privately console but do not always publicly support each other when faced with racist acts. Perhaps believing that other African Americans cannot help us with our needs and ambitions in predominantly White institutions, or knowing that openly confronting oppressive behavior jeopardizes tenure and promotion, we fail to aggressively organize. Our private common complaints only form a superficial and fragile "bonding" when followed by little responsible action. Our egos also create obstacles to building inclusive communities with African American students, staff, lecturers, and faculty: academia's caste elitism and hierarchy are vanities difficult to surmount.

Not being monolithic, we vary in our approaches and connections to academe. Yet we continue to develop ways to talk to each other across our political differences and the great divide of competitive individualism. We have important things to say about learning and education in these times, even as we own or deny our baggage. In academic enclaves we may choose to struggle and live as if embracing and fighting for African communities, disparaged by academe, were our most natural state. The African American legacy of critique and confrontation gives us the gift of power to resist careerism, conformism, and the mystique-hype of academe. This gift also brings the responsibility to carry on a liberating legacy.

In that tradition, to the spirits of our families and ancestors who help us to find our voices with a purpose: Thank you.

Notes

1. Delores M. Saunders, "Tenure for Black Faculty an Illusion in the White Academy," in *Black Issues in Higher Education* (April 12, 1990): 32.

2. For European American women the percentages were: 31 percent, 35 percent, and 48 percent, respectively. Women make up 50 percent of the employees within colleges and universities in the United States. As full time employees, women are 37 percent of the executive, administrative, and managerial professionals, 29 percent of the faculty, and 59 percent of the nonfaculty professionals. Women comprise 64 percent of the nonprofessional employees, including 92 percent of the clerical/secretarial workers, 58 percent of the technical/paraprofessionals and 38 percent of the service/maintenance workers. As part time employees, women comprise 42 percent of the faculty, 52 percent of the executive, administrative, and managerial professionals, 68 percent of the nonfaculty professionals, and 39 percent of the part time research assistants. Source: *The Chronicle of Higher Education Almanac,* September 5, 1990.

3. *The Chronicle of Higher Education Almanac,* September 5, 1990, reports that of the total number of degrees awarded, women of color [Native Americans, Latinas, African Americans and Asians] received approximately 5 percent of the professional degrees, nearly 5 percent of doctoral degrees, and 6 percent of the master's degrees.

4. Yolanda Moses, *Black Women in Academia: Issues and Strategies* (Baltimore: Project on the Status of Education of Women) August 1989.

5. Following the Rodney King verdict, UMass student demonstrations for anti-racist education led to 10 new faculty lines. WoSt student activists demanded: anti-racist courses in the program; and, that WoSt apply for a Native American Women's

Studies line from those positions created by student radicalism. These and other demands were presented in a spirit of frustrated militancy: for months students had participated in meetings with WoSt faculty with little tangible progress towards change. Others shared this frustration. However, the majority of WoSt faculty and staff made choices which effectively isolated and discouraged undergraduate and graduate anti-racist activists from immediate future and full participation in the program. They initially marginalized graduate Teaching Assistants (TAs) organizing against racism in WoSt by denying all TAs (the majority of whom at the time were women of color) a representative vote in the program's Executive Committee. This decision, made by most staff and faculty, White women and women of color, was reconsidered and reversed after a meeting following protests by some undergraduate and graduate students and faculty, again a multiracial coalition of women. Still, later the majority of faculty and staff dismissed as a "perception problem," criticisms by an Indigenous scholar who stated her experiences of the program's indifference to Native American women and activist, antiracist education. Ideology, rather than color, shaped academic-political coalitions working to create, or counter, radical change, while radical organizing provided both the impetus and framework for developing a less exclusive curriculum and program. (See Shanta Rao and Jeanine Maland, "Politics in women's studies: program rhetoric vs. policies and practices," *THE VOICE* (University of Massachusetts at Amherst Graduate Student Senate, Vol VI, Issue 4, February 1993).)

Spirit

1

Mixed Blood, New Voices
Kaylynn Sullivan TwoTrees

Students often ask me to tell them about my background. The inquiries still puzzle me. I see myself as a faceted being—one facet being woman, one artist, one African American, one Native American, and so on. To speak of any one facet more than another dulls the beauty of the whole thing reflecting light.

It has been a long and arduous road gaining this view. Most of my life has been spent in confusion. My looks have made it possible for me to float among many cultures while finding solace in none. I claimed my creative energy as my identifying mark. Even being a woman was secondary to the passion that kept me working.

In my early thirties the need to find tribal links and memories propelled me on a new journey of discovery. My African American heritage was present in the popular culture all around me once I learned the code through which it spoke. It was the Native American part of my soul which languished.

I read much of the modern writings "about" Native Americans ("Indians" felt better to me; it was a word I heard from my grandmother and I felt no malice in it). The books struck some deep chord of disquiet in me. An image or phrase would ring true in my heart but I would feel betrayed at some other level of my being. It was as if I was being teased by the beauty of what I felt but not allowed to labor in it for the beauty of what it held. And each time I met another Native American all I wanted to blurt out was "Who am I? Where is my tribe?" But I didn't do that. I did find friends in many tribes who helped me, taught me, and showed me how to find my way. I walked quietly and listened. I found ways to make the Medicine Wheel a part of my life to walk this Earth Walk in honor of ancestors.

This year I went to Wounded Knee for the one hundredth memorial of the massacre. It was a pilgrimage home—a step in connecting myself with my living relations. But it was also a practical step in reconnecting with my own tribe and family. The journey to Pine Ridge was a stronger connecting than anything that came before. It was the act of trust required of me, facing all the possible attitudes awaiting me. Listening to the Lakota language, watching the ceremonies, and sitting in the silences I realized that humility and sincerity can help one travel far on any road. I am learning courage through each of these virtues, and the Lakota women help me in my search and provide a tribe for me as I find my way.

While my African American heritage was the ground on which I walked as a child, its polyrhythms still provide me with great flexibility and laughter. My grandparents, music on Saturday nights, chicken dinners on Sunday—that was the glue of the extended family which provided for me at my mother's death and cared for my daughter while I pursued my creative passion. Even though an intensely European education separated me from my family in viewpoints, I find my ancestors present in much of what I consider American.

When my quest for spiritual roots began I found that I was encircled by friends and teachers of the religions of Africa which travelled on the slave ships. As I learned more about them, this image of the gemstone of a being—faceted and reflecting light—began to emerge. The similarities of the Yoruba orishas in the kachinas of my friends at the pueblos of the Southwest; the Medicine Wheel of my own Plains People and its reflection in the Dingo-dingo (dance of life) of the Kongo created a picture of a whole which embraced all parts of me. The fractured self of adolescence had become like the colors merging in a stained glass image.

So when students ask questions I know they mean "Tell us how you grew up" or "Tell us rituals you learned." But my tale is more subtle. The facts told as a narrative would be an interesting adventure story. But the essence of it, the process by which I come to know more and more about myself, is a story of mishaps, tripping on the steps of life, and learning. The point of it all was and continues to be learning the tools of self-identification in such a way that self is never separated from the whole. There is no distance between ourselves and the smell of the earth, the people around us, the animals we eat and play with, the forests, oceans, lakes, streams, the sky, the stars, sun and moon, and everything I have forgotten to mention. Identifying ourselves in this way is a creative act.

When I first came to academia I was heartened by the attitude of the universities in their expressed desire not only to expand the base of knowledge to include this view of the whole but also to actively work towards achieving a culturally diverse faculty, student body, and staff. Many thoughts have flown through my mind since then, but several points continue to nag at me concerning this plan.

There is a way of thinking in our culture which separates all things into categories. In our attempts since the sixties to include views other than the predominantly Eurocentric one, we have established Black Studies, Women's Studies, Ethnic Studies, American Studies, and so on. The fight to include these areas and the wealth of information which is available was well worth it and long overdue. Reintegration of indigenous cultures and people left marginalized by the myopic origin myth of the country was a task whose vision spoke to a hopeful future for this country. Collaboration by those people who found themselves here for whatever reason could create something greater than the sum of its parts. But as the years march on and we find ourselves in a country preparing to spend billions celebrating the "discovery" of an already inhabited and civilized country by a man who was lost, questions emerge. Perhaps in separating all our parts we have lost the power of the whole. Collaboration has given way to appropriation and modern colonization, perhaps in the name of "multiculturalism."

Something else to be reckoned with in the separatist view is the way cultural information is assimilated by the young in this country. The basis upon which students build their view of other cultures is through fashion. They are fed so much other information out of context that taking on the clothing, jewelry, hair styles, music, and dances of the world as culture is accepted. It is in reaching beyond style to question our attitude about these cultures, their history and beliefs, that we run into trouble. It is here in the inner realm that the shadows of racism emerge—quiet and unacknowledged. These shadowy feelings are not only held by the dominant culture.

African Americans who have accepted natural hair styles, dreadlocks and the colors of liberation; Native Americans returning to tribal dances and ceremonies as Native American spirituality becomes acceptable; and other members of cultures we class as "minority" in this country, all have another hurdle to face as their cultures become part of curricula. They find themselves in the predicament of being both student and subject—in many cases raising questions in public they have not had the time or opportunity to ask their own people in private. They are, in a sense, remarginalized by the scrutiny with which they are faced, if not by other students then by themselves. Nothing has prepared them for this. They may strike out at the establishment, the teachers, the subject. They may find cause to move closer to the tribe/ family for support and their own information. They may also choose to align themselves with the mainstream and totally objectify the experience.

In any case, what has happened is another separation. The culturally diverse community remains the outsider, however chic the hair and clothing might be. These individuals remain material for a course which might well be called "Exotica 101."

Remedies include our awareness of this predicament and also a willingness on the part of the universities to create internal support/ information/discussion groups for this community which they have sought to create. As a visiting artist I see my role as that of making clear that "culturally diverse" is not "the Other." In speaking of my own journey to identify beliefs and find stories which nurture and heal me, I am identifying where I stand in the mainstream, not on the outskirts. I must be clear in my perception of this since it is not the view held by the majority.

As a teacher I am on my own journey in this territory. I am travelling back to the heart of the tribes of my grandmothers. The way I dress, the jewelry I wear, and how I wear my hair are all part of that journey and part of a picture much larger than the image I create when I walk into the classroom. Two important events come to mind.

I have always loved jewelry and worn it joyfully. My Midwestern upbringing told me that jewelry and clothing were coordinated. The idea didn't sit well with me and I was always losing something—one earring misplaced, a bracelet laid down while washing my hands and forgotten. One day while looking at a book on Africa I came across a photograph of an old woman carrying a basket of twigs on her head and climbing a ladder. She was obviously working, and she had on two large ivory bracelets. I sat looking at the photo, remembering women at the bread oven in the pueblo with their turquoise jewelry gleaming in the sun. I decided then that jewelry was worn for other reasons than to coordinate with my clothes and now I choose pieces carefully and change them rarely. My jewelry bathes with me, works with me, and lives with me.

A similar thing happened with my hair. Ever since I was a child my hair has been the plague of my life. I longed for the silken braids of my father's mother, but what I beheld in the mirror was hair made of iron—curved and twisted like mountain snake back roads and wild and stubborn as kudzu, a weed that grows like an unchecked brush fire. So for years I cut it, kept it short—manicured like a suburban lawn—controlled. Then one summer I listened to a Tewa friend of mine talk about cutting his hair. He told the story of how he had made the decision to cut his braids to symbolize cutting off some old bad habits and changing his life. He went to the kiva with the old men and discussed the rightness of this act, got their blessing. Then he went to the Sacred Mountain of his tribe, cut the braids, mourned and returned, reborn. "What power!" I thought. And how many times had I given away that power to an unknown barber or hairdresser in the name of fashion. It took me awhile to decide what to do. I wanted to make the commitment not to "tame" my hair but to honor it. Thinking of the long braids of my grandmother I decided to have it braided by my daughter. Not the two long braids—neither my hair nor I was ready for that—but a head full of braids growing wild like kudzu—to be rebraided each year or half-year by my daughter, relinking us in a ritual of empowerment. It feels like the best of both tribes. Sometimes I wear feathers on the braids to remember my grandmother and sometimes I tie them up in a turban of brilliant kente to remember the drums and rhythms of Africa.

This is all a part of who I am as a teacher and seeker. This is part of the body of information I bring to a classroom or a workshop. These experiences, like learning with the elders of the tribes, are keys to the journeys of knowledge. The challenge of linking this kind of learning with the traditional systems of pedagogy excites me and frustrates me. I am excited to bring primarily oral traditions, rhythmic cultures, and the song and dance of living into the academic curriculum. I am frustrated by the fact that those who seek me out and hire me have not resolved their own doubts about "doing/living the vision" as an integral part of the critical thinking process of pedagogy. Questions of purpose, content, goals, and evaluation leap up instantly. What remains at issue for me are the areas of focus, intention, question, and commitment. These are the areas that prepare our young for the hero's mythic journey—the search for self after initiation into the tribe. Since we have bypassed not only the initiation but also the oral traditions and tales that build the reality of social structure for the young, our remedy seems to be to use this cry for "cultural diversity" to invite artists, shamans, and other seekers to help bridge the gap. What is missing is the structure within academia to support these bridge-makers, as the shamans were supported by the tribe. And for those of us who accept this job, we are trying to find the circle that holds the square with the circle inside it. A puzzle. We are in a place of seeking/learning, able to pass on what? Information, experience, knowledge, wisdom? Maybe we are locksmiths passing out the keys we have found to remembering.

Part of this task is to remind students and each other that this is a journey of mind and spirit. When the mind is stimulated by information, that intellectual excitement is the sign that a key has been found. Much information fills the academic environment, but when I see it resonate in the mind of a student both of us are standing on the threshold of *knowledge*. The student is looking at the key to remembering and the excitement we both feel is the recognition of this key. It is then the task of the student to take the key and look for the doorway or window which it fits. This fit is a resonance experienced at the center of being—insight, intuition, gut feeling, heart. When it fits we can say we *know* something. It does not necessarily mean that we can analyze, explain or dissect it. That is something else. If this fitting of key to lock is not accomplished, the feeling of uneasiness, of having to hold onto the information—keep notes, fear tests—will continue. But once the journey to fit key and lock is completed or abandoned in search of another key, one is fully engaged in a quest which ends in wisdom. When key and lock fit, past and future memory is jarred and the rest of the details or pieces of that particular puzzle can fall into place with a resounding sigh. If, however, the student believes that I, as the teacher, am responsible for passing on this knowledge and that his/her only responsibility is to listen and record the details of speech then the uneasiness I spoke of previously gains hold. Anger often appears if the student is urged on the journey to find the lock. This is a self-initiating act so I urge as little as possible. But I do try to lay out more keys in case the match is not right. There are keys for watchers, listeners, thinkers and doers. My job is to be sure they all have some to work with.

There are times when I throw out a key and this information goes directly to the place of knowing in the student. The key fits the lock immediately. The first one tried. The spark created when this occurs is the food of many journeys. My reward is in knowing I have been carrying around the right keys. When this happens the mind speaks what the heart knows to be true. The wonder of this kind of knowledge is the fact that it does not separate mind and feeling. It also allows the student full participation in the education process. It is conceptual, active learning. The interconnectedness of things—patterns of thought, systems, living things—begins to appear as more and more keys are fit into the locks of memory inside the individual. This is true of teacher and student alike. As the connections are made I discover combinations which had not occurred to me. The uniqueness of the individual as part of the whole is made apparent in journey after journey. This provides fuel for me to continue my path from knowledge to wisdom. My learning is built on the assimilation of this knowledge into even the most absentminded gestures of my life. When I look at the task of teaching from this point of view of mutual learning/gift-giving, then it is filled with compassion. I am able to deal with the anger aroused by students too frightened to journey, or those hoarding the information as if it were the knowledge, and even by those terrified by the formlessness of what I present to them. And in the best of all possible worlds the students will have compassion for me when I am human.

One professor said to me last semester, "Humility and patience are the two despised virtues in academia." We will all have to put down the shields of "despicability" and honor humility and patience above other qualities if we are to truly learn and survive, because they are the heart of compassion for ourselves and others. Compassion allows us to be fearless in our uniqueness and to collaborate in our diversity.

It was with this idea, this point of view, that I entered the classroom at the beginning of the semester to teach ritual traditions. Ritual has been for me a way of helping to create the focus and silence for the journey to find the lock. The information passed on is the body of details which comprise the activity of ritual. The words or rhythms are the dialogue between the person and the action. The essence of the ritual is the silence at the center, the place past preoccupation, boredom, restlessness, where belief can occur. In the Medicine Wheel it is the hub. In Kongo it is the lake of transformation at the center of the dance of life. When one is able to stand squarely in the center there is clarity. In this place the self is seen face on, if only briefly. So we work towards this by beginning with the act of "making," the creation of identification. We place ourselves in the lineage of every other initiate given the task of identifying themselves for themselves, their tribe and the gods, spirits and/or the unknown. This is the first step towards participation in the social order. It is a step many of us have bypassed, only to be forced to return later.

Last fall, at the beginning of the semester, I stood in front of the students and tried to talk about ritual. My eyes scanned the students, the surroundings, the sound and feel of them, and the place. A theatre, me on stage, them in the seats. The separation had already begun. Even though we moved onto the stage together my first words to them came from a place of separation. I had already been influenced by my environment.

We moved back into the realm of my familiars. Each person came onto the stage and was cleansed with a turkey wing fan (eagle of the south in honor of the child in them). They stepped across the choke cherry branches I had picked and painted to represent the six directions. Then they entered the circle, a Medicine Wheel of twelve rocks from the river bed of the woods near town, rocks collected in view of two deer giving their spirit to the search. I believe in such signs. They form the texture, color and weight of all that I do. The voices of the rock people, the standing people (trees), the wind—all speak in such subtle tones that one must be very still to hear them. These are the things I could have said that first day. But I had read the syllabus and heard subjects defined. I didn't ask the trees surrounding the building what they thought. I didn't ask the rocks filled with fossils for their stories to pass on. I talked to the students about definitions.

Once in the circle, truer voices emerged. They spoke of who they were; each one defining themselves four times around the circle, and each time moving a layer deeper as we passed through the four directions. We all voiced fears of this new environment, our confusion and some of our excitement. In honor of the last two directions we called on our ancestors, I taught them the word for "all my relations" in Lakota—a gift of language.

This feeling of separation from land, sky and experience came upon me often during the semester. So the task I set for the class became mine: redefining ourselves. Using the circle as our guide, we moved from the core around the hub, making medicine bundles and talismans. Studying the images from cultures which had walked this road before us, we made objects which needed only to be seen by our eyes. In class we shared some of the feelings around making a personal power object. With each student I discussed the reasons for choosing the ingredients, the colors, the shapes, and the form. We talked about the exchange or giveaway with Nature when we use the fruit she has given us. We began this trip into the world of symbols, signs, and feelings, expressing the unseen and unheard. I made my own objects and shared with them. I helped with tasks that were new to them (stitching hides, beading, lashing twigs). The doers, thinkers, watchers, and listeners found their own speed and process.

By the time we reached the second stage—the circle farther from center—complaints could be heard. It was not simply fun anymore.

Students didn't like working in a group. They didn't like the time constraints on the projects. What seemed to be at issue in this stage was that, in asking each person to identify themselves in relationship to humanity and their environment in a way that could be displayed, I was asking them to express a vision of the world which they could not define. As we talked it became clear that they were not sure what beliefs they held or whether the vision they held made sense. They were unsure, and this had not been acceptable in a learning environment before. As group and private discussions continued, visions gained shape and confusion became a statement. The next hurdle we encountered was finding the images, materials, symbols and craft to express these visions in a way that could be made public. Those willing to keep the discussion open, even through frustration, became excited by the process. We used the shield of the Native American Plains People as a possible stepping-off place. It is a process which included searching in silence and solitude for a vision then returning to the tribe to express, explore, and visually translate the vision into symbols, and living with that statement visible to all. There was much individual discussion at this stage about translating ideals and ideas into visuals. There was also a growing element of resistance in those students from cultures with this kind of non-European history. This was a good example of where the conflict between public and private identity for that "culturally diverse" population becomes the basis for attacking the system which asks the student to face deeper questions of identity without a cultural support system. This happens with not only students facing issues of cultural identity outside of the mainstream but also those students who find themselves at odds with the ideology of the mainstream culture. It is an issue which I have not resolved for myself in my teaching but which I keep at the front of my consciousness as I approach teaching now.

By the time we reached completion of the shields it was Halloween. We had planned a ceremony honoring our ancestors, displaying their shields and playing musical instruments made in another section of the class. The celebration took place, and the faculty and staff participated and obviously enjoyed the opportunity to actively learn. I taught dances for several African deities and we spoke the names of our ancestors in memory. But the polarization of that group that felt betrayed and offended had come to a full and outspoken offensive.

At the very next stage of the circles of identification there was much vocal opposition to the process. Students were feeling oppressed by the time deadlines and the idea of grades. I was feeling as if all of the teachings that had led me to do this work were not supporting me in this place of isolation and criticism. I could see that some students were making incredible breakthroughs to the memories of their own

European cultures. Others were finding strength in the mastering of visual language. But they were quiet. The voices that raged out in class hid their terror and confusion behind personal attacks.

The redemption of this project was that the altars created for this outer circle of the Hoop by most of the students were testament to the fact that the process was working. They were identifying themselves in relationship to the unknown or the sacred and it was clear in many cases that this was the foundation upon which the other two projects rested. I was heartened to go on.

The final project, a collaboration of two to six students in each group, was really a distillation of the factions that had begun at Halloween. The presentations were statements of growth by those students who had found hope. There were questing confusion with humor. And there were projects by groups who didn't want to do projects—pieces without content. For others it was a last attempt to express anger at those who had pushed them to a place of searching so tender and foreign that it became frightening.

On the last day of class I felt that I owed all those who had struggled and grown and fought a view of this entire process as one that is experienced by all people in different ways in an attempt to find hope and vision. I read them words from the Native Americans who cared for this land and from Africans who hold land, water and sky as sacred. It was my last act of reconnecting it all.

So when I think about the semester and those first questions about my background, I feel that I have answered those questions as I was answered by the elders many times—through stories, tasks, and sometimes silence. I have answered by creating space for them to take their place in the Medicine Wheel, and I have danced so they may watch my feet to find the movement. And when they have admitted to confusion and feeling lost, I have told the stories that were told to me at such times. But they had a harder time than I have had. This world of academia does not offer the surrounding support to the rituals we create together. Fears cannot be put to rest. They are continually summoned up by the analytical mind for scrutiny. Empowerment is not seen as part of the process of critical thinking.

The landscape, however, is confirmation. And as the bridges are built by each attempt to find the marriages of circles and squares, we may find ourselves at a point in remembering where the initiation is complete. This "culturally diverse" country may yet find its way to collaboration and creative vision.

I simply must continue to walk my talk.

2

Carrying On

Joyce J. Scott

Help me Lord! A bit writer like me tackling an entire chapter, what have I done? This could be one of those stream-of-consciousness things that you have to swim up. Oh God! As an African American woman replete with, in fact, a cesspool of stereotypes, I find it a never-ending quest to stay balanced and well-tempered. My lifeline has been my relationship with my family, nuclear and extended. My history is typical. Up from slavery, up from the Reconstruction, uppercut, fed up, the Industrial Revolution, the Depression (talking about depression, how about those lynching trees and night riders? ba boom boom!), world wars, Star Wars. So what's different? Possibly my constant (maybe compulsive) analysis of art as a primal language spoken generationally, and my need to carry it on. Carrying on in my past may have been my ridiculous behavior in the hardware section (get it!, va va voom) at the K Mart. Or needling my friends about issues they already understood. A child of blue-collar workers in the fifties, who had little schooling, but a real respect for knowledge and a belief that work was your way out, I became academically well-heeled.

Mama telling me she wanted to be an artist. Nobody having faith, except the overseer who thought her straw dolls were voodoo. Faith in one day she might swing like a rag doll from a limb. She, too dark, undereducated or whatever they used. Still making picture books of cloth, requiring that extra inch of life. These quilts were filled with her stock and trade of flight from the "isms" society offered. My entry into art-making outside of school's tempora and papier-mâché was magic carpets, wrapping me in slumber. Just how deeply was I dozing?

Recollecting garnet and floral wallpapered rooms, my dolls clad in garments by me with the assistance of mom's knowing hands. Sewing way back beyond the afternoon memories to joyous cabins, where my mom much younger threaded needles under quilts listening to old-time music whipped stitched. Asking why the feeling was so mysterious. Knowing when the point pierces the fabric new melodies are sung about women's work and mending bridges, breaking backs and marriages rolled into a few layers of cotton.

Waxing poetic at exhibitions never gratified. My true potential is fulfilled as I share my gifts. It seems I'm always infusing. My visuals and performances are seldom abstract, but power-packed because life is power-packed.

Big Mama's got it, too fine, fine plus. So big and the butt's SO wide, the world bows under her weight. SO indigo, her shadow feels competition. Midnight calls from mock beaus too highstyle for daylight rendezvous, too hungry to abstain. This babe is bumping. SO totally MISS THANG that the traffic lights pop out-traffic jammed. She's jamming. Mama's BIG!

Every time I think I've made a clean getaway something pops up and I'm back in the fray. Art is the most potent formula for info-giving I have. The ideas of joy and risk are central to my work and instruction. I can't get enough of making . . . things. It's magical (not like the rabbit out of a hat), staying close to that feeling and sharing the heat involves risk. Being on the edge is facing fear, even passing through it. Students generally question how I achieved this openness. As if I've been through millions of hours of therapy/primal screams. I learn a lot from my parents but, am I a natural braggart with a measure of refinement? That's not it. I realized the liberty in going for it, because most of our scariest fears don't happen. We believe the worst will. Like being caught proposing marriage to Wayne Newton at a big Southern church with lots of older Black women looking at you like you have surely lost your mind. Or standing naked in the supermarket comparing fruit to your body parts.

None of that stuff happens, at least not to me. Maybe I'm doing something wrong. The worst was my making bad art. The best was the knowledge of achievement through adversity. Like listening to cosmic, yet stupid appraisals from artists who weren't even drinking. Those blatant guffaws served as rungs in my ladder of understanding and link with my students, regardless of age.

It is up to me to help change the world. Don't think I don't know how that sounds. Artists armed with gilding tools in defense of the

Joyce J. Scott, "Big Mama" 1991. Beads, Wire, Thread 27″ × 8″ × 10″.
Photo Credit: Kanui Takeno

"greater good." Jessie Helms would have us believe that the "greater good" deserves the exclusion of many artists. But we are the parents, siblings, and children of our society. Solid citizens. Our chronicle combined and separate represents the annals of everyone. I teach for valiant, altruistic, monetary, and outright selfish reasons. If we don't establish and protect freedom of expression, we will meet on the street those who create with bullets not paintbrushes.

Joyce J. Scott, "Rodney King's Head Was Squashed Like a Watermelon" 1991. Beads, Wire, Thread 13½″ × 8½″ × 7″. Photo Credit: Kanui Takeno

My slide lectures represent three generations of art-making in my family. Students are intrigued. They speak about their original impulses for art, how it's primacy comes from a unity of the aesthetic and visual, the dream manifest.

Saying my grandmother's quilts are sheet music is more than a slick description. I discuss strip weavers of West Africa, their ability to improvise rhythms, and how the hits just keep a-coming through my mother and me. After this research, I admitted I was a player in a much bigger picture. No forgetting those televised forecasts of the lives of civil rights workers (my own neighborhood was surrounded by the National Guard). Firehoses shooting with such velocity, helping wash the blood away. Blood from bodies attacked by dogs and nightsticks. That choreography helped determine my turpsickery with a joke "Rodney King's head was squashed like a watermelon" speaks to how slowly things change. I chose the watermelon because I believe in messing with stereotypes, prodding the viewer to reassess. The same goes for teaching. Everytime I feel a student, class, or subject is too comfortable, I mess with it. I fool with the mix and hopefully motivate reexamination.

Freeze-frame to yet another slain child juxtaposed beside communion, prom, or graduation photos; however voyeuristic, these views transformed my ideas from hippy beads to moccasins to sarcastic sculpture and self-deprecating collages. I'm not a tenured faculty member. I enjoy the shotgun approach (with today's problems, I maybe should have chosen a better term) of a visiting artist. Giving as much as I can in a short period of time, deeply serious and cutting the fool, getting to everybody's saturation point then one more step is provocative. I think teachers are saints. The endless meetings, paper and homework can be torture. The challenge is to keep joy in art-making for both teacher and student. I remember being the student who experimented with new techniques. No matter how belittling the outcome, I felt safe. That environment allowed for mad scientist antics without humiliation. Which is what I'm hoping to do. I devised a program while an artist in residence (after reading this you'll know it's not for creative writing) called "Turning the tables on 'em." Classes from elementary and middle schools were sponsored by the Maryland State Art's Council and the Baltimore City Public Schools. This generally meant the budget was bigger, providing a larger variety and quality of materials. When I presented the title to administrators, they usually thought I was trying to pull something. They were right. Comforting the spirit through limited or at least student-inspired competition was my way of turning the tables. Setting myself up as the person to surpass for silliness was seldom sought or achieved. This allowed for a less formal, risk-taking environment.

Not just talking about, but being the art was motivational. Dressing multiculturally, meaning no jeans or exercise togs, invited conversation about style, material, technique, and customs of the makers. It also allowed me to tell stories about my travels, making teaching less anonymous, more alive.

I actually turned the tables upside down and warped them like frame

Joyce J. Scott, "Something Going On" 1987. Glass, Beads, Wire, Fiber.
6″ × 5″ × 3″. Photo Credit: John Dean

looms. They were the perfect height and size for students to pull up a
chair and weave. It was like a Joan Rivers hour, gossip, fashion, even
politics. I requested a cross section of students. So along with the "art
stars," I got the "discipline problems." In a classroom setting small
enough to handle without stun guns (fifteen students, with diverse
personalities) I found an interesting switch. Instead of the art stars
lording over, most judged each other by skill and good humor. I believe
the different levels, and lack of "our gang" peer pressure, coalesced in
students who would never mix after school! They really let down
their guards. This was not heaven. There were problems. The younger
children seemed to be much more involved with who was really good
at weaving and sewing, while the older (middle school) ones were goal
oriented. A workspace where the students have more involvement,

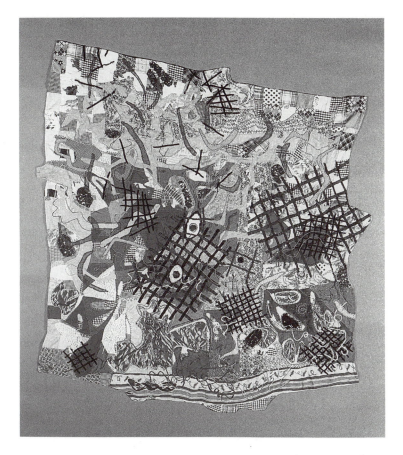

Joyce Scott, "3 Generation Quilt" 1988. 6″ Photo Credit: Kanui Takeno

even power, in the project from start to finish develops solid pride and security. These projects were enormous wall hangings, sometimes six to eight feet long. After installing an extremely large hanging at the top of a stairway, I was cautioned by a principal "That's going to fall on a child and kill it." I was taken aback and responded "This is probably the least dangerous thing an inner-city child has to worry about." But I think that statement implied that art is dangerous, like freedom of thought and speech. Shut my mouth. You know I won't.

Whether in my studio, on stage, or in the classroom, I'll always be messing. It's a family tradition. My mother, Elizabeth T. Scott, is a nationally known quilt-maker. She creates story quilts the old-fashioned way, without patterns. We have collaborated as teachers in public schools. My mother is not a weaver so we taught Quilting and Molawork (Panamanian reverse applique). Mom was the good cop, warm and grandmotherly. I was the bad cop, directional, academic. It was once again three generations (including the students) working on sewing projects, as my mom had sixty-five years ago. Shall the circle be unbroken?

3

African Philosophy, Theory, and "Living Thinkers"[1]

Joy James

Mbungi a kanda va kati kwa nsi ye yulu: The center (cavity) of the community is located between the above and the below world. The reality of the cultural heritage of a community, i.e., its knowledge, is the experience of that deepest reality found between the spiritualized ancestors and the physically living thinkers within the community.

—Kongo proverb-philosophy[2]

I think, therefore . . .

Notes to myself when teaching pile up as fragmented but connected thoughts. They remind me that I am attempting to return to something and somewhere in order to reconnect with a traditional wisdom foreign to academe:

Ours is a spiritual tradition. So, I want to begin class with meditation. . . .

We must continue to thank our ancestors, our spirits for the ground upon which we stand, for their struggles enabled us to survive genocidal wars, enslavement, and dehumanizing oppression.

First I thank our ancestors, elders and those who prepared the space for us . . . then, I tell my story. . . .

Ours is an oral tradition.

We tell stories to illuminate the paths we travel and to share humor, courage and wisdom in this liberation struggle. Our storytelling is our theorizing. And so an "introduction" into theory is an introduction into spiritual, political struggles for peace and freedom.

31

> I consciously began "theorizing," as Barbara Christian calls it, when I was nine and my father, returning from Viet Nam, brought the war home.

As I try to share these fragmented thoughts, which help me through teaching, they are most meaningful when set within traditional African cosmology, philosophy, theory, and radicalism for liberation.

Philosophy, Theory and "Living Thinkers"

In traditional African cosmology, as expressed in Kongo philosophy, living thinkers are initiates in a philosophical system in which they channel between the metaphysical and the physical. Key to traditional African cosmology, which guides the philosophy of living thinkers, is the understanding of the uniform of reality, particularly the nonduality of time and space. Traditional philosophy bridges artificial and socially constructed dichotomies: between sacred and secular, spiritual and political; within time (past, present, and future) and space.[3]

Philosophy serves both the spiritual and physical needs of the community. Community extends through time and space to include the ancestors, those now physically present, and future children. All collectively comprise "community," which refers to the ancestors, those now living, and those not yet born.[4] Community here is not bound by physical or temporal limits. Africans belong to the African community even when they do not reside in a Black community. Belonging is not determined by physical proximity. It is determined when one is born. Born into a community you may later decide whether to become an active or alienated member. You may move out of the state or the old neighborhood to "escape" your family or people, but you carry that family, the neighborhood, inside yourself. They remain your family, your people. You determine not whether or not you belongs but the nature of the relationship and the meaning of belonging. The quality of those familial and communal relations is set by practice.

Relationships are determinant. Philosophy is defined by its relationship to cosmology. Theory is defined by its relationship to philosophy. All three are determined in relationship to community. The nature of freedom, of a good spiritual and material life, and the place and responsibilities of human beings in the universe are philosophical issues or questions. Yet the core of philosophy is the cosmology or worldview which gives birth to it. Here, cosmology is the metaparadigm. Philosophy, the study of the truth and principles of being, knowledge and action, is the core of theory. Theory describes and explains phenomena while shaping propositions into principles. Encountering any social theory first ask: What is its philosophical assumptions or paradigm? Then seek the metaparadigm or cosmology which hosts that philosophy and paradigm. Afracentric worldviews maintain community or the collective as central; their transcendence or spirituality is inseparable from the mundane or secular.

Philosophy and theory intend the vitality and health of community. The community needs cosmology to guide it towards development; cosmology requires community as its realization. Relationships are central. Native American womanist writer Lee Maracle, in *Oratory: Coming to Theory* (using "theory" in the sense of the definition given here for philosophy) points to a traditional Native American cosmology similar to that encasing traditional African philosophy. Within this worldview, philosophy functions as "oratory" and prayer:

> Oratory: place of prayer, to persuade. We regard words as coming from original being—a sacred spiritual being. The orator is coming from a place of prayer and as such attempts to be persuasive. Words are not objects to be wasted. They represent the accumulated knowledge, cultural values, the vision of an entire people or peoples. We believe the proof of a thing or idea is in the doing. Doing requires some form of social interaction and thus, story is the most persuasive and sensible way to present the accumulated thoughts and values of a people.[5]

Within traditional African cosmology, philosophers travel full circle to realize metaphysical ideals—freedom, beauty, and harmonious order—on the physical realm; they think and act in service to the community. Connecting spiritual and material worlds merges ideals with action. Here, philosophy is not viewed as an idle luxury of a privileged sector or as alienated mental abstractions. Philosophy is practical. Its pragmatic function is service. Philosophy, in this worldview, is a necessity, for it embodies active service for the good of community and individuals within community. Tsenay Serequeberham, in the anthology *African Philosophy*, describes the role of the African philosopher as developing within and through service to the community:

> [T]he calling of the African philosopher . . . comes to us from a lived history whose endurance and sacrifice—against slavery and colonialism—has made our present and future existence in freedom

possible. The reflective explorations of African philosophy are thus aimed at further enhancing and expanding this freedom. . . .[6]

This "call" of the African philosopher is here defined as "theory." African philosophy and the call to it existed before European imperialism and profit from African enslavement. Predating the European colonization of Africa, philosophy stems from community (and the cosmology that gives meaning). Africa's ancestral tradition identifies philosophy and knowledge as acquired through a collective phenomenon. Philosophy and knowledge are collective creations, although they may be articulated by individuals. When knowledge is "the experience of that deepest reality found between the spiritualized ancestors and the physically living thinkers," it can only develop in relationship, in community. When strategizing and thinking on behalf of community liberation, everyone theorizes. When reflecting on the ideals which guide and guard our humanity, we philosophize.

Every people's praxis (theory and action)[7] is an expression of their collective philosophy reflecting and articulating its worldview and cosmology. Because service is indispensable to philosophy and theorizing, praxis is essential.[8] Defining philosophizing and theorizing as activist and communal does not mean the disappearance of the individual. Theory is done from the standpoint of the individual—in relationship to community. Where you stand when you philosophize and theorize determines who benefits from your thinking. The point is to stand at the crossroads, at the center within community. There the world of your horizon—family, friends, community, and people (nation) and the vertical climb and descent where spirit links you through time to those preceding you (ancestors) and those to follow you (the not-yet-born) intersect. Stand at the center, within community, and you will see the four corners of the world. From the vantage or viewpoint, in African cosmology, we theorize to live freely as human beings. From that vantage point we philosophize with our lives and in our life stories.

Autobiographies, Theory, and "Living Thinkers"

Autobiographies record the oral tradition of theorizing. Often the theory of African American women, particularly community activists, is oral and so remains largely unwritten. Like Kongo proverbs, political struggles are also "concrete sayings conveying practical wisdom." Since the political autobiographies of African American women are rarely referred to, or sought out, as political philosophy and theory, they may seem incongruous entries under the rubric "philosophy" or "theory." However, their theorizing reflects traditional African philosophy, for it exists on behalf of our ancestors and ourselves. In the wedded complementarity of life struggles, it remains both collective and singular, political and spiritual. These writings share more than autobiographical details; they express highly politicized commitments to praxis on behalf of liberation, with an understanding of the essential nature of spirit(s). Kongo proverb/philosophy echoes in these autobiographical writings as the women mirror the reality between ancestor-spirits and the physically living thinkers. Philosophy appears in the autobiographies as the women write within an ethic for human liberation; theory unfolds as they strategically analyze state and social systems that create and maintain oppression. Cosmology provides the floor, walls, and ceiling of the stories of women working as theoreticians to meet the call of liberation.

Principled living rooted in community makes possible autobiographies reflecting traditional African cosmology. This is the identity of the "living thinker" where storytelling as oral or written literature carries theory and philosophy. Such stories carry collective wisdom, responding to the African philosopher's call to think and act for the necessary conditions for freedom and humanity. Storytelling, theorizing in proverbs dedicated and responsive to the community, is essential for living thinkers. This is the medium of communication that binds the individual to the communal. It is perhaps the most effective means of instruction in philosophy and theory. Maracle succinctly states the relationship: "There is a story in every line of theory [philosophy]."[9] Philosophizing and theorizing in autobiographical storytelling are practices, in which we live our thoughts and recount our lives, reflecting this.

Thinking works to resist erasure and genocide as we present ourselves in stories-autobiographies.[10] There is an agency and immediacy in African (American) autobiographies where individuals respond to the conditions of freedom and oppression in the community which shape them. African American autobiography mirrors a communal ethic. According to Toni Morrison:

> The autobiographical form is classic in Black American or Afro-American literature because it provided an instance in which a writer could be representative, could say, "My single solitary and individual life is like the lives of the tribe; it differs in these specific ways, but

it is a balanced life because it is both solitary and representative."
The contemporary autobiography tends to be "how I got over—
look at me—alone—let me show you how I did it." It is inimical, I
think, to some of the characteristics of Black artistic expression and
influence.[11]

When African (American) autobiographies balance both the solitary
and representative, their equilibrium rests upon traditional African
philosophy: living for the community, working as a conduit from the
past through the present to the future; channelling desire and will into
praxis and principles for African liberation.

Political autobiographies present political philosophy through stories. Storytelling instructs development and resistance. Using storytelling as a means of instruction to honor ancestors and serve the community expresses an understanding of spirit, political courage. It is a
commitment to community as well as self or "I." Philosophy and
theorizing in the autobiographies of African activists reject the concept
of inherent opposition between individual and community. The rejection of individualism, and its ideological irresponsibility to community,
is itself a form of African resistance to oppression. When the central
opposition is not with the community but with the dominant, colonizing culture and state, the goal is not individual freedom from society
or community but *freedom of the individual through the liberation of
her/his community*. When freedom is achievable only through the
liberation of the community, then community freedom is the precondi-
tion for personal freedom, although not synonymous to it. One's life
belongs simultaneously to oneself and the community. In autobiographies the writers construct no identity outside of or in abstraction
to community. For being "within community" requires more than
residence, it requires moral action and political praxis. In autobiographies, living thinkers develop their identities through praxis within
community.

Autobiographical oral or written literature is one of the many vehi-
cles transporting political philosophy. Using proverbial storytelling,
these political autobiographies work as treatises, manifestos, poetry,
and songs, to influence identity and politics. They call their readers to
initiation as living thinkers. Although we may read political autobiographies of African American activists for their philosophy and theorizing, we may also read them for historical data. However, autobiographies by African Americans in revolutionary struggle are rarely read
frivolously. Such autobiographies are unsettling rather than entertain-

ing, subversive rather than assimilable to hegemonic thought. These autobiographies are disturbing because of their radical analyses of domination, and their stories of resistance in which there are personal risks, and painful punishments and victories. Those who read these writings may read them as political theories and/or for reflections on spirit and personal integrity and insight of women and men in liberation struggles.

For example, the study group of Free My People, a youth-led political organization in Roxbury, Massachusetts, reads African American political autobiographies to better understand and shape their conditions and identities as community activist-thinkers, confronting racism, sexual violence, drug addiction, police brutality, inferior schools, deteriorating housing, and murderous "health care." African American youth read to find other living thinkers. Generally, African Americans study autobiographies by men, for instance, *The Autobiography of Malcolm X* or *Blood in My Eye* by George Jackson. These autobiographies play an indispensable role in promoting reflection and theorizing in community; however, it is important that we equally examine the autobiographies of revolutionary African American women whose contributions are more obscured by this culture. Women, who represent half of the African population, have played an essential but too infrequently recognized role as living thinkers. They have given us their stories, reflecting their lives resisting the intertwined oppressions of racism, sexism, and sexual abuse. Our ancestors have been and are aware of our power to confront oppression and create a new world. African American educator-activist Anna Julia Cooper asserts in her 1892 autobiography *A Voice from the South:*

> Only the *black woman* can say "when and where I enter, in the quiet, undisputed dignity of my womanhood, without violence and without suing or special patronage, then and there *the whole Negro race enter with me.*"[12]

In that spirit, the autobiographies of revolutionary women activists present images of African American women as powerful actors rather than passive victims.[13]

Autobiographical Theorizing and Revolutionary Women

Autobiographies create a partnership, no matter how warm or cool their reception. Dance with the thoughts of the living thinker and you dance within community. Spurn the living thinker, and you reject the gifts of this form of theorizing. One priceless gift is that of the archetype of African (American) woman as philosopher. Presenting African American women as warriors, workers, lovers, and theorists in revolutionary praxis creates both model and conduit. In describing their development through an activist commitment to African liberation, women outline the vision and balance of just order, while defining the spirit and space of human survival and liberation. This is the function of philosophy. The descriptive nature of these autobiographies conveys both proscription and prescription.

Autobiographies such as Angela Davis' *Angela Davis: An Autobiography*, Anne Moody's *Coming of Age in Mississippi*, Bernice Johnson Reagon's "My Black Mothers and Sisters—Or on Beginning a Cultural Autobiography," and Assata Shakur's *Assata: An Autobiography* present revolutionary praxes and archetypes.[14] These four African American women activists, born into and growing up in the South during the post-war 1940s,[15] were members of progressive-radical organizations such as the Student Non Violent Coordinating Committee (SNCC), Soledad Brothers Defense Committee, and the Black Panther Party (BPP). In these autobiographies, their lives flow within African tradition: commitment to community's metaphysical and physical needs for freedom. The women embraced community even amid the internal violence and external dangers of organizations targeted for violent and illegal state repression by the Ku Klux Klan, the FBI's Cointelpro, and police.

Revolutionary political perspectives shape both the women's lives and hopes; they describe reality. Bernice Johnson Reagon defines "revolutionary" in the context of the lives of activist African American women:

> The roles that Black women have played in making a black space in the United States of America in which Black life can grow have been nationalistic, cultural, and also revolutionary. Revolution, as I understand it, is the stopping of something, the turning around of something, the radical change of direction. It involves a lot of violence, and it has to be a cleansing process . . . we were brought here to do certain kinds of work, to carry out a certain kind of function. That function and responsibility did not have with it a concern with our continuance or existence as a people through time. Sometimes I think by the time they made the cotton-picking machines, we were just not supposed to be here anymore. The continuing process of stopping that, the act of turning that around, this kind of nationalism

is revolutionary; and Black women have played a major role in that particular struggle.[16]

Women assumed the responsibility for "our continuance or existence as a people through time" and worked as both cultural nationalists and political revolutionaries. Continuance of the community as a whole, predicated on its self-determination and liberation, was and is the standard for evaluating the relevancy and worth of philosophy and theory. Revolutionary praxis and knowledge of historical and contemporary practices assaulting African people characterizes these autobiographies. They are also formed by the radical commitments of women risking their lives to connect theory to action. When reading these autobiographies, we may respond to the roles and lives of *revolutionary women* channelling as theorists in a communal, nonhierarchical fashion with antipathy or acceptance. Images of African American female power are unfamiliar to most of us raised outside a militant African female tradition of uncompromising resistance to oppression.

The political understanding of revolutionary women that social change comes from the power of the community leads them to portray themselves as "unexceptional" women connected to many others. Their rejection of elitism is tied to a class analysis and democratic understanding of leadership (class analysis in and of womanist or Black feminist theorizing is not common). For example, Angela Davis writes in the preface to her autobiography:

> Many people unfortunately assumed that because my name and my case were so extensively publicized, the contest that unfolded during my incarceration and trial from 1970 to 1972 was one in which a single Black woman successfully fended off the repressive might of the state. Those of us with a history of active struggle against political repression understood, of course, that while one of the protagonists in this battle was indeed the state, the other was not a single individual, but rather the collective power of the thousands and thousands of people opposed to racism and political repression.[17]

Angela Davis' autobiographical (and nonautobiographical) writing remains centered on the lives of African American people, liberation and political activism. It also argues the indispensability of community. Neither history nor philosophy or theory are products of "great individuals," according to Davis, who writes:

The real strength of my approach [in writing the autobiography] at that time resides . . . in its honest emphasis on grassroots contributions and achievements so as to demystify the usual notion that history is the product of unique individuals possessing inherent qualities of greatness.[18]

Although not themselves archetypes, the women participate in collectively realizing potential and actual, archetypal, African, female, living thinkers. They also conjure up ancient archetypes of the mother Yemaya, the Oshun, goddess of friendship and eros; Oshun of the Gelede, ancestral energy of women elders' nurturing community. These archetypes of resistance and love antedate and coexist with archetypes of a Harriet Tubman battling enslavement. They present not only models for theorizing and organizing but also a conduit. As a passage for reflection and development, archetypes can organize our thoughts and direct or channel our theorizing into transformation or a revolutionary praxis.

I found this particularly true in reading *Assata: An Autobiography*. My first encounter with Assata Shakur's autobiography, one of the most controversial among African American women's autobiographies, was through book parties held by African American community activists at the Harlem State Office Building and at an African Caribbean art gallery in Loisada, Manhattan. At these gatherings African American poets, activists and artists reflected on the importance and relevance of the autobiography to the ongoing struggles of African American communities. After recommending the book to my friends and organizing study groups, I introduced the book into my university classes.

It is difficult to teach about revolutionary African American women within institutions that appropriate and commodify knowledge about people of African descent. Because the lives of these women contradict rather than fit into academe,[19] their work is marginalized. Where a colonizing culture cannot appropriate revolutionary theorizing for Black liberation, it tends to trivialize or ignore it as irrational (although, in traditional African cosmology, theory irrelevant to community survival is irrational). It is easier to appropriate African art, literature and language than the political theorizing of revolutionary African American women. For example, the following passage from Shakur's autobiography inhibits appropriation:

I wasn't one who believed that we should wait until our political struggle had reached a high point before we began to organize the underground. I felt that it was important to start building underground structures as soon as possible. And although I felt that the major task of the underground should be organizing and building, I didn't feel that armed acts of resistance should be ruled out. As long as they didn't impede our long-range plans, guerrilla units should be able to carry out a few well-planned, well-timed armed actions that were well coordinated with aboveground political objectives. Not any old kind of actions, but actions that Black people would clearly understand and support and actions that were well publicized in the Black community.[20]

This theorizing is not fully comprehensible outside of its context—African liberation struggles against oppression during brutal racist and state repression. Historical and contemporary political knowledge of African American liberation struggles is a prerequisite. To engage this theorizing requires understanding or at least recognizing the conditions and sources of oppression, both specific to one people and universal. To whatever degree I accept or reject, embrace or distance myself from her, I respond to Assata Shakur as a living thinker who serves community. Shakur was and is a model and a conduit. Her theorizing, bound to the community, forces a response not only to her struggles as a revolutionary but to those of the community as well. Reading her autobiography provokes me to reflect on why she thinks this way and the implications of her praxis.

These autobiographical writings, theorizing for contemporary revolutionary praxis, provide a living history in which the past is tied to the present and future. To encounter the women as "living thinkers" prohibits reading their stories as entombed in a moribund history. Since time is not compartmentalized within traditional African cosmology, neither is the liberation struggle: the past freedom movements are connected to present organizing, and shape future liberation. The autobiographies of living thinkers embody revolutionary praxis for African liberation. Although autobiographies by African American women may be taught in academia, it is not usually for their prescriptive and theoretical content. This is partly due to the general disassociation of "philosophy" with African Americans and the academic presentation of African women as nonphilosophers. It also stems from the political conservatism and liberalism of academe threatened by contemporary radicalism. Angela Davis, although better "educated" in European philosophy than most European (American) academics, is more generally categorized as a "Black feminist" or "activist" than as a theorist. Academic elitism and racism, coupled with a denigration of radical political activism, creates an academic environment that devalues the theoretical contributions of activist-writers.

If the autobiographical writings of revolutionary African American women activists are read at all in academia, they tend to be read not as political philosophy and theory representative of a community, but as personal "slave narratives." Obviously, "slave" narratives present(ed) African American women not as mere victims but as survivors and warriors in a resistance tradition. However, compartmentalized, the writings are reduced to painful personal narrations of "past" (therefore abstract) historical struggles against racial-sexual atrocities. This compartmentalization severs time and community, and African women, from theory and philosophy; it sanctions academia's denial that revolutionary African women carry theory whose philosophical core encases the gem of an ancient cosmology. Our responses to academic denials shape the parameters for African- and community-centered thinking in academe.

Academic Responsibility and "Rootedness" to African Philosophy

In *The Divine Horsemen: The Living Gods of Haiti,* Maya Deren's description of a destitute Haitian hougon's failed exploitation of Voudun for tourist dollars depicts our dilemma as African academics:

> It was the ancient loa deities who, with divine accuracy, understood ["[that] the exploitation as folklore attraction constituted a degradation of the religion"] and perceived also the falsification and corruption implicit in the fact that the songs would be sung, the dances danced, and the rituals performed not in the service of the loa, nor in the exercise of obseisance and discipline, but for the purpose of self-exhibition and self-aggrandizement.[21]

Commercial academic hougons know that objectifying the community for print promotes tenure. Theorizing responsive to community is costly in academe. Alienation, a signature of academia, pays. In belonging to a people seeking freedom from colonization, African American academics face issues of responsibility and accountability, unrecognized by White colleagues. African (American) stories can be told, songs sung, dances danced not for the benefit of the community and ancestors but for purpose of exhibition and self-promotion, to entertain employers. Paradoxically, students may learn from these shared stories and culture, albeit in an estranged form, where we as academics act as estranged people.

Despite our estrangement, our allegiance to academic institutions is part of the job: corporate survival demands loyalty and careerism. African American communities do not hire, promote, tenure, or fire. Yet the "slaves" to community, in praxis, carry the culture which permitted our entry into academic jobs. They also create the culture which gives us something other than "pathology" about which to write. That culture is of course rooted in community, of which a central part is the spirit world of ancestors. As Toni Morrison wryly observes:

> When you kill the ancestor you kill yourself . . . nice things don't always happen to the totally self-reliant. . . .[22]

To choose to live outside our traditions, apart from our ancestors and people, means losing: the roles of living thinkers, servants to the spirits, community activists; and, the deepest realities they reflect. Ancestral spirits and community people perceive and create realities academic intellectuals may deny, ignore, or (mis)interpret. In the absence of relationships with community, ancestors, youth, we may become ignorant about the deepest realities of our individual and collective lives. Wisdom requires initiation. Initiation means practice. To practice one needs community. Only by belonging to community can we say we "know" and speak with competence.

However, as an academic it appears sometimes that my primary objective is to become "totally self-reliant" without responsibilities to community or spirit. I seem often to buy, after first customizing, the worldview that corporate academia sells: self-reliant isolation and competition, hoping to somehow avoid the consequences of an alienated existence. To escape self-alienation as an African American academic I may develop the desire and discipline to become a living thinker: although this will provide no academic status or economic rewards.

In academia, where individualism manifests as a prerequisite for success, remembering our connectedness to other more expansive worlds, and warnings to never neglect them, are quickly forgotten. I too often forget the ancestors, when what is foremost and "real" in my mind are accolades for my mental ego. I remember and forget my own roles in academia, proselytizing ignorance. Forgetting and remembering are like drifting and waking in day/nightmares where sleepwalkers peddle "knowledge" without apology or confrontation.

I remember to routinely wake up and forget not to drift back, anesthe-
tized by pedantic lullabies shredding people. I remember that I have to
stay awake as an academic aberration in order to theorize within
traditional wisdom. I never forget that asleep or awake Africans in
academia are anomalies. In the Kongo philosophical tradition, where
knowledge is "that deepest reality found between the spiritualized
ancestors and the physically living thinkers within the community,"
we are everyday folk. Trying to forget the propaganda of "specialness
through Ph.D." and attempting to not settle for tenured survival as
some sort of "honorary White skin privilege", I recall that within
community, in the alchemy of political theorizing and struggle, living
thinkers routinely, ritualistically step above mere survival. Remembering to try and pass on what the ancestors tell me through my god-
mother, I see that the intent is to move beyond survival—the intent is
to be free.

Notes

1. I thank Ernest Allen for his suggestions for this chapter.

2. K. Kia Bunseki Fu-Kiau, *The African Book Without Title* (Cambridge: Fu-Kiau, 1980), 62.

3. John Mbiti, *Traditional African Religions and Philosophies* (London: Heineman, 1969).

4. There are a number of similarities between traditional African cosmology and traditional Native American cosmology. Particular to both is a concept of commu-nity that extends through time. For examples, see the philosophy of the Native American concept of "seven generations"; and Paula Gunn Allen, *Sacred Hoop: Recovering the Feminine of American Indian Traditions* (Boston: Beacon Press, 1986).

5. Lee Maracle, *Oratory: Coming to Theory,* North Vancouver, BC: Gallerie Women Artists' Monographs, Issue 1, (September 1990), 3.

6. Tsenay Serequeberham, *African Philosophy* (New York: Paragon House, 1991), xxii. For a collection of philosophical essays on the connections between philosophy and politics in African American theorizing, see *Philosophy Born of Struggle: An Anthology of Afro-American Philosophy from 1917,* edited by Leonard Harris (Dubuque, Iowa: Kendall Hunt, 1983).

7. Although this article offers no full analysis of praxis, I reject the assumption that "theorizing" is synonymous with praxis. My understanding of praxis within the lives of revolutionary African women, discussed here as theorists and living think-ers, is that praxis entails concrete physical activity beyond the activity of theorizing to realize philosophical ideals.

8. See Barbara Christian, "The Race for Theory," reprinted in *Making Face, Making*

Soul: Haciendo Caras, edited by Gloria Anzaldua (San Francisco, Aunt Lute Foundation, 1990).

9. Maracle, *Oratory.* Maracle also critiques the Eurocentric claims that only Europeans produce philosophy (theory): "We differ in the presentation of theory, not in our capacity to theorize. . . . It takes a great deal of work to erase people from theoretical discussion."

10. The United Nations Convention on the Prevention and Elimination of Genocide (1948) defines "genocide" as any intent to destroy, in whole or in part, a national, racial, ethnic, or religious group including "causing serious bodily or mental harm to members of the group" as well as "killing members of the group."

11. Toni Morrison, "Rootedness: The Ancestor As Foundation," *Black Women Writers (1950–1980)* (New York: Anchor Press, 1984), 340.

12. Anna Julia Cooper, *A Voice from the South* (Oxford: Oxford University Press, 1988), reprint (originally published, Xenia, Ohio: Aldine Printing House, 1892).

13. Deborah King, "Multiple Jeopardy, Multiple Consciousness: The Context of a Black Feminist Ideology," in *Signs,* 14:1 (Autumn 1988).

14. Anne Moody, *Coming of Age in Mississippi* (New York: Bantam Doubleday, 1968). Bernice Johnson Reagon, in *Feminist Studies,* 8:1 (Spring 1982), reprint from *Black Women and Liberation Movements,* editor, Virginia A. Blandford, Institute for the Arts and the Humanities, Howard University, 1981; Angela Davis, *Angela Davis: An Autobiography* (New York: Random House, 1974), reprint International Publishers, 1988; and Assata Shakur, *Assata: An Autobiography* (London: Zed Books, 1987).

15. Anne Moody was born in 1938 in rural Mississippi and organized with the NAACP and SNCC during the civil rights movement in one of the most violent and racist states. Moody at one time headed a KKK assassination list because of her SNCC organizing.

    Bernice Johnson Reagon was born October 1942, in Georgia. She was a SNCC activist and a member of the Freedom Singers, 1962–1963. She is currently Curator at the Smithsonian in Washington, D.C., and founder and director of Sweet Honey in the Rock, the acapella, African American, women's musical group.

    Angela Davis, born in 1944 in Alabama, was active in SNCC, Black Panther Party, Soledad Brothers Defense Committee, and the Communist Party, and was a political prisoner in the 1970s. She is a professor of Women Studies and Philosophy in California.

    Assata Shakur (Joanne Chesimard) was born in 1947 in New York City and raised in the South. She was a member of the Black Panther Party. Shakur was forced underground in 1971 after being targeted by the FBI's Cointelpro. She was captured in May 1973, during an alleged "shootout" on the New Jersey Turnpike during which she was shot, while her companion Zayd Shakur was killed; one state trooper was killed, and another, Harper, wounded. Assata Shakur had nine trials during 1973–77, ending in three acquittals, one hung jury, three dismissals, and one mistrial due to her pregnancy. Her conviction in 1977, by an all-White jury, was tied to possession of weapons (none of them proven to be handled by her) and attempted murder of state trooper Harper. Harper, who sustained a minor injury during the shootout, had testified that Assata Shakur shot him although there was no gun residue on her fingers, and no evidence that Shakur ever fired a shot or handled any weapons. Harper admitted later during cross-examination that: he never saw Assata Shakur with a gun; she never shot him; and that he had lied under oath. Nevertheless, Shakur was convicted of killing a state trooper and sentenced to life plus 26–33 years. In November 1979 Assata Shakur escaped from her New Jersey prison. She is in political exile in Cuba. (See Attorney Lennox Hinds' introductory remarks to *Assata*.)

16. Reagon, 82.

17. Davis, viii–ix.

18. *Ibid.*

19. In feminist/womanist theory classes, often students find this theorizing a disturbing catalyst for their own thinking and development. The autobiographical theorizing of revolutionary African American women shakes personal identities enmeshed in materialist, sexist, and racist distortions. To meet the women, students must offer their thinking and also risk and reveal their own life-stories. Autobiographical theorizing affects students more than most other progressive academic writings; for African women as living thinkers offer not just their thoughts but their lives. Some students embrace the individual women of the autobiographies while rejecting the revolutionary politics and theorizing that is the most challenging. Paradoxically, their desire to appear nonracist and/or antiracist also leads them to assume "revolutionary" rhetoric.

20. Shakur, 243.

21. Maya Deren, *The Divine Horsemen, The Living Gods of Haiti* (New York: McPherson & Co., 1953 and 1970), 80. Deren writes of the serviteur's relationship to religion: "His [her] invocation [calling upon the loa] was the genealogy of his [her] own divinity, and, condensed into the shorthand of this nomenclature, contained the record of the race, of all that which, flowing like a river forward in time, was to be funnelled now into this single individual so that, in his [her] own person, the accumulated force of moral history would be pitted against contemporary circumstance." Deren, 81.

22. Morrison, 344.

Space

4

American Studies: Melting Pot or Pressure Cooker?

Elizabeth Hadley Freydberg

In order to remedy the lacunae in American Studies, we must examine and include a wider range of authors with those quirks of personality which make living scholarship possible. And we must do so by any means necessary, examining the biases which have kept African American women, as both subjects of study and as scholars, out of the field. Admittedly, many of the recorded documents of African American women are considered more than applicable to categories of history and literature. However, many of the writings dismissed as improperly historical or literary are genuinely reflective of African American women's struggles to become part of America's mainstream. African American women have transcended both legal and extralegal means to produce works in any genre—and in many cases have excelled in doing so.

The problem may lie in the fact that in order to include these materials, the gatekeepers of American culture would have to consult African American Women's Studies scholars to determine what constitutes a canon in these disciplines. And, as the lament goes, "there *are* no qualified candidates for this position." African American women in academia are few and far between, statistically speaking. Those who are around tend to be tied up with committees (being the "minority presence" on an endless succession of committees) and working overtime mentoring young African American scholars (to ensure that there *is* a next generation of Black scholars in academia). If one African woman scholar is available, she's inevitably "hostile": dark glasses, wild dreadlocks, and an *attitude*—one which no doubt stems from seeing herself systematically excluded from the American landscape.

Indeed, systematic exclusion is not unique to American Studies. My areas of specialization include Theatre and Drama, Women's Studies, African American Studies, and American Studies. Throughout graduate school at Indiana University-Bloomington while attending classes in these disciplines, I consistently found myself asking: "Where are the Black women in your syllabi—where am *I?*" During my first year, I bravely forwarded a bibliography to the Chairperson of American Studies, who was also professor of my required seminar in American Studies. He responded to the "woman question" by including Catherine Esther Beecher's *American Woman's Home, or, Principles of Domestic Science: Being A Guide to the Formation and Maintenance of Economical, Healthful, Beautiful, and Christian Homes* (1869; 1975), and to the African American question with the inclusion of *Ragtime* by E. L. Doctorow. In Women's Studies I examined and compiled an annotated bibliography of canonical works, in which I indicated whether or not each work mentioned African American women. My professor mildly reprimanded me by pointing out that I had rendered a critical review of books rather than an annotated bibliography which was my assigned task. Regarding African American Studies, although the majority of classes were dominated by male subject matter, under the employment of Dr. Herman Hudson, and later Dr. Portia K. Maultsby, I was permitted the freedom as an Associate Instructor to expand my assigned courses to include women in the syllabi. I included women from the same periods in "Black Autobiography," and developed "Black Women in America" in which I included a section on lesbians.

I was also fortunate to study and teach with Dr. Phylliss Rauch Klotman, Director and founder of the Black Film Center Archive at Indiana University-Bloomington. There I became familiar with films by African American women, and was granted the freedom to meet, write, and teach about these women and their films. My specialization in Theatre and Drama is American Theatre. Throughout graduate school, we consistently read theatre history books that most often excluded African Americans and always excluded African American women. No matter what the focus of discussion was, I located African Americans and specifically African American women relevant to the subject to write about. And finally I did my dissertation on Bessie Coleman (1896–1926), with the objective of representing the four disciplines of my concentrated studies by presenting the history of an African American woman who performed aerial feats while flying airplanes. The Department of Theatre and Drama granted the degree because my other areas of concentration were considered "nontraditional," without degree-granting authority.

I frequently found that, instead of my professors embracing and encouraging my tenacity toward developing additional areas of study, they groaned in concert with many of my classmates, who had no interest in hearing yet another report from me on the contributions of African American women. I was branded racist, hostile, and polemical because of my single-minded preoccupation with one subject. Graduate school evolved into a combat zone for me—I was fighting for my life.

The battle continues as a faculty member. Only now it has escalated. Before, I was threatened with the loss of my doctorate, now I am jeopardizing my livelihood. In determining which area I wanted to be employed in as a professor, I chose African American Studies because I believed the department I was joining would provide the opportunity to develop courses related to Black women. While the department appears to be amenable to my ideas, there is a great deal of bureaucracy to wade through in order to get courses accepted by the university. Perhaps it is too early to make a judgment call, but the atmosphere throughout the university is volatile, engendered by "downsizing." Everyone is preoccupied with demonstrating that the university cannot survive without their particular discipline; would-be proponents join the lengthy list of adversaries. Gone is the excitement of scholastic, intellectual exchange among peers, replaced by insecure, backbiting, hostile colleagues, protecting their turf.

Women's Studies, for example, is dominated by White, women, part-time adjuncts to "programs" rather than "departments," who designate their canon, which is almost always void of works by and about women of color. One of the ongoing misconceptions by some White women is that all feminists have one common enemy: the patriarchy. They do not address race or class issues, or homophobia. After having been involved in several organizations dominated by White women, I did not wish to expend energy in skirmishes that usually concluded in White women accusing African American women of making them feel guilty whenever issues of racism in the Women's Movement were broached. In short, I chose not to apply to Women's Studies Programs because I did not want to make White women "feel good about themselves" at my expense. I clearly recognized that their agendas radically differed from those of women of color. Women of color tend to address communal issues that include women, children and men in the entire community, even when the focus is on lesbians (see works by Audre Lorde, Barbara Smith and others). The African American community's homophobia does not preclude lesbians from confronting the issue within the community. African American women confront racism not only within the White, Male, patriarchal society, but also within White women's communities and organizations, advanced by those who embrace the behavior of the patriarchy whenever expedient.

The paradigm of exclusion is consistently played out in academia. Although it can and has been argued that hostility toward "outsiders" compels the disowned toward innovative works, the constant battle exacts a price. Some of the symptoms seem akin to post-traumatic stress syndromes. There are numerous and increasing stories related by and about my sisters experiencing mental breakdowns, attempted suicides, paranoia, neurological infirmities, and hypertension caused by stress in the extreme. Perhaps the less apparent consequences are that many careers suffer from the absence of creativity in a "publish-or-perish world" where the majority of our creativity is consumed by writing papers that are reactions to someone else's negative treatise on African Americans. By the time some have succeeded to full professor, they have acquiesced so long that their own words ring hollow; they have not written their *magnum opus;* they have arrived, but they are embittered. They exorcise their animosity by making academia excessively difficult, but void of intellectual challenge for their students—often creating more rules and regulations than the founding fathers of the university have. All the while our attention is diverted into writing reaction papers, new disciplines (multiculturalism) are embraced and new bodies of work are published by people opposed to inclusion in the academy. And, moreover, they are writing treatises which establish them as the "experts," as evidenced by the proliferation of edited works on African American women's literature and the swelling body of works on multiculturalism.

Having to fight for entrance into the classroom after having proven myself by vaulting the hurdles created by the gatekeepers of academia contributes to a hollow feeling of "homelessness" in the academy, and insecurity regarding my worth compels me to aggressively elbow my way into the classroom, and occasionally shout "I have something to say." I get tired of arguing for the inclusion of African American women's history in the classroom; tired of presenting the argument that I am not suggesting replacing the canon, but that I am recommending that we expand the canon; and tired of demonstrating how the exclusionary practices of academia have meted out a grave injustice to all students of United States history. Fatigue engendered by warfare causes a person to retreat, resign, or regroup. So far I have chosen the latter; to regroup and fight while praying that I do not join my sisters on the list of casualties.

American Studies as a discipline has traditionally been concerned primarily with the contributions of White, American males. However, this focus has gradually undergone a metamorphosis since the introduction of "nontraditional" disciplines to the academy. African American Studies and Women's Studies are two disciplines that have provoked curriculum revisions in academies throughout the United States during the past twenty-some years. The history and literature of African American women, however, continue to be neglected in both disciplines and are therefore the primary focus of this paper.

Modification of the American Studies curriculum has in some cases evolved naturally because of a numerical increase of African American women in the classroom since the early seventies. Their presence and contributions to academia have naturally necessitated a curriculum transformation. More frequently, however, this change has been involuntary, facilitated by agitation and formidable scholarly research and publications by African American women, whose contributions are only recently being recognized. These are contributions which should now be integrated into new curriculums if the academy is to continue to strive for truth and honesty in the representation of "Americans" in American Studies.

The remainder of this chapter will focus on the necessity for including African American women in the American Studies curriculum and the ways in which American Studies can and must expand its curriculum by including works which have not been considered properly germane to the field. I offer suggestions as to how American Studies can forge a viable liaison to other "nontraditional" disciplines, such as Women's Studies and African American Studies, without either infringing on their autonomy, or overextending itself to the point of undermining its own credibility. The suggestions presented will serve as a constructive paradigm for the inclusion of additional "nontraditional" groups and subjects germane to American Studies—such as Native American, Asian Americans, Latin Americans, and other marginalized cultures.

American Studies as a field promises to examine the whole fabric of national identity, from the founding of a unique socio-political experiment, through stages of growth and expansion that have frequently been tumultuous and painful, to a present in which citizens are the body politic giving the mandate to a world superpower. In practice, however, American Studies has been primarily concerned with and defined by the perceptions of privileged White males, such as Benjamin Franklin, Andrew Jackson and Horatio Alger. Even these three names invoke a superstructure far greater in the national mythology than their individual deeds and contributions. They embody a spirit of self-reliance, heroism, and volition which could only have emerged from a rough-and-ready defiance of obstacles in an untamed frontier landscape, and from a parallel agnostic struggle against European cultural dictates.

When it first became a subject to be advanced for serious consideration in the 1940s, American Studies challenged prevailing notions of literary canon and historiography in longer-established academic units. During its early years, American Studies was in the truest sense "multidisciplinary," although that buzzword had yet to acquire its *sine qua non* aura of desirability in the proposal of new directions of study within the academy. It posited a holistic fabric of national culture, in which history informed literature in the face of flagrant New Critical praxis and in which politics and popular culture shared the same bedroom, if not as strange bedfellows then at least as roommates. Thus did American Studies address itself to the task of mending a world gone mad with war and struggling back from the brink of chaotic annihilation. In other words, American Studies offered an infusion of courage and good cheer to the United States which was, as Ezra Pound phrased it, "an old bitch gone in the teeth / . . . a botched civilization."

Methodologically, American Studies, continues to be interdisciplinary, grounded in history and literature, and frequently merged with mythology and sociology. A cursory view of any syllabus today offers if not all, at least several of the following titles: Anthony F. Wallace's *Rockdale: The Growth of an American Village in the Early Industrial Revolution;* Henry Glassie's *Pattern in the Material Folk Culture of the Eastern United States;* Henry Nash Smith's *Virgin Land: The American West As Symbol and Myth;* John William G. McLoughlin's *Revivals, Awakening, and Reform: An Essay on Religion and Social Change in America, 1607–1977;* William Ward's *Andrew Jackson: Symbol for An Age;* and Benjamin Franklin's *The Autobiography.* These titles reflect a variety of pedagogical concerns: the impact of industrial development on one particular community; how individual artifacts influence folk culture based on their structure, their form, and their use; how symbols and myths fuse concepts and emotions into an image; religion as a catalyst for social change in America; and concentration on the life of a single individual, in order to demonstrate various qualities of the period in which he lived.

The method of study, although interdisciplinary, is primarily paradigmatic as opposed to empirical. (Paradigm here might be understood in a broader sense than in T.S. Kuhn's work, to include any pattern selected by a theorist in advance of one's study.) That is to say, the study of America must have underlying, theoretical presuppositions which govern the study, and empirical data and other information; lived experience and particularities are only to be considered later.

So the paradigm is searching for a certain kind of relevance; the historian or theorist has his proceeds with research knowing in advance what kinds of material will put flesh on the difficult abstractions. He or she has in mind certain organizational patterns and structures which determine the nature of his research. McLoughlin, for example, in his discussion of religion as social change in America, maintains that "five great awakenings have shaped and reshaped American Culture since 1607." He consistently refers to what he calls a "culture core" which is based on the cultural myth (this is his paradigm, and is closely related to the story of the Israelites in the Bible) that "Americans are God's chosen, leading the world to perfection."[1]

Each of these books, to be sure, employs detailed empirical studies; nevertheless, the shapes that these studies take are determined in advance by theoretical and methodological concerns which I have called paradigmatic—a term derived from the Greek word which refers to a pattern. The pattern for which these authors are looking has been largely decided in advance. These works, despite this common feature, tend to digress in specific ways.

Smith's book *Virgin Land,* for example, proceeds primarily as an encounter with American historiography, and more particularly with explicating Frederick Jackson Turner's view of the West in terms of the symbol of the garden, and America's westward expansion serving as the myth of the possibility of America. This work is content to unfold the historiography of the past and to show the world the place the American West played in it. Glassie's work, instead of taking large ideas, takes individual artifacts and unfolds his thesis on folk culture; he draws generalizations based on their structure, their form, their use, and so forth. William Ward's *Andrew Jackson* and Benjamin Franklin's *Autobiography* concentrate on single individuals, in order to demonstrate various qualities of the period in which each lived. McLoughlin in *Revivals* emphasizes a specific manifestation prominent in American life and history, namely Protestant "awakenings." And although he brings many disciplines to bear upon the study of the events collectively referred to as awakenings, this phenomenon constitutes at once the point of departure and the point of return for the entirety of his interpretation. The awakenings become not merely a sequence of events marshalled into a framework, which in turn exists within a larger

American society; rather they become the central informing feature of American history from its inception to the present.

What this means in reference to my interpretation of American Studies is, first of all, that both the identities and the differences among these works form a quintessential American pattern through which all American phenomena must be perceptible. If the experience of a people or a group—such as African American women—does not register on the calibrations set by these works, then the experience simply does not exist. If the experience does not exist, then it cannot be written about or admitted for serious consideration in any legitimate field of study. Those scholars who persist in tackling such forbidden areas of knowledge fail to meet tenure requirements because they have not published "rigorous" works (if indeed they have managed to find a publisher at all), and are cycled out of the academy. The fact that such scholars do not exist in large numbers is not, in the commonly-accepted reading of the situation, proof that they have been blocked by institutional hegemony. Instead, their failure to thrive in large numbers is allegedly *prima facie* evidence that paradigms they propose are skewed misrepresentations and misunderstandings of valid scholarship.

It is not, I must hasten to add, that scholars presently within the comfortable fold of the American Studies canon are engaged in some kind of massive, conscious conspiracy. There are many genuine, earnest and thoughtful works meritorious for their contributions to our overall understanding of what America is all about. Probably not one of the authors I have listed as examples has consciously sat down to write a treatise damning all Black women everywhere, for all times, to nameless oblivion. However, it is also true that when Black women are conjured into existence at all, their appearance is an afterthought, an uncomfortable wraith from a part of America circumscribed out of the author's main interest, a mechanical accident in the causality of America, an aberration rather than a well-reasoned and reasonable part of American patterns and structures.

If American Studies scholars do not all tacitly believe that they can have their cake and eat it too—perform theory and practice at once—then the exclusivity of our reading lists suggests that they have been constructed as omnipotent, omniscient monsters. The bald truth is that although they do carefully define methodologies and delimit their subjects and scopes, scholars write about what interests them personally. We all do, whether we admit such a naked lack of objectivity or not. Nor does such a revelation entail disability or lack of rigor; rather, it acknowledges that the free reign of quirks of human personality will continue to endow the field with richness and depth. A variety of writers will illumine various phenomena of American life which otherwise might have remained concealed. The one thing we must remember is that lists of writers accepted as pacesetters have been constructed through the interplay of departmental politics informed by racism, sexism and classism.

Inclusion of works not previously considered true to the American Studies approach requires a complete overhaul of the American Studies canon. In other words, instead of belaboring the same issues, and propagating the same myths, we as American scholars will have to reexamine our canons, and read works that have been previously ignored with an eye toward reparation and expansion of the canon.

A major problem facing American Studies as a discipline is that proponents of American Studies have not arrived at a common definition of what constitutes American Studies. I take my cue from the definition advanced by Malcolm Bradbury and Howard Temperley in *Introduction to American Studies;* they define American Studies as:

> a form of cultural studies in which the essential problems of analyzing the complex nature of a modern technetronic, ideologically plural, ethnically mixed, artistically vigorous society arise. And hence much of the best work done in it has not come from the application of a single meta-discipline, with clearly defined rules and resources, but from the efforts of individuals, variously trained, to obtain insights by relating aspects of various fields of study: history, sociology, cultural anthropology, social psychology, political science, law and institutions, economics, literary and artistic studies.[2]

This definition recognizes the eclecticism of American Studies, much like the eclecticism of America itself. So then, in pursuing this path of analysis, much of African American women's literature by its very nature is germane to this discipline. The development of African American culture had by necessity to be "eclectic"; it is a synthesis of African and Euro-American cultures, originating in the social constraints initiated by Whites during the enslavement of Blacks. Because of the particularities under which the syncretism we call African American culture has evolved, it has features which are discrete from mainstream Euro-American culture, yet at the same time are in part derived from that base. For example, as Houston Baker asserts, regarding the culture of African Americans:

> Black American culture is characterized by a collectivistic ethos;
> society is not viewed as a protective arena in which the individual
> can work out his own destiny and gain a share of America's benefits
> by his own efforts. To the black American these benefits are not
> attained solely by individual effort, but by changes in the nature of
> society and the social, economic, and political advancement of a
> whole race of people. . . .[3]

Both the Bradbury and Temperley excerpt and the Houston Baker
reference, it is worth pointing out, converge in their insistence that
American culture—whether the larger American culture or the African
American—are characterized as eclectic and interdisciplinary. Proceed-
ing from these points of agreement, a viable canon for the study of
both cultures side by side can be established.

Furthermore, although Americans may speak the same language,
dress the same, and are mass-educated to think and behave the same,
they are culturally different. Any discipline which would purport to
study America must be interdisciplinary, eclectic, and above all daring
in its ability to reconcile apparent polarities, contradictions, and conceptual oxymorons. Americans are a composite of involuntary and
voluntary immigrants—people of different colors, races, creeds, national origins, languages, and cultures from all over the world who
have refused to divest themselves of their cultural differences. This
assemblage of people living together in the same country, sharing
a common language, dress, and culture is commonly referred to as
America's "melting pot"; but it is the retention of individual group
customs that betray this image. This recognition prompted the late
Bayard Rustin to declare that, "There never was a melting pot, there
is not now a melting pot, there never will be a melting pot, and if there
was it would be such a tasteless soup that we would have to go back
and start all over."[4] It is also this mixture of people with diverse and
shared ethnic cultures however, that has contributed to the evolution
of what is quintessentially American.

Any concentration on the "self-made man" should include the stories
of Sarah (Madame C. J. Walker) Breedlove (1869–1919)—the first
American woman millionaire (White or Black) to get rich through her
successful business acumen—and Maggie Lena Walker (1867–1934)
(no relation)—the first African American woman to be president of a
bank—two exceptional stories of American History during the early
1900s. Religion has been and is the backbone of African American
culture, therefore it would be inconceivable to cover a course on reli-

gion in America and exclude the autobiographies of Jarena Lee (1836), Zilpha Elaw (1846), and Julia A. J. Foote (1879). Courses focusing on national missions, should include *Sojourner Truth: God's Faithful Pilgrim;* Ida B. Wells-Barnett's *Crusade for Justice: The Autobiography of Ida B. Wells-Barnett,* and *A Red Record: Tabulated Statistics and Alleged Causes of Lynchings in the United States, 1892–1893–1894;* Mary Church Terrell's *A Colored Woman in a White World; Mary McLeod Bethune;* and Shirley Chisholm's *Unbought and Unbossed;* and those highlighting folklore must include Zora Neale Hurston's *Mules and Men.* This list is meant to be inclusive and not exclusive.

American Studies as a discipline will continue to remain specious as long as these and other works—which are genuinely reflective of what has been delineated as American Studies objectives—are excluded from its course requirements. Yet, to date, American Studies professionals identify certain authors and works as stalwarts in the discipline, and proceed to teach these works as prescriptions for a holistic study of America, rather than as descriptions amenable to further exploration, elaboration and change. The prescriptive approach has proven to be a circuitous one; predictably it engenders little but stagnation, as researchers seem to have in advance a notion of what will satisfactorily constitute the construct or paradigm to be discovered, and then select texts in which to make their discoveries. This is perhaps the reason why almost every journal on American Studies includes at least one article raising the question of methodology in the field.

If we are to remain a vibrant, viable component of academia, we must continue to evolve just as America has. One way of doing this is to include at least a representative sampling of works by and about the majority of Americans in all introductory level American Studies courses. It is also equally urgent that we stimulate, support and reward scholarship, especially that performed by junior scholars, which does not merely tread the same ground, and regurgitate the same concepts, in an endless hall of mirrors.

The hall of mirrors is a closed system, which reproduces and authenticates its own legitimacy by drawing upon the same terms it seeks to prove. The canon of texts becomes tautological: texts are explained in the terms which they themselves have generated. Further, a hall of mirrors hermeneutic not only undermines its own empirical claims to epistemological integrity, but it also reproduces the infrastructure of imperialism. For as surely as the hall of mirrors creates the illusion of an authenticated "center"—the so-called "core" texts of American Studies—so too does it construct a colonized "not-center," which is either marginalized as "other" or completely expunged as unassimilable and alien. An additional consequence of such an imperialist infrastructure is that marginalized groups are pitted not against the center, but against each other: "divide and conquer." There is not enough (funding, food, power) to share around. As Toni Morrison has so eloquently written:

> Canon building is Empire building. Canon defense is national defense. Canon debated, whatever the terrain nature and range (of criticism, of history, of the history of knowledge, of the definition of language, the university of aesthetic principles, the sociology of art, the humanistic imagination), is the clash of cultures. And all of the interests are vested.[5]

It is important to note that American Studies must also include representations of all the "Americas"—North, South and Central—within its disciplinary boundaries, if it is to continue to use this broad title. This fact was brought home to me during an American Symposium colloquium of which, as a Fulbright Lecturer, I was an invited participant in Nairobi, Kenya, East Africa, in 1990.

Finally, it is not my intention to suggest that American Studies be the panacea for the enlightenment of the academy regarding African American Women's Studies. Nor do I wish to suggest that African American women (and by extension, African American Women's Studies) should bear the burden of broadening the field of American Studies. Either postulation would be erroneous and impossible. Black women for too long have been excluded, or attended to only marginally (which is sometimes worse, as a little knowledge can be a dangerous thing), in both African American Studies and Women's Studies units. African American Studies units tend to focus on Black men; Women's Studies units on White women. Both are slowly but surely mending their ways—at the same pace and for the same reasons that American Studies is finding it necessary to explore new possibilities: demands which are sometimes polite, and sometimes strenuous, but always urgent. Neither field has yet developed a fully articulated methodology or core of texts which embody the complexity of African American women's lives and experiences; but both contain key components which are mandatory to the construction of such a methodology.

It is my recommendation that American Studies include rigorous and scholarly examination of Black women and their experiences as subjects of study in existing course requirements, in order to stimulate new and fresh scholarship. Such inclusion will prompt, direct, and pique the interest of students and junior scholars who wish to specialize in Black women's studies, but who have not been able to find an academic "home" which will permit them to do so. Such an idea is neither profound nor original, since this is precisely how American Studies has functioned for literature, history, folklore and many other disciplines that were once "nontraditional." That is, American Studies from its inception has taken academia's "tired . . . poor . . . huddled masses yearning to breathe free" of the restraints of traditional scholarship in other disciplines.

More important than functioning as a logical base for specialized study, however, inclusion of Black women's studies will serve as a paradigm for the process of inclusionary scholarship. We have been, for nearly two decades, in the midst of what some have called a Second Renaissance; Black women's studies, in particular Black women's literature, has become visible enough that, if it does not always generate the kinds of scholarship we would wish, then it at least claims a modicum of guilty inclusion. In other words, we have reached a critical mass of both dedicated scholars, and politically motivated interest in Black women's studies. Another way of stating the matter is that the wheel which squeaks the loudest is starting to get the academic grease.

But if we as scholars are to make an honest assessment and establish an honest view of American Studies, then it is necessary to continue and extend examination of the works in the diaspora of American contributions made by *all* indigenous people in the melting pot. Anything less is scholarly dishonesty and will fuel the factions and forces fighting against each other for academic credentials and funding, in a pressure-cooker situation which will inevitably explode. The inclusion of works by African American women in the American Studies canon will not only restore an omitted history of one segment of the American population, but will illuminate the history of all Americans and the making of America in general.

Notes

1. John William G. McLoughlin, *Revivals, Awakening, and Reform: An Essay on Religion and Social Change in America, 1607–1977,* 8, 19.

2. Malcolm Bradbury and Howard Temperley, eds. "Introduction." *Introduction to American Studies* (New York: Longman, 1981), 16–17.

3. Houston A. Baker, Jr., "Completely Well: One View of Black American Culture,"

Key Issues in the Afro-American Experience, Nathan I. Huggins, Martin Kilson and Daniel M. Fox. Vol. 1 (New York: Harcourt Brace Jovanovich, Inc., 1971), 32.

4. Quoted in Harry A. Johnson, ed. "The Afro-American in the Melting Pot," *Ethnic American Minorities: A Guide to Media and Materials* (New York: R. R. Bowker Company, 1976), 1.

5. Toni Morrison. "Unspeakable Things Unspoken: The Afro-American Presence in American Literature," *Michigan Quarterly Review,* Winter 1989, Vol. 28, No. 1:8.

5

Teaching Comparative Social Order and Caribbean Social Change

Helán E. Page

Introduction

As a womanist African American anthropologist, I strive to help my students, who may or may not intend to pursue studies in advanced anthropology. My aim is to help them learn to analyze the social order and understand how it evolves. Each named aspect of my identity plays a crucial role in formulating the curricula I design, because in my identities are rooted my expectations about how my curricula should impact on my students cognitively, emotionally, and behaviorally.

From the start of my career, I found myself teaching at predominantly White institutions (PWIs). My mainstream European American students normally come to me with a narrow Eurocentric understanding of social order. Despite the best intentions of their previous educators, most students who take my classes are fundamentally unaware of how social order is constantly being constructed. At best, they have some understanding about how the mainstream or dominant view of social order is reproduced, but typically, they are ignorant about the implications of social difference. In fact, they only seek out perspectives on social difference either when they are required to do so or when they are eccentrically curious. Rarely do they realize that an understanding about difference is essential to their ability to function well in today's world, which is more explicitly multicultural than ever before.

When they first come to me, mainstream European American students are not normally able to recognize the role that Westerners have played, and continue to play, in perpetuating the global problems facing most people of color today. Nor do they easily realize how those problems—which they so often think are unique to people of color—

actually and consistently intersect with many of their own problems. Initially, most of these students proclaim and adhere to a view of the world that legitimates only a Eurocentric, Western viewpoint, but after the first few weeks in my course, they start to recognize its limitations, only because they are suddenly exposed to what the world looks like from the other side of the coin. If they are initially unfamiliar with how people of color view the world, they quickly start to learn how a preponderantly Western perspective has expurgated the viewpoints of people of color from the curricula to which they have been exposed before entering my class.

Whether they are White or not, most students who have been exposed only to mainstream curricular offerings before taking my courses admit to being blinded by an information gap, which makes them especially ignorant about people of African descent. Rarely do they realize how similar the African American experience is to that of other people of African descent elsewhere in the world. But I help them see how their recognition of this information gap is instructive. Their recognition that information about African people is missing shows them how the mainstream curriculum has deprived them of basic knowledge about the central roles played by people of African descent in the evolution of social order. To the extent that this information gap precludes their ability to grasp contemporary patterns of social change, I seek to close it.

To help my students get a better grasp of their changing world, I design the Caribbean course in a way that compels them to take a diasporan perspective, that is, to look at how African people experience the Western social order, on a comparative basis. I invite them to discover themselves by crossing over a perceptual threshold. Taking that step enables them to confront the relationships they share with African people in the diaspora that are situated in the intimate connections between gender, race, and class. By learning to use information about those relationships in their efforts to analyze the evolutionary history of Caribbean social change, my students acquire conceptual tools that can help them better comprehend the experiences of Africans in the Americas; and this, ultimately, helps them better comprehend themselves.

I was inspired to design my Caribbean course when I realized how apathetic mainstream Americans are about the plight of Africans in the Americas. That is why I start this essay by reminding you, dear reader, just how serious that plight is becoming. Next, I urge you to consider what it might mean to the mainstream, Western world if the vitality of African American cultural production continues to be choked off by restricted access to resources. Finally, I urge you to recognize that such a course is sorely needed, because Western conceptions of social order condition students to uncritically judge patterns of African American adaptation as being inherently pathological. For this reason, most students do not see such behavioral patterns as African American efforts to rationally respond to the structural violence that is so characteristic of their experience of the Western social order. The Caribbean course resolves this problem by emphasizing the processes of coerced and voluntary migration which have forged intimate connections between African American and African Caribbean peoples.

An awareness of how social order evolves can help any student find explanations for things that might otherwise seem inexplicable. For example, I do not consider it strange that African American women are resorting to female-headed households, but most Americans do. Nor do I consider it strange that most Americans think like this. After all, most have never visited places outside the United States in any capacity other than tourist, or read much about such places; thus, they are generally unable to grasp an anthropological view of the African American situation, mainly because they are unable to contextualize the choices that African American women are making. Therefore, most Americans cannot see that African American women are perceptive and are responding to what they perceive. That is, whether they do so consciously or not, African American women seem to be reorganizing their households in order to make them more resilient under growing social pressures that are linked directly to the consumption and production habits of the Western world. What is interesting is that African Caribbean women have always responded the same way to structural violence, so the implication of this parallel is clear. Even though African Americans and African Caribbeans certainly have sufficiently distinct histories, the similarities of their otherwise unique experience reflect similar pressures and similar adaptive strategies.

In this chapter, I show how my Caribbean curriculum connects the experiences of Africans in the Caribbean and Africans in the United States. Furthermore, I discuss how my students respond to this curriculum, emphasizing how they are influenced by the recognition of such connections. Thus, readers will see that my course is a strategy that makes space for the analytical perspective of a womanist, African American anthropologist. It elegantly opens up the narrow straits of mainstream awareness with conceptual precision in order to make global politics personal—for my students and myself—in the largely conservative, intellectual arena of the academy.

Mainstream Disconcern and the African American Plight

In an anthropology course, where mainstream European American students at PWIs normally prefer to learn about African Americans, information about the racist nature of the social order can be more easily communicated in courses about the Caribbean. Not only do European American students find Caribbean people more interesting, perhaps because they seem more exotic, but the same students also want to believe that casting their gaze on the Caribbean as opposed to the United States makes it easier for them to keep themselves out of the analytical picture.

However, by taking my course, which focuses on the experiences of Africans tied to the evolution of Caribbean social order, students are compelled to closely examine the nature and mechanisms of social oppression in its international dimensions. In addition to learning that the long existence of racial oppression in the United States cannot be extricated from Caribbean history, which cannot be extricated from the history of African and European contact on the African continent, students also learn that racial oppression cannot be extricated from the issues of gender and class oppression. By helping them see the interlocking development of gender, race, and class oppression in the Caribbean context, it becomes easier for them to see how that analytical picture mirrors or reflects their own United States experience. When they notice their own image in that mirror, most students are then ready to ask questions about the African American experience. At that point, I can reveal the link between the apathy and the defensiveness they often assume and their insulated sense of safety. Such a discussion is necessary if we want our students to recognize that apathy cannot extend the safety they seem to need.

Apathy in Defense of Safety

When my students get defensive in response to the new information I present, they often have trouble saying why. It takes a while for them to see that they are defending an artificial sense of safety by trying to remain apathetic. Because they are conditioned to see the new information as a threat to their apathy, they come to my course not having realized that apathy is really the greatest threat to their safety, and that apathy thrives on ignorance. They believe that if they can remain ignorant of how social issues are rooted in the processes that govern social order, then no change in their behavior, as individuals, is required.

Thus, my students typically behave in a way which confirms Haki Madhubuti's assertion that mainstream America has no vested interest in diligently searching for solutions to central-city problems. My students are surprised to learn that recent national opinion polls categorize them as mainstream young Americans of voting age who could really care less about social problems, as long as they are made to feel relatively safe. As one of those reports explains:

> the indifference of the new generation—to politics, to government, even to news about the outside world—is beginning to affect U.S. politics and society, helping to explain such seemingly disparate trends as the decline in voting, the rise of tabloid television and the effectiveness of negative advertising.[1]

My students often don't see the connection. They have trouble seeing that each of them either is already or soon will be a mainstream consumer, seeking to have his or her attention distracted so as not to notice, or feel responsible, for chronic social problems or evidence of acute social injustice. When problems directly concern the well-being of African American communities, the diversion of attention that is needed to feel safe works well for some of my European American students. This is especially true for those who have been encouraged to identify faulty African American cultural production as the real problem.

In other words, many of my students bring to the classroom a mainstream American attitude which presumes that the root of African American social problems lies not in the faults of the social order which privileges Whites over non-White others, but in the inept cultural production of African Americans. Katz concurs with this conception of the mainstream attitude, arguing that it helps mainstream Americans feel safer by suggesting that, for all its menace,

> the underclass was a comforting discovery. . . . Its prominence not only refocused attention on [African American] culture and behavior, [but] deflected it away from the more intractable, growing, and

potentially subversive problems of the working poor: increasing income inequity and the bifurcation of America's social structure.[2]

Katz is suggesting that mainstream America's discovery of the underclass made it possible for them to blame African Americans for their own lack of success, American style, but laying blame on African Americans is only an escape. It relieves European Americans of the obligation of having to pay attention to growing class stratification in the United States, and our highly exaggerated disparities in income.

Unfortunately, my students also learn that apathetic disinterest is not restricted to the European American mainstream. Strong kinship ties once imbued African America's traditionally well-organized, upwardly mobile households with a felt sense of obligation that compelled them to work at improving central-city ghetto life during the 1960s, but those bonds are rapidly disintegrating today. In their absence, a breakdown in communication has occurred between African Americans who have learned how to "make it" and those who have not.

Even African American critics of the central-city ghetto often engage in victim-blaming. But, whether Black or White, few seem to realize that members of the ghetto culture of the 1960s had a very good chance of excelling, but were undermined, not only by economic decline, but by structural impediments, disintegrative social policies, and the state-induced annihilation of many who had been leaders of social movements. The loss of leadership has proved a fatal blow, mainly because it represents the loss of role models. The upward mobility of the African American middle class is not specifically to blame, however; their apathy is legitimated by the larger society's apathy. Their lack of solutions is a measure of the larger society's refusal to invest in problem-solving modes of government intervention.

The decision to revive African American central-city culture by improving the conditions of ghetto life is not taken seriously. Instead, some advocate that African Americans abandon the ghetto mode of African American cultural production, as if it were nonviable, irretrievable, or irreparable.[3] Instead of fighting for those central-city communities, some argue that African Americans should be trying to succeed, like other immigrants, ignoring findings (e.g., Mullins 1978), which prove how differently access to resources has been structured for most African Americans (coerced immigrants) and those whose migration was voluntary ("genuine" immigrants).

Lehman is one critic who legitimates mainstream apathy by concluding that ghetto culture is its own worst problem. He is one thinker who expects upwardly mobile African Americans to reject the ghetto mode of cultural production and escape central-city spaces. To facilitate their escape, he advises mainstream Americans to give up their apathy, to support policies that ignore African American wishes and push them out of the central-city. He does not encourage mainstream ideologies to challenge their apathy by seeking any truth other than his own.

Lehman's thinking on the inviability of central-city African American cultural production ignores the fact that mainstream factions in the Western world will defend their sense of safety. They do this most often by retreating to an apathetic position where their confusion about the action necessary often becomes their excuse for habitual inaction, which accommodating African Americans often pretend not to notice.

Restricted Access Equals Choked-off Vitality

African American apathy is rooted more in a sense of powerlessness than simply in disinterest. Middle-class African Americans remember, and students should know, that the African American masses wanted jobs that did not exist for them in the 1960s, and never materialized. Students should also know that by 1980, a twenty-year history of restricted resource access choked off whatever mainstream vitality could be mustered up by African American cultural production.

The situation in 1980 was one in which 60 percent of all central-city African Americans had become 30 percent of all America's poor, and there were proportionately three poor Blacks for every poor White in America.[4] This downward trend is due largely to the fact that antipoverty programs of the 1960s were designed to quell civil unrest, promote welfare dependency, and offer job preparation opportunities, but they were not designed to create jobs for the African American masses.[5] As early as the late 1970s, mainstream-sanctioned "antipoverty" activities were supported by the federal government, but these may as well have been read as "no-job" programs. It's not that the creation of jobs was impossible; it's that mainstream society never saw jobs for African American masses as an answer to the unrest of the 1960s and 1970s. Consequently, the legitimacy of the social order prevailed over the demands being made during that era.[6]

Furthermore, the rules of the upward mobility game changed. Access to decent jobs and other opportunities began to require even more education; and even more African Americans workers were dislocated, due to a number of factors: lost manufacturing jobs; the new proliferation of poverty-wage jobs in industrial and service occupations; demographic changes in city centers (which became mainly non-White territory due to White flight); and the growing inaccessibility of affordable housing near jobs.

"With traditional structures crumbling and mobility blocked, urban adolescents turned increasingly to crime, conflict, and drugs."[6] Household residence patterns shifted, with young adults living apart from parents, and with the aged living less frequently with relatives, while children were raised in female-headed households.[7] Because of this decline in the quality of central-city life, and because new urban and suburban space opened to them, the propertied Black middle class fled central-city communities as soon as open housing made it possible for them to do so, creating a vacuum where their skill, experience, and success were lost as a local resource.

Meanwhile, most central-city residents remained propertyless, and many of them followed the Black middle class into nicer residential areas, normally occupying rental housing considered too run down to rent to anyone else. Unfortunately, the unsteady employment of poorer African Americans made it difficult for them to maintain the properties they rented; and this, in turn, led to their frustration and the rapid decline of upwardly mobile, Black, central-city neighborhoods.

The subsequent emergence and prominence of female-headed households followed the mass exodus of middle-class African Americans, but this radical departure from an ideal two-parent family model exemplifies neither a peculiar African American quirk nor a feminist preference. Instead, it points to the impact of impoverishment and stress that consumed central-city environments as teenage mothers and jobless youth inherited postindustrial urban spaces in the eighties and nineties.[8] Consciously or not, many African American women are compelled to select a pattern of household organizations that works best, given their situation, even though it seems detrimental from a middle-class viewpoint. Thus, the ideal constant residency of men in urban African American households has been called into question due to the impact of our distressful social order. That distress is quite evident in the constantly declining number of Black men in African American communities; and it is just as evident in African Caribbean communities. Except in the case of cargo cults, anthropologists avoid explaining cultural production as a response to a distressful social order, but African cultural production in the Western hemisphere can be explained in no other way. The evidence of distressful social order is locked in the historic process and can only be retrieved by looking at how a new society evolves. The Caribbean case is ideal for this kind of focused examination.

Historical Process and Societal Distress

Much of African America's cultural production is a conditioned response to social distress. Could it be that the cultural production of Africans in the Caribbean follows similar patterns and that apathy aims to protect mainstream safety in the Caribbean just as it does in the United States? Could it be that the restricted access to resources has the same effect on African cultural production in the Caribbean as it does in the United States? Would greater awareness of the intimate connection between African American and African Caribbean culture and more emphasis on the unity of African diasporic culture inspire new modes of resistance throughout the Western hemisphere? The response of my students to this course suggests a resounding "yes".

Similar African Responses to the Western Social Order

The central-city problems so characteristic of African American urban communities are no different than the problems that can be observed in Kingston, Port-au-Prince, or Georgetown. Whether in the Caribbean or in the United States, Africans have had to make the transition out of slavery, to move from agrarian economies and into new ones based on consumerism and wage labor. While that three-pronged process is nearly complete in the United States, it is still happening in the Caribbean, but that does not mean that Africans in the United States are more advanced. In fact, it only means that Africans in the United States were subjected to the forces of de-agrarianization and proletarianization much easier than those in the Caribbean. It may also mean that being subjected to such forces later may enable Africans in the Caribbean to retain more of the agrarian root values, which could help them develop more adaptive responses that could bring about different outcomes in the future. For now, in each place, the details of that transition differ, but the main trends and outcomes are not so different.

As in the United States, middle- and upper-class Caribbean people are those with the most educational and resource access. Darker-skinned "underclasses" in the Caribbean and in the United States are similar in having relatively less access to education and other necessary resources, like adequate food and housing. While access to education is often seen as the most appropriate way to overcome restricted resource access, the Western model of education brings to the illiterate its own set of problems that tend to inhibit the adaptation of most underclass people in the Western hemisphere, mainly helping an upwardly mobile few. Indeed, educational success has often alienated many Africans from their communities and made them willing puppets of European elites.

In the same way that educated Americans tend to blame uneducated African Americans for failing to succeed, uneducated Africans are similarly blamed by educated classes in the Caribbean. In the Caribbean, as in the United States, the ghetto culture is not seen as an indicator of a distressful social order that must be reorganized, but as a failure among Africans in the Caribbean to adapt to modern urban life. There, as here, it is assumed that the successful African Caribbean will assimilate the values of White society and will act in the long-term interests of the dominant society as much as possible.

As in the United States, the absence of jobs in the Caribbean brings about social decay; but the availability of jobs also brings about the same endemic kinds of consumerism that exist in the United States. In both cases, heretofore unsuccessful Africans may chase the jobs that promise wages, or successful ones may chase the Western goods that wages can buy. In neither case are Africans learning to forego that chase in order to pursue the degree of self-sufficiency that made so many of them free after slavery.

I try to help my students detect African Caribbean cultural adaptations and to explain how they are responses to a distressful social order. To do that, my students learn that a racist social order uses the issue of race to rationalize gender and class discrimination. They learn to recognize how racism, and African Caribbean responses to it, are rooted in a global pattern of economic insecurity, and in legitimate fears about how well people of African descent might be able to compete with people of European descent in highly competitive Western worlds. In our class, we don't accept the inevitability of a competitive social order either; in fact, we demonstrate the possibility of one in which competition is severely decreased and reorganized into more cooperative forms where it does occur.

Conceptual Change and Curricular Design

Because mainstream students are normally frightened of me on the first day of the course simply because they feel uncomfortable with my difference, my first goal is to make them feel safe. I accomplish this by trying to relieve grade pressure and decrease their fears about how I might use my power to grade them in order to punish them for disagreeing with my point of view. In part, I overcome this by assuring them that they are free to express oppositional opinions. That is, I invite their debate and do not expect them to agree with me. Likewise, I expect them to defend whatever positions they take by using data and theory to back up their arguments.

But another part is how I minimize grade pressure in this course by disregarding the mainstream canon on grading. I stress their ability to think critically and I want them to demonstrate it in writing and also in classroom debates or discussions. Their primary grades are the exam and the final paper, but they can also earn credit by working in class with others in a team that will present a topic, and they can involve themselves completely in classroom work. If the exam and paper are 70 percent of their grades, it does not leave them very much more room for safety. That is why I intentionally added an additional 10 percent to their grades. Those who participate most constructively in class are therefore able to cushion their grades, making the student feel safer while allowing me to critique their essay exams and their research just as rigorously as their fellow students critique their in-class participation and presentations.

The first topic discussed is the social construction and psychology of oppression. Under that topic, we discuss the origins of Caribbean colonization as an aftermath of the Spanish Reconquista, a reaction to the Moorish domination of Spain. The aim is to identify assumptions about the Western social order that are transferred to the Caribbean initially and how those assumptions become a template for future development. Just as slavery was part of the Moorish social order, it is transplanted and reinterpreted in the Caribbean, although the Christian version of slavery is much more dehumanizing than the Islamic version was.

I also introduce the conceptual format under the topic, encouraging students to think about the Caribbean social order as the evolution of a slave society which is similar to the same process of evolution in the United States. Thus, they are compelled to understand how the emergent social order is designed to oppress in order to subjugate and dominate. To understand the psychology of oppression and its dual impact on the oppressor and the oppressed, we consider the works of Mannoni, Fanon and Bulhan. I urge the students to always keep in mind the intricate connection between emotion, cognition, and behavior, and I encourage them to think of Caribbean culture reproduction as a process which makes most people forget what they are really capable of accomplishing, so as to keep them subordinated. In our class, we define the subsequent struggles for liberation as efforts to overcome the constraints imposed by the pseudo-reality (consisting of "oughts" and "ought-nots" instead of "cans" and "wills"), that pose as reality itself.

The main theme of the next topic is to establish the African viewpoint as our primary point of reference for looking at scholarly discourse about Caribbean social order, but we don't look only at Africans or what African Caribbean scholars have to say. Rather, we try to understand how Africans fit relationally into the social order and how African and European scholars approach the topic from different disciplinary angles. We concentrate on how the relations of African to other groups affect their modes of adaptation.

We are particularly interested in the role of religious ideology, comparing its role in the Caribbean to the role it plays in African American communities. The primary point of comparison is not just the ideological structures of religious belief and practices, but the actual organization of religion as a mode of ideological production that parallels material modes of production. The students are encouraged to think about how ideological change accompanies or influences changes in the mode of material production. They should be able to identify which forces operate to bring those changes about.

In the third topic, we discuss the economic development of the Caribbean. In particular, we examine the idea that Europeans rationalized colonization by their perceived need to "follow the sun." The implications of that are rooted in their need for food and in the consumer markets fed by Caribbean agricultural exports. I try to help students recognize that Western approaches to this problem of how to organize modes of production have varied historically, ranging on the European side from freebooters, to buccaneers, to piracy, to the reign of "King Sugar," and to the subsequent rise of industrial multinationals, some of which were initially agrarian based; and ranging on the African side from slavery, to runaway maroons, to common-land peasants, to freehold peasants, and to paid agrarian labor.

Students are shocked to learn about the oppression of the European working class who either benefitted from African oppression or participated in it in other ways. They were especially shocked by how the working class of Europe was intentionally made addicted to sugar in order for the elite to increase their profits from the production of sugar and other commodities being imported from the Caribbean, and produced there on the backs of African Caribbean and other laborers. They are further shocked to see more contemporary versions of that same adaptive pattern in the use of audiovisual imagery to sell overseas production and consumption through the image of a Carmen Miranda or through the cultivated consumer desire for blue jeans.

Next, we look at the political development of the Caribbean, focussing on *The Black Jacobins,* by C. L. R. James. In those discussions, students are asked to analyze the relations of production that were characteristic of the slave society, and to contemplate the ensuing changes in how people experienced that social order emotionally, cognitively, and how they responded behaviorally. Students come to better understand the notion of class stratification, and they see how it relates to ownership, legislative control, and revolt. It is especially useful for students to see that change in the Caribbean is intimately connected to change overseas, as in Europe, where C. L. R. James explains how the revolt of Paris Masses is linked to the Haitian revolt.[9]

It is also useful for students to critically assess the role of Toussaint L'Ouverture, not only in his heroic aspect, but also in his human aspect. We try to understand how his position in slave society conditioned him emotionally, cognitively, and behaviorally, as depicted by James. We are critical of James too, and base our critique on his position in the Caribbean social order, so that students see that the same analysis that can be applied to Toussaint L'Ouverture also must be applied to James. No position is privileged. Moreover, their position in the social order links up the greater access of men over women with the greater access of Whites and mulattos and the greater access of rich over poor. The complexities of social change are opened up to the students, who begin to contemplate such intricacies and to see similarities in their own experiences in the United States. In connection with this, students are asked to consider how they are oppressed as White people of a particular ethnic background, gender or class in the United States.

The Caribbean family and society is the next topic of concern. Here we look at how religious ideology and African practices sustain cultural production among Africans who remained self-sufficient after some time. We consider the implications of Miller's "Gender and Low-Income Household Expenditures in Jamaica" in order to get an idea of how gender is related to class, but the major piece here is *Masters of the Dew,* by Jacques Roumain. By reading this novel by Roumain, students can learn something about the role he played in Haitian cultural production. Roumain accomplishes this by trying to rectify the image of the Caribbean peasant in his interpretations of the Haitian peasantry.

Students are impressed to learn that Roumain studied anthropology and established an ethnological society in Haiti in order to document and preserve Haitian culture. They are also frightened to learn that he belonged to the Communist Party and was exiled from Haiti for many years. Some of them are suspicious of his motives and assume he is attempting propaganda about the virtues of socialism, until we map on the board how he was really suffering from his own elite position in the social order. We see Roumain as a mulatto with conscience, a man searching for his roots, and we learn that he is really only comparing individualistic wage seekers with collective agrarian life in order to remind the peasantry of its potential to determine its own destiny. We learn from his depiction about the central Caribbean conflict: that is, the heroic struggle for self-sufficiency versus what seems like the inevitable dependency on wage labor. Students learn in this novel about the notion of internalized oppression and they see it expressed equally in the novelist, in the protagonist, and in the antagonist, who each have a different vision of what Haiti and the Caribbean should become.

Next, we read Michelle Cliff's *No Telephone to Heaven*. Ironically, the same themes are reiterated in a novel about contemporary Jamaica. Students see the same contestation between the successful and the unsuccessful, between the Whites and Browns and Blacks, between the individualists and the collectively oriented. Also, for the first time, we tackle the question of gender head on, recognizing that Cliff is suggesting that gender somehow gets distorted by relations of racial and class dominance. In the novel, the failure to rebel is attributed to impotence, and the impulse to rebel or to do whatever is needed is invested in women, or in a transsexual who assumes the role of such a woman, when no other woman is available for the job. Similarly, this novel also makes it possible for students to concretely observe the intimacy between Africans in the Caribbean and Africans in the United States. The central Jamaican characters belong to a family with both experiences across the generations. The inculcation of internalized oppression in Jamaica results in similar adaptive responses in other locations. Regardless of location, Cliff insists that people of African descent are compelled to struggle to regain their sense of identity and their capacity to bond with other Africans that their experience of structural violence in Western worlds has decimated.

Finally, we think about contemporary pressures that impinge on family life, by my reading of Faye Harrison's *Three Women, One Struggle: Anthropology, Performance, and Pedagogy* and by viewing the film *Voyage of Dreams,* which depicts the plight of Haitian boat people whose family life is completely destroyed by their flight from oppression and poverty. In each case, we see that African women are insightfully aware of the nature of their plight, and are beginning to explicate the connections between Caribbean society and the United States in ways that have never been so obvious before. We also see that Caribbean people are becoming very angry, no matter how quaint they have seemed to so many students in the past. We also see that the anger is no different from the anger that led to the rise of the Black Power movement in the States after the frustrating disappointments of the Civil Rights Movement. In the same way that the Black Power movement was put down by the assassination or imprisonment of its leaders, we see the same efforts to suppress Caribbean leaders with similar goals, such as Maurice Bishop of Grenada and his New Jewel Movement.

Next, we return to the notion of religious ideology, and try to situate it more contemporaneously in the context of modern capitalist penetration. We see how labor today still draws from the central conflict between the beliefs of the oppressors and the beliefs of the oppressed to forge liberation ideologies that often end up in liberation movements. In the next topic, the goal is to establish a connection between ideologies and the role of language socialization and education. We look at Fisher's *Colonial Madness* as a way of trying to understand how obsessed some Caribbean people become with either fitting in or opting out of the White world. The normal person is believed to straddle the fence; but abnormal people will either suffer from studiation which is believed to lead to madness, or will actually become mad. In either case, the normal people believe that such people have lost their balance by failing to fit in with established norms that define a community that does not strive for change, but stasis.

In my lecture on Brackette Williams' chapter from a new manuscript called *War in my Veins; Stains on my Name,* I look at the same problem. Notions of upward mobility get conflated about notions of ethnicity and the presumed right that some groups have to greater access over others. Williams depicts how different groups strategize by using ethnic markers either to promote themselves or to denounce others who promote themselves too well. In another lecture, I explain how Williams describes the use of humor and linguistic ambiguity in community-based Guyanese disputes where ethnicity and class are often invoked. From a theoretical perspective, I have the students consider the efforts made to legitimate the language use of Third World people, and I have them note how important their indigenous theoretical point of view is to our analysis. Postcolonial writing is proposed as a good way to gain an understanding of colonialism and its impact then and today.

The migration issue emerges as a potential topic when we read *Masters of the Dew,* because Roumain depicts the early migration of Haitian peasants in search of wage labor to the Dominican Republic, where they are currently suffering impoverishment. *People on the Move,* by du Toit, gives us a theoretical and empirical understanding of the migration problem, and we see how it connects intimately with Caribbean women and family life in the essay by Enlow called *Just like One of the Family.* To bring home the point, I play for the students a song by Mutabaruka called "H2 Werka." Even if they do not initially understand the theoretical and empirical literature, this song clarifies the theoretical issues, and makes it possible for the student to connect abstractions to the concrete experiences described by the singer. The exploitation of the classified migrant Caribbean worker in the United States is an unavoidable conclusion. Students often have personal experiences either in Jamaica or in the U.S. that verify this conclusion.

The next topic concerns our consideration of the Caribbean Basin Initiative. Following the advice of colleague Franz, who collaborated with me on the design of this course, I ask the students if it would be better to think of it as the Caribbean Basic Initiation. The question is whether the politics of the initiative were meant to inculcate dependency or self-reliance? I invite to speak another colleague, Carlene Edie, who is well-versed in Caribbean political science. After presenting a series of case studies, the students are asked to consider Dr. Edie's propositions about how the initiative actually works and to assess her assumptions that efforts are made by the internationalist elite to keep it operating that way. In conjunction, we view the film *Manos a la Obra: The Story of Operation Bootstrap,* and students see for themselves that much of what Edie has to say has relevance. Inevitably, they ask about the relation between U.S. foreign policy and U.S. domestic policy; they question why Jesse Jackson was so forcibly rebuked for proposing a new foreign policy for the Caribbean during his presidential campaign; and they wonder if a high standard of living can be maintained in the States and engendered in the Caribbean, without continued exploitation.

Has crisis become a way of life for African Caribbean society as it has for so many African Americans in the U.S.? No answer is offered to that question, but it is discussed in the context of how Caribbean people are positioned to constantly react to crises that they do not seem positioned to avoid. By means of Zalkin's *National and International*

Determinants of Food Consumption in Revolutionary Nicaragua, we look at recent changes in food consumption at the local level that are intimately linked to the international economy. Students realize that if they are just beginning to recognize such linkages, then it would be hard for African Caribbean people, who have much less access to information and resources, to recognize and rectify them.

Using Cuba and Grenada as case studies where women have played central roles, we turn our attention to what alternative models of development have been attempted. In addition to discussing how and why the alternative movements in Cuba and Grenada were mounted, and what the outcomes have been, we also look at what Ellis has to say about how the media portrays or depicts a certain role for women in the development process. On the one hand, we see that the hope for alternative change probably lies in the dreams and aspirations of women, but on the other hand, we see that women, and their hopes and dreams, may be interpreted by higher powers that enable those already in power to co-opt any potential they might bring to an opposi-tional movement. The suppressed role of women in the Civil Rights and Black Power movements is the obvious comparison, and students are asked to think of other ways that images of African women's development can be communicated in the media.

I urge the students to think about what a fresh approach to interna-tional politics might do for the Caribbean. In this discussion we con-sider the link between consumerism, capitalist production and the quest for nationalism. In the article by Peggy Antrobus, "New Institu-tions and Programs for Caribbean Women," we both see the adverse impact of development that disregards the needs of women, while also contemplating how a more comprehensive development program must include women's needs. We also see, in the piece called, *Who Will Control the Blue Revolution? Economic and Social Feasibility of Carib-bean Crab Mariculture,* by Rubino and Stoffle, that it is very important to consider how communities will respond to the plans for national development, and that such plans work best when communities can be assured of their feasibility. The advantages of disengaging from development that requires dependency on Western powers is reviewed in the film called *Grenada: The Future Coming Toward Us.* That film deals with how the New Jewel Movement used popular education at worksites as a way of helping workers understand their role in redirect-ing the flow of their labor energy away from overseas markets, while keeping that energy circulating in the Caribbean. That kind of informa-tion helped workers understand the value of developing their own food processing industries, rather than having food exported overseas and then sold back to Grenadians at import cost as processed food commodities that profited Westerners more than anyone involved in the process on the Grenadian end of the process.

Making Politics Personal in the Academy

At every part of this rather unusual curricular approach it is possible to help students recognize how gender, race, and class interests correlate with relations of domination and oppression. Students see how gender relations often get hidden in certain historical periods and rise to the forefront in other historical moments. They can see how class relations and gender can make a critical difference in the way that the Caribbean social order is presented by Caribbean scholars, and they come to understand why more substantive connections are not normally made between the colonial United States and colonial Caribbean. They come to see that they share, as people of European descent, in White privilege that was constructed in the colonial context, and they see how the efforts of Blacks and lower-class Whites to unify have always been disrupted by the interjection of racial rhetoric by the White and Brown people in power, who have much to lose by lower-class unification.

The class is revolutionary in the sense that students learn to recognize internalized oppression. They come to realize that subjugation requires a degree of consent, and that the internalization of oppression manufactures this consent, which hegemonically legitimates the relations of domination. They see that the internalization of oppression relegates White people to inaction just as it does Black people, and they learn that internalized oppression must be studied more and overcome before the relations of domination that sustain oppression are undone.

Students also learn to see the classroom as a battleground, where ideas that would sustain relations of domination are deconstructed, so as to liberate the potential for more creative thought that would bring about more humane relations of production in the social order. The premise is that a kinder social order is possible that does not necessarily require the rich to abdicate their all, but does require some restrictions on their normally untrammelled quest for profit. The course also shows how women of color are most inclined to pursue alternative modes of social order, because it is they who suffer most at the bottom of the social order. At the same time, students come to realize that really insightful leadership is often undermined by the pettiness that internalized oppression often invokes, or that such leaders may also be bribed or assassinated. In other words, students learn that change is not haphazard, but most often requires insight into social order and the courage to take great risks.

Notes

1. The two studies were conducted by a research and lobby organization called People for the American Way and by The Times Mirror Center for the People. Based on these two reports, people under thirty were characterized by Michael Oreske in the *International Herald Tribune* (June 29, 1990) as being indifferent, self-concerned, disengaged, and informed through cultural sources, like concerts and popularly designed local news programs, rather than through traditional news sources. Participants in the Times Mirror report talked incessantly about their own stress and cited the weakness of their political education. Consequently, young adults report a desire to avoid bad news. The Times Mirror survey director, Mr. Kohut, explained that because "those under 30 are separated by their lack of knowledge and interest from those over the age of 30" there is a tendency for the electorate to rely more on popular sources of information.

2. M. Katz, *The Undeserving Poor: From the War on Poverty to the War on Welfare* (New York: Pantheon Books, 1989), 196.

3. It has been argued that: ". . . the distinctive culture [of ghettos] is now the greatest barrier to progress by the black underclass, rather than either unemployment or welfare. . . . The negative power of the ghetto culture all but guarantees that any attempt to solve the problems of the underclass in the ghettos won't work—the culture is too strong by now. Any solution that does work, whatever it does about welfare and unemployment, will also have to get people physically away from the ghettos" N. Lehman, "The Origins of the Underclass," *Atlantic Monthly* (June 1986): 36.

4. Michael R. Greenberg, "Black Male Cancer and American Urban Health Policy," *Journal of Urban Affairs*, 11 (2): 127n.

5. Katz.

6. In response to the demands of the 1960s, America began to deemphasize the importance of possessing or controlling material wealth as a guarantee of mainstream legitimacy, while more insistently marginalizing the African American masses, and other resource-poor Americans, by emphasizing symbolic nonmaterial wealth, in the form of income, benefits, jobs, occupational licenses, franchises, contracts, subsidies, use of public resources, and services (Katz: 108). Taking advantage of these newly emphasized opportunities required incredible access to information, either through education or by purchasing the time of people who were thus informed. The right to obtain and make use of these informational opportunities were thus cordoned off on behalf of the highly educated middle class who would acquire the necessary credentials more easily than any underclass group.

7. Katz, 97.

8. *Ibid.,* 129–132. W. J. Wilson and L. J. D. Waquant, "The Cost of Racial and Class Exclusion in the Inner City," *Annals of the American Academy of Political and Social Sciences,* Vol. 501: 8–25; M. Dear and J. Wolch, "How Territory Shapes Social Life," in Dear and Wolch (eds.) *The Power of Geography* (London: Unwin Hyman, 1989); E. W. Soja, "The Socio-spatial Dialectic," in *Postmodern Geographies: The Reassertion of Space,* in Critical Social Theory (New York: Verso, 1989), 76–93.

9. C. L. R. James, *The Black Jacobins: Toussaint L'Ouverture and the San Domingo Revolution* (New York: Vintage Books, 1963), 118–144.

6

Making Room For Emancipatory Research In Psychology: A Multicultural Feminist Perspective

Kim Vaz

Multiculturalism in Psychology

Who am I in academe and what do I do? I teach a course called the (a?) psychology of women and I am not considered a psychologist. Having conducted research in Africa is enough for some academicians to label me an anthropologist. Having received a doctorate in educational psychology from a school of education makes me suspect to others. Still, filling a multicultural position in a Women's Studies program makes me an ill-specified being, that is, a colorist. I am committed to carrying out research on disenfranchised populations. I use techniques that aim to report their conditions from their perspectives, based on the premise that people should participate in finding solutions to their own problems. This makes my research "political." My reliance on qualitative data analysis makes it nonscientific. And my reluctance to use extant models that do not take into consideration sociohistorical contexts, and indigenous explanations of behavioral and emotional phenomena, renders it atheoretical. This is almost an existential crisis.

I am intrigued by the number of African American women who drop out of psychology because they can not "understand" it. Surely it is difficult to find one's reflection in the stilted writing and analyses that social science offers. Coupled with the largely pathological approach to the study of people of color, as a student, an African American woman may be left wondering about the relevance of psychology for her life. It has only been through a great deal of self-study of Black women novelists and literary critics that I have begun to think about a canon in psychology that puts women of color in the foreground in a nonpathological sense. To do so, I also have looked outside the narrow confines of the discipline, first stopping on the margins, and then on to other disciplines whose research methodologies hold great promise for changing the lives of women of color. I look to the contemporary movements in psychology, namely social constructionism and hermeneutics. In the social sciences more generally I have become acquainted with the African-based participatory research project and sociological grounded theory. Multicultural feminism has assisted me in finding meaning and relevance for the psychological study of the lives of women of color.

When I began the search for relevance in psychology, Gloria Hull, Patricia Bell Scott, and Barbara Smith's anthology, *All The Women Are White, All The Blacks are Men, But Some Of Us Are Brave,*[1] made its much needed appearance. African American women's issues were put up to view. The gauntlet that had been thrown down by our foremothers demonstrating their resistance was reaffirmed and extended in that volume. Because of their commitment to making "primary the knowledge that will save Black women's lives" I developed a sense of where I needed to be moving in my intellectual quest for understanding our problems and achievements.

As orientations, social constructionism, qualitative and emancipatory research, and Third World feminism intermingle for me. They represent a special attitude toward how knowledge is derived and used, and have begun to form the bases of my contemporary epistemological position. Each is discussed in turn below and is followed by some of my goals in changing students' perspectives on the definition of psychology, research strategies, and the use of research findings with respect to the psychology of women.

My discussion of the place of culture in psychology is two-pronged. First, there is the issue of psychological research as it is carried out in Third World countries. Secondly, the impact of an investigator's "values" on her or his epistemological position has created in psychology various theoretical orientations[2] or cultures[3] that influence one's research problem selection, methodology, and interpretation of results.[4] Let us briefly turn to psychology outside the United States.

I have a definite interest in the concerns of Third World psychology. I conduct research in southwestern Nigeria. I seek a variety of indigenously developed, interpretative frameworks that would be most relevant to explaining the conditions of my research participants. Third World countries import psychological theories and methods from the United States for reasons almost purely related to economics.[5] F. M.

Moghaddam suggests that indigenous psychologies would expand the field of psychology in general, through redefinition of constructs, such as individualism and collectivism.[6] Whereas these are viewed as opposite tendencies in the West, in developing countries they need not be mutually exclusive. In other words, the individual need not be pitted against the group.

The individualistic nature of the human being is valued in Western society, and lies at the root of empirical psychology's perception of the person as research subject. In empirical psychology, knowledge is derived from observations of the world we live in. These observations are data or facts about the world, collected in a way that is supposedly free of value, that is, objective. Value-free data are bits of information that are gathered without regard for a way of explaining them.[7] My mentor, Chizuko Izawa, a cognitive psychologist, used to tell me that when the data and theory do not match, it is the data that are holy and the theory that is wrong. So the idea of observable facts existing without reference to the context from which they are derived is a key notion in modern empirical psychology.

A second aspect of empirical psychology is that the individual and the environment interact with one another. But the individual and the environment are not interacting in a random manner. Rather, these interactions are guided by a straightforward working out of the laws of causality. That means for every action, it is possible to detect the mechanisms at work which produced it. The underlying assumption is that the environment and the individual are made up of isolatable elements that interact, but can be studied separately. Thus, researchers manipulate variables and record their observations as the individuals respond to standard stimuli, such as the tasks used in laboratory experiments, or items on questionnaires.[8]

R. K. Unger notes that positivist empiricism defines the relationship between investigator and subject as an impersonal one. The ideal subject of the experiment is a "narrowly calculating human being who adapts, conforms, engages in self-interest behavior, rather than in action that has social as well as personal meaning."[9] Such an approach, she maintains, prescribes prediction and control, limits the behaviors studied to those that are amenable to simple observation and/or categorization, eliminates the possibility of alternative behavior, and totally disregards those actions that involve ideology and values. Given that (a) only certain behaviors are deemed valid for psychological inquiry, (b) the inquiry is preferably carried out through experimental procedures, and (c) an ideal subject is implicitly specified, Unger notes that control, by definition, is the key to understanding the impact of conceptual frameworks on epistemological commitments.

Who is most likely to be comfortable with a positivist empirical method of conducting psychology? From the available information, objectivism seems to be more in concert with Anglo-American culture than are alternative approaches, and is more likely to be adhered to by researchers whose backgrounds are more socially acceptable in American society.[10] For example, J. Sherwood and M. Nataupsky found some evidence that the conclusions investigators reached about whether the differences in intelligence of African Americans and Anglo-Americans were innate were related to various characteristics of the researcher's backgrounds.[11] Investigators who concluded that African Americans were innately inferior to Anglo-Americans tended to come from backgrounds where their grandparents had been born in this country. They had parents who had completed years of schooling, were of high academic standing as undergraduates and were younger when their findings were published than were investigators finding no differences, or attributing differences to environmental factors. Not only does coming from the appropriate background encourage an acceptance of mainstream methodology early in one's career, one becomes even more wedded to the status quo because acceptance of it brings occupational success. N. Caplan and S. D. Nelson note that psychologists enhance their own careers by conducting research that their colleagues see as relevant. Helping the socially disadvantaged become self-determining lies outside the definitional boundaries of traditional psychology and is not likely to enhance one's career. The preoccupation of psychology with person-centered variables (characteristics that lie within the individual) as opposed to situational factors, irrespective of the type of problem or the intent of the researcher, Caplan and Nelson argue, facilitates a chain of events that lead to "blaming people in difficult situations for their own predicament."[12]

Control over the definition of social problems determines how these problems will be addressed. For example, if African American poverty and its attendant problems of deviancy, nonachievement, and high unemployment are defined as being the result of female-headed households, the authors point out, discriminatory hiring practices and other system factors will not appear as blameworthy as the African American woman herself. African American women, whatever their level of education, are keenly aware of the devastating blow of the myth of the black matriarchy. Even though this issue is no longer of much interest to mainstream social scientists, African American women are still coping with its implications.[13]

Moreover, the marriage between mainstream researchers and established empirical psychology gives birth to social change programs. Within these programs administrators and others have a vested interest in maintaining established definitions, since their very jobs and status may depend on the hegemony of those definitions and vested interests in maintaining them. A cycle of definition, research, and program implementation originating in Anglo-American, middle-class, male values is passed on as standard psychological practice. Anyone not adhering to these laws is not a psychologist.

Social Constructionism

The concern that some psychologists have with values in research has given rise to a movement in psychology called social constructionism. Social constructionism invites us to suspend our beliefs that categories (for instance, gender) have been objectively and empirically derived. For example, those who study the social construction of gender are debunking myths of the existence of two genders. Traditionally in other cultures women have been able to take on the roles of men and live as social males.[14] The female husbands among the Nnobi of Nigeria are an example.

Furthermore, the categories are derived through a process of negotiation of persons who have access to literacy and information dissemination. These individuals can determine the nature and the content of the categories and select the metaphors that represent them. All of this in turn makes an impact on public policy, and treatment and educational programs, that serves to reinforce the status quo. R. Hare-Mustin and J. Marecek note that men's perspectives have long been dominant in the university, where the meanings of social categories have been constructed and as such reflect male values.[15] They point out that in social constructionism, scientific facts are viewed as values, passing as answers for questions posed by individuals with definite political interests. Unger, in the area of the psychology of women, highlights the transforming possibilities for social constructionism in view of its receptiveness to feminist analysis.[16] Her point is that since social constructionism requires that psychological phenomena be interpreted with respect to the historical or situational context in which they occur or are studied, current social arrangements are required to enter the analysis of psychological data.

While social constructionism allows us to highlight the political agendas of all research paradigms, it does not provide a method for conducting emancipatory research in which women of color figure predominantly. I find starting places for this in a variety of methodologies.

Hermeneutics and sociological-grounded theory are at once orientations to knowledge, as well as methodologies for data collection. Packer describes hermeneutics as an effort to describe and study meaningful human phenomena in light of practical (everyday) understanding rather than beginning with preselected theoretical assumptions. Researchers study the everyday activities of individuals while they are engaged in them, as opposed to interrupting them to obtain their speculations about what they are doing. Interruptions would include interview situations, paper-and-pencil tests and laboratory tasks. The goal is to find out which human purposes and interests are being served by the individual's actions, and these actions are never considered without reference to the context in which they occur. Once the information on everyday activities in their natural settings is collected, the researcher develops an interpretation for it which is reported through narrative accounts.[17]

Grounded theory adds to the hermeneutic approach, for me, the view that the research focus "emerges" as the investigator increases his or her involvement in the naturally occurring setting.[18] The power of grounded theory lies in the researcher's need to be sensitive to the language and concepts that are important to the individuals participating in the study. Ideally, the researcher suspends his or her beliefs, to learn to listen and observe the aspects of the research environment that are the most salient to those who are living the experiences being studied.

The participatory research approach invites eclecticism in methodology but demands that researchers have a subjective commitment to the people being studied.[19] In this approach researchers become closely involved with the members of a community. The researcher and the study participants engage in a dialogue, whereby the researcher uses her or his knowledge to stimulate a new awareness in the community. Research is primarily carried out to resolve problems by discovering the conditions that stand in the way of a pragmatic solution. Both the researcher and the community members are active learners in this process of social change. A final aspect of the participatory research approach is that people's own capability and potential to produce and analyze knowledge is respected. Although social constructionism and the interpretive research methods allow us to develop theories and methods consistent with the needs and interests of disenfranchised groups, it is only feminists of color who seek to make primary the needs and achievements of women of color. In her article, "Feminist Theories and the Politics of Difference" Donna Langston offers a useful summary of the major points of feminists of color, such as bell hooks, Audre Lorde, Cherríe Moraga, Gloria Anzaldúa, Cheryl Clarke, and Barbara Smith. These points include a critique of false universalization, a model of simultaneous oppression, and antiseparatist position, and a critique of racism. False universalism occurs when one set of experiences serves as the universal model of the human experience. The model of simultaneous oppression recognizes that the major systems of bigotry (for instance, racism, sexism, homophobia, classism) are interlocking and can not be compartmentalized. In adopting an antiseparatist position, feminists of color band in solidarity with oppressed men on the basis of race, ethnicity, and class, and join with other women because of shared class and/or sexual identity issues. The critique of racism has led women of color to demand that White women take responsibility for their own racism and not require women of color either to educate White women on issues of race or to applaud their efforts at becoming less racist.[20]

The final aspects of my emerging epistemological position derive from the stories of survival passed on to me through my mother and grandmother, as well as from my work experiences.

Thelma and Madame Glover: On the Political Significance of Nondisclosure

For many years, beginning in the 1950s, my grandmother Thelma worked as a domestic and caterer for a Jewish family who owned a furniture store in the Midwest. Thelma was born and reared in New Orleans, where she completed high school and worked as a public school teacher, before marrying and moving North in the 1940s. At the end of each day her employer would drop her off in front of the house in which she lived. My grandmother would enter this two-story house with an upstairs apartment through the back door. The first Christmas my grandmother worked for this family, the female employer gave her a Christmas present which consisted of a set of tea towels and pot holders. My grandmother opened the gift, looked at it, folded it up, and returned it to her female employer. My grandmother said politely, "Thank you, but I have dozens of these." After that incident, my grandmother was allowed to select anything she wanted from the store as her Christmas present. Years passed, the rides home continued, always ending at the curb.

My great-grandmother, Madame Glover, a masseuse, beautician and Southerner, came from New Orleans to visit her daughter, who had long ago migrated to the North. Once, my grandmother's female employer came unannounced, looking for my grandmother. Not knowing which door was my grandmother's, the employer knocked on the one for the main entrance. My great-grandmother opened the door, the woman introduced herself and relying on her social graces from the South, my great-grandmother invited the woman in. "Who lives here?" the woman asked as she spied the baby grand piano, the fine living room furniture, and the separate and well-furnished dining room. My great-grandmother, the Southerner that she was, provided details, including those of my grandmother's tenants. The woman was shocked, and so was my grandmother when she came home to find the intruder in her living room. The female employer told my grandmother. "I always thought you had a room in the back of the house." My grandmother was polite and said, "Now that you are here would you like to see the rest of the house?"

This is one of the many stories of survival, which have been passed on to me from my mother and grandmother, about when to speak and when not to, about how people so easily construct an image of you based on their own limitations. My grandmother's story and attitude toward nondisclosure took on added significance when I went to work as a research associate in a department of psychiatry in a Southern medical school.

Excursion into Madness: A Womanist Analysis of Office Politics

My job was to interview women who were severely socially disadvantaged, to gather information about their mental health. The questionnaires were of the traditional survey type, and required over five hours to administer. The head of our immediate research offices was an Anglo-American, middle-class, middle-aged man. He and the Anglo-American, woman, social worker who had an adjacent office were the representatives of "normalcy." Their status was reinforced by their titles and the fact that they had individual offices. Those of us who occupied the middle office were gay and/or women of color, the traditional other of the other.

Curiously enough, the small office held four of us, and there were some musings from the "normal" group that hopefully we would be joined by an Asian American to complete their collection of liberalism. Our small office was also designated as the social arena. Any time those in the upper echelons of the hierarchy came to the office this was where the socializing took place. The analogy of White heterosexuals representing the developed world and the women of color and/or gays representing the underdeveloped world is irresistible. We were overcrowded, our workspace and activities could be encroached upon at any time, and we could be called out of our names with impunity. The heads routinely called their research associate, a White, gay man, a "fairy." And they would yell out to this man from their offices, "Faggot, get your ass in here." He would oblige, and go shuffling along. His irritation would surface about once a week when he turned up to full volume his boom-box and played classical music. They nicknamed the African American female secretary, BW, which stood for Black Woman. Eventually, she asked why the women of color called her by her name but the whites did not. She directed the question to the White, heterosexual woman, and said if it continued she would call her WB, for White Bitch. Her nickname stopped, but the disrespect did not.

In the beginning of my short tenure there, I took as a confidant a man of color with some rank in the hierarchy. He also was my immediate supervisor. I told him that I was looking for a permanent position (this one was funded by a grant), that I would be returning to Africa to continue my research and that I would soon have my dissertation completed. I did not see him on a daily basis, but interactions were pleasant and cordial.

After a while, I became concerned that the women I went into the local community to find were in desperate need of more than the small research remittance we were providing. The majority of women were African American. The information from the survey was largely irrelevant to their most pressing and immediate needs, and they participated in the study because they thought they would be helping others, as well as getting some help themselves. I was to bring the information back to a team of White, middle-class, male and female, mental health professionals. In our research meetings they threw around typical pathological notions to account for the reasons the women (women they had never met) were in these conditions. From my own experiences, the rendering of each subjects' account provides emotional relief for both the subjects and researcher, and serves as the foundation for mutual participation in changing life conditions. I, the overeducated colored girl, was expected to contribute what I had learned and then to sit back and let them theorize and better yet, when the really top people were in the meeting, I was dismissed.

I began to name this activity "the twenty-five dollar hustle." I approached my supervisor about our (African American) participation in this hoax, when women truly needed and thought they were getting real assistance. He approached another African American woman of still higher rank, who responded by replying that this was the name of the game. She meant that our job was to obtain pilot data to use in securing large government grants that bring prestige to the university and additional income to individual researchers.

Luckily for me there was a woman of color who shared my research orientation, and we became allies. My supervisor suggested that we were compatible because we were both isolated, and he never accepted my feelings of having been mistreated. Isolated implied being a separate division of something, but I felt included. My ability to develop and sustain rapport with very poor African American women was seen as important. I believed that my ally and I were mistreated because we were inappropriate and unsuitable according to Anglo-American middle-class sensibilities. We lacked Whiteness, a penis, class privilege, and the ability to conduct therapy that could be charged to insurance companies. We were mistrusted because we did not seek Whiteness, nor reinforce capitalistic patriarchal attitudes about poor women as eager participants in their own self-destruction.

I reached a simple and obvious conclusion. We did not need to conduct research to understand how and why these poor women became mentally ill and economically disenfranchised. We only needed to examine our research unit. The blatant racism, sexism, classism, and homophobia, the allegiance to oppressive research paradigms, and the issuance of a sum of money to desperate women fit into a long line of treatment for these women. They had been used as sexual partners for relatives and strangers in exchange for necessary goods and services. We were giving nothing back, aside from the therapeutic relief offered by a single, detailed, information interview. Nor were there any pragmatic ideas to bring about change in their lives, only vague notions of bringing them into the laboratory for periodic observations.

When my supervisor felt threatened by the research team's questioning of his participation in the project, he told of his own woes and also about my plans. Suddenly, I was seen as having value—albeit limited to getting subjects, of course (the Black woman laborer in the field continues). I felt betrayed by his disclosure, as my grandmother had by her mother.

Integrating the Curriculum

After my experiences with this research group, I gained a fuller commitment to understanding the story from the actors' and actresses' point of view, and including them in the construction of theory and the development of social change. Toward this end, my efforts in integrating the curriculum have been directed toward course work that will change students' perspectives on the "proper" area of inquiry, methodological tools, and interpretative frameworks as falling under the purview of psychology. One example comes from my recent experiences teaching a course in the field on the psychology of women. My goal in teaching a psychology of women from a multicultural feminist perspective is to stress the diversity of women's experiences.

The very idea of "who is a woman" is problematic for the discipline and for some of the students who are encountering multiculturalism for the first time. Some White students voice their concern about who is a woman by saying "we did not know the course was going to focus so heavily on minority women." It would appear that Sojourner's question, "Ain't I a woman," is still pertinent. Or, "when you talk about minority women, we feel guilty, we feel our suffering is not as important as the suffering of women of color." Of course, who is a minority is dependent on one's frame of reference. Thinking locally, that is, in terms of the United States, then women of color are a minority. Thinking globally, Anglo-Americans and White European women become a minority. I am making a simple point. A psychology of women must speak directly of, to and about women: brown, white, black, rich, poor, healthy, the physically, emotionally and intellectually impaired, straight, and lesbian.[21]

The ability of our discipline to separate individuals into variables of race, gender, and class is directly challenged by Third World feminists and psychologists of color, who refuse to choose between being women and being persons of color.[22] The artificial dissection of fields of study with definite boundaries laid down long ago by a small number of White men has deemed psychology as the study of "us" White people, and anthropology the study of "them," the colored others. When White students study the psychology of women they expect to learn primarily about themselves, and are content with the special focus on African American women during one lecture only. I continue to find problematic the special chapter/issue approach, which continues to treat women of color as appendages to an area of study. It perpetuates the notion that the field is really universal, when all we know is about a specialized population parading as the universal and "real" human experience.

Many students find it cognitively disconcerting that women of color can be integrated so deeply into the psychology of women. Starting from a colored core and working out to see the universality of the experiences of women of color poses real difficulty for some White students. Women of color feel extremely validated when readings about their lives are included. They take the lead in the discussions and those with an interest and openness to other experiences also contribute. Those uncomfortable with multiculturalism tend to try to reduce the experiences of women of color to simplistic notions that we are all the same. Such students are invested in the empirical point of view in psychology that individuals exist with elements that one can isolate and observe independently of one another.

After one class meeting, a student and I had a discussion about what is the primal form of oppression. That student's point was that gender constitutes the most basic form of oppression for all women irrespective of their class and ethnicity. This point would be considered valid from an empirical perspective, which deems that elements of the individual can stand in isolation from all other aspects of that individual. Yet the writings by women of color that we read stand in direct contradiction to this empirical notion that individuals consist of isolated elements. They speak to the simultaneity of oppression.

In my psychology of women class the first set of readings are on the images of women. We use a standard psychology of women textbook. The additional readings communicate to the students the understanding that women's false representations are not mere reflections of their gender. Rather, the way women are represented is a direct reflection of the stereotypes that prevail about their racial group in addition to the stereotypes that are in existence for Anglo-American women. Many standard textbooks trace the images of women as drawn by the intellectual traditions of Anglo-American Christian culture. That is, women as mythic, mother nature, enchantress/seductress, necessary, evil and mysterious, and virtuous are allowed to stand as the expressions of all women in America. These categories take on additional meanings when the variable of ethnicity is introduced.

I have found helpful the writings of Rayna Green, Irene Fujitomi and Diane Wong, Paula Giddings, and Cherríe Moraga.[23] From Paula Giddings we learn that Black women have always worked out of economic necessity. Yet because this behavior does not conform to American middle-class values, male sociologists have labeled us as matriarchs. From Fujitomi and Wong we learn that Asian American women who wish to assert themselves and become leaders in American society must be willing to challenge traditional gender roles and the American myths of the Asian American woman as humble and nice. From Rayna Green we see that the ways Native American women have been depicted historically are a direct result of the desires of White men. When the New World had to be conquered, the Native American woman symbolized both the treasures in and the dangers of the Americas. When the colonies were established, the Native American woman began to be seen as someone who was civilized and a defender of American democracy. Cherríe Moraga tells us that Chicanas who choose to align themselves with White women politically and sexually are seen as traitors to their race.

Textbooks alone make the mistake of false universalism. As bell hooks points out, false universalism occurs when authors are allowed to speak about women, when they really mean White women, but add a prefix when they speak of women of color. Collectively these articles maintain that one's gender, race, ethnicity, class, and sexuality are part of the individual and can not be separated. Women exist in a certain class, with a certain race and ethnicity, with a specific sexual preference in a particular historical and social context.

The flip side of lumping all women together on the basis of gender is grouping all minor(ity) women under one minor(ity) experience. For example, in many texts we read about the minor(ity) experience. That minor(ity) experience is the African American one, but what about all the other minor(ity) women in America and the world over. There is not one minor(ity) experience. Essentialism is not limited to ideas about gender differences. Each of us speaks from a place in our community. My experiences as an African American woman do not reflect the experiences of all African American women; nor does any one individual speak for his or her entire group.

Conclusion

What I am working toward is a multicultural feminist perspective in psychology. The problems I have with an empiricist perspective concern the notion of individuals and environment as having elements that are isolated. As individuals we do not live our lives in isolation from the elements that are essential to who we are. Rather, we live as individuals who are constellations of race, class, gender, and sexual preference, existing in particular social and historical contexts. My concerns about the empiricist perspective include: Who has been given the opportunities to define the categories in social sciences that up until recently have defined women and people of color as less than White males. Finally, it is vital that information collected from subjects be made available to them, and programs designed with their input, in order to enhance their own efforts to change their lives.

Because psychology looks toward the natural sciences as a model for conducting research, United States' psychology is primarily experimental and survey, as well as quantitative in orientation. The abundance of laboratories, sophisticated research equipment, trained personnel, and an infrastructure that can support this type of research cannot even be imagined in developing countries, where resources are scarce. Unless we create a climate in psychology that is more amenable to alternative methods of carrying out research that are not heavily dependent on technology, our information about women in developing countries will be almost nonexistent. Our psychology of women becomes the study of women's behavior in the developed world, not a true psychology of women. If we are content with accepting that gender oppression is the most fundamental, and ignore how other factors come into play, such as sexual preference, class, and ethnicity, the psychology of women remains White, middle-class, and heterosexual.

If psychology begins to develop its affinity with the interpretive disciplines rendering accounts of human meaning systems, the definition of psychology as a science which seeks to predict and control behavior gives way to a psychology which seeks to gain greater and more differentiated sensitivity to the everyday concerns of multidimensional individuals. By expanding the parameters of psychology to include methodologies that are amenable to the resources of Third World psychologists, we empower their ability to conduct scientific research. Field studies where investigators actually spend time in the naturally occurring settings of their research subjects is one alternative to laboratory research. When practiced by researchers in the United States, these methods provide researchers with the opportunities to gain the necessary value perspectives of their subjects. Thus we can move from a psychology of control to a psychology of empowerment; a psychology which seeks to assist individuals in improving their ability to become self-determining. Psychology becomes the field of study whose goal is to describe and understand human behavior, and to control those aspects of behavior that wittingly and unwittingly disempower people. As an area of specialization in psychology and in valuing difference, a psychology of women becomes the study of women in all our diversity, and the goal is to break down the behavioral barriers that stand in the way of our emancipation.

Notes

1. Gloria Hull, Patricia Bell Scott, and Barbara Smith, *All the Women are White, All the Blacks are Men, But Some of Us Are Brave* (Old Westbury, New York: Feminist Press, 1982).

2. L. Krasner and A. C. Houts, "A study of the 'value' systems of behavioral scientists," *American Psychologist* 39: 833–839.

3. G. A. Kimble, "Psychology's two cultures," *American Psychologist* 39: 840–850.

4. R. K. Unger, "Through the Looking Glass: No Wonderland Yet! The Reciprocal Relationship Between Methodology and Models of Reality," *Psychology of Women Quarterly* 8: 9–32.

5. R. W. Russell, "Psychology in its World Context," *American Psychologist* 39: 1017–1025.

6. F. M. Moghaddam, "Psychology in the Three Worlds: As Reflected by the Crisis in Social Psychology and the Move Toward Indigenous Third-World Psychology," *American Psychologist* 42: 912–920.

7. M. J. Packer, "Hermeneutic Inquiry in the Study of Human Conduct," *American Psychologist* 40: 1081–1093.

8. *Ibid.*

9. R. K. Unger, 1983.

10. *Ibid.*

11. J. J. Sherwood and M. Natupsky, "Predicting the Conclusions of Negro-White Intelligence Research from Biographical Characteristics of the Investigator," *Journal of Personality and Social Psychology* 8: 53–58.

12. N. Caplan and S. D. Nelson, "On Being Useful: The Nature and Consequences of Psychological Research on Social Problems," *American Psychologist* 28: 199–211.

13. "Scapegoating the Black Family: Black Women Speak," *The Nation* July 24/31, 1989.

14. K. J. Gergen, "The Social Constructionist Movement in Modern Psychology," *American Psychologist* 40: 266–275.

15. R. Hare-Mustin and J. Marecek, "Gender and the Meaning of Difference: Postmodernism and Psychology," in *Making a Difference: Psychology and the Construction of Gender* (New Haven: Yale University Press, 1990), 22–64.

16. R. K. Unger, "Imperfect Reflections of Reality: Psychology Constructs Gender," in *Making a Difference: Psychology and the Construction of Gender* (New Haven: Yale University Press, 1990), 102–149.

17. Packer, 1985.

18. B. Glaser and A. Straus, *The Discovery of Grounded Theory* (1967).

19. Y. Kassam and K. Mustafa, *Participatory Research: An Emerging Alternative Methodology in Social Science Research* (Khanpur, New Delhi, India: Society for Participatory Research in Asia, 1979.)

20. D. Langston, in J. W. Cochran, D. Langston, and C. Woodward (eds.) *Changing Our Power: An Introduction to Women's Studies* (Dubuque: Kendall/Hunt Publishing Company, 1984), 10–21.

21. I am encouraged by the fourth edition of Janet Shibley Hyde's introductory textbook on the psychology of women, entitled Half the Human Experience (Lexington, Massachusetts: D. C. Health and Company, 1990) as moving in the right direction.

22. P. Reid and L. Comias-Diaz, "Gender and Ethnicity: Perspectives on Dual Status," *Sex Roles* 22: 397–408.

23. R. Green, "The Pocahontas Perplex: The Image of Indian Women in American Culture," in *Unequal Sisters: A Multi-cultural Reader in U.S. Women's History,* E. C. DuBois & V. L. Ruiz (eds.) (New York: Routledge, Chapman & Hall, Inc., 1990), 15–21.

   Irene Fujitomi and Diane Wong, "The New Asian American Woman," in *Asian-Americans: Psychological Perspectives,* S. Sue and N. Wagner (eds.) (Palo Alto: Science and Behavior Books, 1980), 252–263.

   Paula Giddings, *When and Where I Enter: The Impact of Black Women on Race and Sex in America* (New York: William Morrow Company, Inc., 1984)

   Cherríe Moraga, "From a Long Line of Vendidas: Chicanas and Feminism," in *Feminist Studies: Critical Studies,* T. deLauretis (ed.) (Bloomington: Indiana University Press, 1986), 173–190.

7

Deconstructing, Reconstructing, and Focusing our Literary Image

Nagueyalti Warren

African American women at Emory University constitute less than one percent of the administration. None hold the position of dean or vice-president. There is one associate dean in the Office of Admissions. The Assistant Dean for Multicultural Programs and Services (formerly the office of Minority Student Affairs) is an African American woman. Faculty representation is not much better. The English Department has one recently acquired professor. Educational Studies has two African American women, both at the associate professor level. Sociology has one tenured full professor. Four African American women constitute the total number of African American women on Emory's college faculty. Needless to say, there is restricted space for growth and development of African American scholars, educators, and administrators. Emory is not unusual; in fact, Emory probably represents the norm in American higher education.

On the average, African American women constitute less than three percent of higher administration and faculty of Emory University. Most of the women on any campus are students or secretaries, if they are White, service workers, or custodial staff if they are Black.[1] In general, preferential treatment of men exists throughout our society. The academy is no exception. Men occupy high-status roles. Bias has been empirically identified in evaluations of intellectual products, credentials, authority, and leadership, allocation of resources, and interpretations of success and failure. Therefore, bias can, and, particularly for African American women, does, influence hiring salary, and promotion and tenure decisions, as well as colleagues' evaluations of daily routine contributions, students' evaluations of courses, and editors' evaluation of work publication.[2]

Consensual misperceptions that hinder Euro-American women are especially negative for African American women. Studies show that unconscious bias influences the perceived quality of suggestions, opinions, lectures, course content, and handling of administrative responsibilities.[3] Academic committees formed to guard against bias by relying on group consensus end up with misperceptions, all distorted in the same direction. This is not surprising when the group consists of homogeneous members. Many committees are indeed homo (man) genus (kind: Euro-American), and will continue to be so until the incorporation of women and other groups changes the academy.

Given the current state of the academic environment, African American women involved in higher education must perforce revive their spirit in a liberating pedagogy and carve a space for themselves to survive.

Because images are crucial to the replication of stereotypes, and stereotypes operate as tacit knowledge that influences conscious and unconscious bias, this chapter focusses on images, with specific regard to the way African American women are depicted generally in the humanities but most specifically in the literature taught in college and university classrooms. The canon, that group of books authored by Euro-American men, which every college-educated person is presumed to have read, presents negative stereotypes of women and especially damaging portrayals of African American women, or no image at all. This literature informs the majority of the educated population over thirty-five. The core curriculum or so-called general education requirements of recent decades promotes the inclusion of "other" writers—diversifies (to some destroys is more accurate) the canon. In this literature African American women still do not fare well. Feminists, mostly White, have done an excellent job unravelling the stereotypic image of Euro-American women. It is not surprising, nor is it expected, that African American women would benefit from their efforts. They have not. The African American woman's experience of sexism differs from the White woman's experience.[4] White women operate within the matrix of racism and White privilege. The solipsistic arguments of many feminists pose race and gender as Black *or* female, effectively erasing the Black woman. Thus, African American women have remained invisible. Euro-American feminists, preoccupied with their feelings, as they should be, often are unable to connect with the experiences of others. But as bell hooks points out, feminism is really about empowerment[5] and, as such, Euro-American women cannot empower African American women. Empowerment results from understanding one's own experience. No one can do that for us but us; nor should we want them to. Therefore, African American women must address the task of changing our image. African American literature nudged its way into the curriculum and ironically produced a recognized canon. African American men, namely Wright, Ellison, and Baldwin, constitute the triumvirate which might, because of the authority close association brings, be even more detrimental to the image of African American women than the image erected in the Euro-American canon.

Consequently, there is a need to exorcise the images and erect new ones. This chapter includes methods for achieving a more accurate literary image in hopes that positive or neutral types will filter into tacit knowledge, thereby changing the racial and gender bias that now affects the African American woman's space, spirit, and survival in the academy. Cheryl Wall's introduction to *Changing Our Own Words* states the imperative for African American women academics. She writes:

> We bring to our work a critical self-consciousness about our posi-
> tionality, defined as it is by race, gender, class, and ideology. The
> position or place we are assigned on the margins of the academy
> informs but does not determine the positions or stances we take.[6]

Our task, then, is to challenge traditional humanism, that is, humanism which embraces only White, Western, male culture, promoted under the rubric of classics, introduction to philosophy, and so on, and call to question academic authority that ignores the culture of the majority of the world's human beings.

The African American Woman: Image of the Arts

The image of the African American woman in the arts, that is, in music, dance, film, painting, sculpture, has either been erased or egregiously distorted. Rarely aggrandized, her image is no image that is acknowledged. "No Image," a poem by Waring Cuney, speaks to the conundrum in literature and in life regarding the image of African American women. The crux of the problem is articulated by Nikki Giovanni in her foreword to *Images of Blacks in American Culture*. The last line of Cuney's poem states: "dishwater gives back no image." Giovanni insists, "A woman standing, whether tall and proud, or heavily leaning, over dirty dishes, *is* an image. The dishwater is not required to reflect it; we are required to acknowledge it."[7]

Gilman's cogent delineation in "Black Bodies, White Bodies" of the nineteenth century's image of Black women is a good place to begin the examination of images. Informed by the language, taking cues from the word "black," the scholars closely adhered to the etymology of the words "black" and "female." "Female," deriving from the old English term, "to suckle; attend; after male," served as a double negative for the Black woman. The *Old English Dictionary* lists a litany of adjectives for "black," including sinister, evil, wicked, harmful, disgraceful, sorrowful, suffering, villain, morbid, cynical. When juxtaposed against the adjectives for "white," which include pure, spotless, innocent, harmless, caucasoid, honest, fair, decent, morally upright, it is no wonder the Black woman is castigated and portrayed as lascivious.

The Black woman served as sexual icon for Black sexuality. Scientific literature produced statements such as that Black women copulated with apes,[8] and sought to prove that Black women were physiologically different from White women. *The Dictionary of Medical Science* (1819) by J. J. Virey stressed the relationship between the Black woman's "hideous form" and her physiognomy, her horribly flattened nose. He also wrote: "Voluptuousness developed to a degree of lascivity unknown in our climate, [the Black woman's] sexual organs are much more developed than those of whites."[9] Obsession with Black, female genitalia is striking considering that no mention is made of Black males during the same time. Gilman points out that William Turner dissected three Black men in 1878, 1879, and 1896. He does not mention the male genitalia. The uniqueness of the sexual organs and buttocks of the Black person thus is associated primarily with the female and is taken as a sign of an anomalous female sexuality.[10]

In 1905 Havelock Ellis provides, in volume four of *Studies in the Psychology of Sex,* a detailed example of the Great Chain of Being. He believed there was an absolute scale of beauty which was totally objective and which ranged from Europeans to Blacks. Thus men of the lower races "admire women of the European race more than their own. And women of lower races attempt to whiten themselves with face powder."[11]

Charles Darwin's *The Descent of Man and Selection in Relation to Sex*[12] did its share to promote the sexual icon of Black women. Gilman demonstrates how the presence of Blacks in nineteenth-century art signifies the sexual availability of the White females pictured in art. Furthermore, he writes, "When the Victorians saw the female black, they saw her buttocks and saw represented by the buttocks all the anomalies of her genitalia."[13] Both G. W. F. Hegel and Arthur Schopenhauer believed that Black people represented the most primitive stage of humankind—unbridled sexuality. So much for academic authority.

The origin of syphilis sounds much like the explanation concocted to explain AIDS. Scientists said it was not introduced to Europe by Christopher Columbus' sailors. They claimed it was a form of leprosy which had long been present in Africa and had spread into Europe in the Middle Ages. Black women were especially associated with syphilophobia during the late nineteenth century. Thus the Black woman comes to represent not only the sexualized female, she represents the female as source of corruption and disease. The White male, Gilman admits, is the progenitor of the vocabulary and images through which Black female icons developed.

The "Hottentot Venus" is a primary example of "hegemonic othering" of the Black woman.[14] Sarah Bartmann, used as the Hottentot Venus, and put on display in Paris for Europeans to view her steatopygia (protruding buttocks), died in Paris in 1815. She was twenty-five years old. Henri deBlainville performed and published the results of an autopsy he performed on Sarah. In his report he compared her, an example of the lowest human species, with the highest ape, the orangutan.[15] Each discipline has its catalogues of distortions for the Black woman. Gilman's article served as a useful example of how painting and the developing science of the latter century intersected, reinforcing negative images.

African American Women: The Literary Image

The literary image of African American women has developed in both the European and American traditions from negative terms. Influenced by nomenclature that depicts black as evil, dirty, unenlightened, and that utilized such terms as "negress" to identify Black women as one identifies a tigress, writers who chose to concern themselves with Black women characters accentuated their so-called animal nature. Considering this history, Henry Louis Gates asks those of us in the academy who carry the weight of such historical baggage, "Is our fate one of perpetual negation? Are we doomed merely to 'oppose,' to serve within the academy as black signs of opposition to a political order which we are the subjugated?"[16] Gates argues cogently for African Americans to analyze the ways that writing relates to race, and I might add, to gender. We must examine how attitudes toward racial and gender difference generate and structure literary texts by us *and* about us.[17] While I would argue that Gates' agenda is necessary, a clear understanding of the institutions in which we operate is the first step to change, one step conducive to the kind of research Gates posits.

In his 1978 essay "Academicons—Sick Sacred Cows," Ray B. Browne states precisely the problem of the academic environment. Browne writes: "Academics maintain a set of icons in their higher education temple that are private, self-serving and generally as impervious to re-examination as those in any other section of our society."[18] He thus delineates the holy icons, which constitute a holy trinity, as it were, in the ivory tower. Foremost is the idea that the academy is "separate and distinct" from the world in which it resides, which supports it, and which it is supposed to serve. This rather odd perversion is identified in what Parker Palmer reveals as ironies between "epistemology" and life. That is, Palmer believes, and rightly so, that the system of higher education in the United States is dominated by a pseudo-science that claims "objectivism."[19] Thus, the separateness emanates from the effort to be objective, to put distance between the academy and that which it examines.

One of the great fallacies in American higher education is that the academy is objective. That an effort has been made to keep knowledge from the contamination of subjectivity, prejudice, and bias is beyond question. What is also beyond question is that the effort has failed miserably. I need not catalogue how, just through the sins of omission, knowledge becomes prejudice. However, the point that concerns Palmer is the whole idea that divorces knowledge—a part of the world—from personal life, creating, as it were, "a world 'out there' of which we are only spectators and in which we do not live."[20]

Second in the holy trinity is the sanctity of the curriculum. For many academics the curriculum is chiseled in granite. Therefore, criticism of the curriculum is tantamount to an assault on the Ark of the Covenant.[21] The goal of the liberal arts curriculum is to produce well-rounded human beings, aware of the world around them, and well-equipped to improve it. Of all the disciplines, the study of literature should be the most humanizing. Yet the fight to include literature of the majority of humanity continues. The effort to expand the canon appears as an invasion of holy terrain.

Denying the humanities to humanity is an elitist agenda articulated by many well-known scholars including Maynard Mack, director of the Humanities Institute at Yale University. "The humanities are not really something you can democratize [he said]. It's like democratizing surgery. Who wants someone picked up off the street to operate on him? Well, it's the same thing in the humanities."[22]

The third icon, which supports the previous two constituting the trinity, is the cry for standards. The cry for standards, more often than not, simply masks the belief that new and different equals inferior. Or, if it is not the same old thing, it must not be of high quality. The doors of America's academy, of all places, are closed to new ideas as well as to old ones that are nontraditional. When the academy's doors have swung open, as they did during the late 1960s and early 1970s, the academy has been eminently successful in metamorphosing the common larvae from ghettos, barrios and simply "up off the street" people into elite butterflies all too willing to deny old gods and embrace the new religion with its new icons. Old gods, those ancestral spirits that abide in ethnic traditions, the oral traditions, the extended families, the centrality of art to life, its utilitarian nature, are discarded for new traditions which do not reflect the historical experiences of the newly initiated. The new icons, detached, unemotional, rational symbols of Western materialist culture, forbid the expression of a deeply spiritual, nonmaterial culture. Instead of embracing that which inhibits us, our task is to reconstruct images until they reflect our presence.

Given the history of the academy, the title of this book, *Spirit, Space, and Survival,* is an implicit challenge. As African American women, we are reminded that

> Our reality is not that we are "neither white nor male," *our* reality is that we are *both* black and female; and it is in the belief that our narratives can be transformational that we begin.[23]

Daryl Dance, Professor of English and noted African American folklorist at Virginia Commonwealth University, delineates the rise and fall of African American literature, stating that the readership for this literature fluctuates between peaks and valleys. Yet, during its peaks, the Harlem Renaissance and the 1960s, the contributions of African American women remained deemphasized and only rarely acknowledged. Dance recalls that, when Black Studies courses were first introduced, White students were eager to learn. However, too soon White students were intimidated as African American students found their identity in their own literature.[24] The result has been not simply a shift in readership but a resistance on the part of White students to study African American literature.

The comments of Sandra Govan, Professor of English at the University of North Carolina, are not unique when she recalls her own experience with students. Govan notes, "sometimes the greatest discouragement comes from the students themselves. I've had problems with closed-minded, White students who resent and resist the literature. They'll write on teacher evaluations, "If I wanted an African American class, I would've signed up for one." And this is only after you've introduced two Black writers."[25] Even more resistance is encountered when the literature of African American women is introduced.

Criticism comes from both White and African American male students. Responding to a course that I teach, entitled African American Women's literature, an African American male student informed me he was going off campus in order to take a course on Black male literature. I informed him he could get the identical course on campus. It was simply called African American literature. The description for this course read:

> Major literary traditions of black people in the United States, both oral and written, with special attention to such writers as Toomer, Hughes, Wright, Ellison, Baldwin, Jones, and Reed.[26]

The problems are many, but the issue of including African American women in the curriculum is one that is slowly gaining attention. At least ten universities are currently participating in a project sponsored by the Ford Foundation, called, Incorporating Women of Color into the Curriculum.[27]

Deconstructing the Images

Deconstruction challenges, in our "scriptocentric academy,"[28] conventional assumptions made about literary texts. The deconstructionist argument has the potential to undermine the foundations of Western thought and culture, or, given White male hegemony, it can have no practical consequences whatsoever. At this point it is hard to tell what the consequences will be. In the able hands of African American scholars and critics, however, deconstruction offers a way to move from margin to center, that is, provided "deconstruction" is operationalized to address African American philosophical needs.

The elements of deconstruction most applicable to the African American experience both within and outside the academy are *demicroyance,* a DuBoisean idea of double consciousness, and "narcissistic self-regard," although not in the sense asserted by Harold Bloom; that is, not as postmodern feelings lost in the face of history and powerless to alter our potential to self-destruct.[29] The idea of magical properties of the word is also compatible with Black philosophy, as African Americans have long been aware of the magical power of the word, both spoken and written. Thus, to embrace magical theory articulated by Bloom, is simply to recover what we have always known.

The fallacy of deconstruction as theory for African American literature is its tendency toward linguistic nihilism, its effort to disavow that words are acts, its effort not to impose meaning on experience and its effort to present history as an illusion.[30] In essence, deconstruction, as articulated by Paul de Man, Jacques Derrida, and Geoffrey Hartman, rationalizes the Euro-American collective guilt from their historical experience. For those for whom history has been and continues to be a continuous sequence of oppression, no theory, deconstruction included, can disconnect history from reality.

Deconstruction is useful, then, not as theory but as strategy for revising or getting inside the word of the text, of examining the double-coded language defining the image of the African American woman. Leaving a lot to be desired of theory, deconstruction still challenges the scholar to examine presuppositions taken for granted and to problematize issues traditionally taken as given.

As African American academics, it is our duty to transform the teaching of literature in higher education. My experience suggests that one useful way to approach the task is through historical analysis. By that I mean that many of the students we teach have little or no awareness of historical imperatives. These students, both Black and White, are unaware of stereotypes, false images, and constructs that have defined the literature, and are thus unable to reconstruct or even focus on issues of change. When discussing a particular literary work, I am often struck that my students do not recognize a character as a type, or view it in any relevant historical context. It occurs to me that one cannot reconstruct unless one is aware of the construction of an object, character, or text. Therefore, context is crucial foreground for the study of African American Women's literature. That context is political is no excuse for avoiding it. As it is unthinkable to teach American literature without contextualizing it in terms of the Revolutionary War, westward expansion, Civil War and other social and political movements, it is equally ludicrous to expect to somehow explicate African American women's literature from an apolitical perspective.

The 1982 publication of *All the Women Are White, All the Blacks*

Are Men, But Some of Us Are Brave set the agenda for Black Women's Studies for this century and the next. It should serve as a handbook for anyone attempting to teach not just African American Women's literature but Women's Studies in general. The Introduction, "The Politics of Black Women's Studies," is a succinct rendering of our political position in the academy and in America. Hull and Smith use a literary example to illustrate how African American women have been portrayed in literature. They write:

> In 1932 William Faulkner saw fit to include this sentence in a description of a painted sign in his novel *Light in August*. He wrote: But now and then a negro nursemaid with her white charges would loiter there and spell them [the letters on the sign] aloud with that *vacuous idiocy of her idle and illiterate kind.* [Italics Hull's and Smith's][31]

Faulkner's assessment of the African American female intellect, stated as merely an aside, not only typifies American literature, but the oppressive images emanate from what is considered an American masterpiece. Ironically, the images depicted in the works of another recognized master, Richard Wright, are hardly less virulent. In Wright's novels African American women emerge as "intractable bitch" (Gladys in *The Outsider*), "the hysterical breed" (Dot and Myrtle in the same work), or "whore" (Gladys in *The Long Dream*). Wright's most Faulknerian passage, however, appears in *Lawd Today*.

> "Lawd, I wish I was dead," she [Lil] sobbed softly. Outside an icy wind swept around the corner of the building whining and moaning like an *idiot* [italics mine] in a deep black pit[32]

Wright is signifying. Not only have African American women been unabashedly used as negative signifiers, they are signified upon by the men closest to their lives.

Theory and Praxis

"We do not teach literature, we are taught by literature"[33]
Odette Ewell Martin in an unpublished dissertation posits a valuable approach to the study of African American women's literature. Her

work contextualizes the literature and delineates the images for facile recognition and classroom discussion.[34]

There are two sets of images that characterize African American women. One category constitutes a set of pathological images. This category can trace its roots back to the nineteenth-century idea of the Hottentot Venus, and includes the African American woman as negative signifier, cause of deconstruction, castrating matriarch, destructive mother, and masculinized woman. These pathological images spawned complex concepts gaining strength from social science and creative literature. The other set of images which run counter to the pathology images are the icons posited in the theory of the "Black Madonna," the messianic role assigned to Black women, the mammy, the strong superwoman ideal, and the sexualized healthy African American woman. These constitute the defining images in literature, and most are reinforced in social science.

Nineteenth- and twentieth-century social science placed the burden of responsibility for the home and family on women. In turn, the African American woman was held accountable for the disorganized state of the African American family. E. Franklin Frazier's *The Negro Family in the United States* (1939) affected profoundly the concept of the African American family. Using White, middle-class standards, Frazier characterized the African American woman as a threat to the American social structure. Because he accepted the idea of feminine as passive, dependent, and nonaggressive, Frazier found the African American woman wanting and deviant in her posture toward autonomy. Frazier describes the African American, middle-class woman as preoccupied with power. He further postulates that her need to escape the frustration of an unsatisfactory sexual life produced her unhealthy need for power. Finally, what we have in Frazier's image of the low-income African American woman is a matriarch who rules her household with an iron hand.[35] This study, which was not comparative, was nevertheless generalized in literature and popular culture to include all African American women.

Continuing where Frazier left off, Daniel P. Moynihan called the African American family "a tangle of pathology."[36] To the concept of Frazier's matriarchy he added the term emasculator. With the addition of the emasculation theory to social science's imaging of the African American family, the portrait of the African American woman acquired new meaning. Her acknowledged self-reliance and strength were negated. Viewed as masculine modes of being, the African American woman's strength was her undoing. Through her strength she was accused of destroying her family, the very fabric of the community. For the African American woman power was negatively defined. She was thought to have the ability to advance herself and, simultaneously, to control, limit, and destroy the power of others.[37]

As incredulous as the negative power theory is, African American men expressing open hostility toward African American women embraced the pathology model held by society at large. Price Cobbs and William Grier, in *Black Rage,* accept the theory of the "failed black family."[38] Embracing the pathology model, they reconstruct the slave experience to explain the African American female psyche. The slave mother, they posit, created a slave child and mediated the world for him (the focus is on the relationship of mother and son). As a result of her role as mediator, Cobbs and Grier found that African American men felt hostility toward their mothers.[39] An even more bizarre rendering of the African American woman's psyche is Cobb's and Grier's postulation that feminine narcissism is "closely linked to intellectual achievement."[40] Since African American women cannot achieve the blond, blue-eyed ideal of feminine beauty, they cannot become, according to Cobbs and Grier, healthily narcissistic. Thus, the African American woman's intellectual achievement is limited.

Other negative images of the African American woman include the promiscuous, amoral female driven by her biological impulses, who undermines the family and disrupts social organization. Chick, the vamp in King Vidor's *Hallelujah,* is an early example from the motion picture industry. Frazier's research gives credence to the idea in sociology. Hortense Powdermaker supports the impulse theory in her work. Instead of sex, Powdermaker focuses on religion. Her 1939 book, *After Freedom: A Cultural Study in the Deep South,* defined the low-income African American woman as fundamentalist about religion and expressive emotionally and physically.[41] Nearly thirty years later, Cobbs and Grier support Powdermaker's claims in their publication of *The Jesus Bag.*[42] The impulse theory adds up to the image of African American women as biologically anchored rather than intellectually motivated.

These pathological images merge with the complex concept of strength. Given a pathological slant, strength connotes brutal hardness, coldness, and the capacity to emasculate. The African American woman represents a crucible of conflict.[43] Blamed, rejected, condemned, and resented, she is at the same time idealized as a symbol of survival, achievement, and liberation.

In opposition to the pathology school are the images forwarded by believers in the strength of the African American family. In 1941,

Melville Herskovits's publication of *The Myth of the Negro Past* opened the door to an alternative view of African American behavior. Recognizing difference as difference and not deviance, Herskovits reasoned, "aspects of Negro life which diverge most strikingly from patterns of the white majority are seen to deviate in the direction of resemblances to West African family life."[44] West Africa was characterized by polygynous families with what appeared to be female-headed households. However, these households were merely one small part of a larger family group. Each wife had her own house and managed her own household. This was no matriarchy, however, because her husband ruled the entire compound.

As one might expect, it took the pioneering research of an African American woman sociologist to analyze sensitively and carefully the pathological image of African American women. Joyce Ladner's *Tomorrow's Tomorrow* placed the idea of strength back in its positive context. In her work, matriarch becomes creative mother. This mother becomes a survival symbol, and the carrier of culture for the African American community. Regarding promiscuity, Ladner's work posits a sexually healthy woman.[45]

Ladner was not alone in her assertion of a basically healthy African American family theory. Jacqueline Jackson,[46] Andrew Billingsley,[47] and Robert Staples[48] resist the pathology theory. Jackson asserted, "A Black female-headed family maintaining itself over time is not unstable. It is stable. To put it another way, the presence or absence of a male head is an insufficient criterion for family stability."[49]

W. E. B. DuBois in *Darkwater*[50] introduced the Black Madonna or messianic symbol. The goddess or Black Madonna exists as literary archetype. Defining archetype, Catherine Starks says, "it embodies an idea that attracts conscientious response . . . recurs as a thematic motif in its subsequent manifestation and acquires mythic dimension as required by cultural needs."[51]

The Black Madonna myth is a covert image of powerlessness. The canonizing of virginity and immaculate conception is a deception that removes from the woman the power and control of her body. From the archetypal figure of the goddess/mother flows images of "good mother," "surrogate mother," and "mammy." A subtype, "strong woman" image is subsumed in this category. The strength of the positive, strong woman is not emasculatory, rather it appears to render the woman invincible. Thus, the African American woman's strength is mythicized to the almost total exclusion of her victimization.

The ambivalence of the African American community toward African American women partly reflects the community's powerlessness. The image of the hardworking, independent and autonomous Black woman is at variance with America's stereotyped definitions of the feminine as passive, dependent, and nonaggressive. The African American woman is found wanting, and the Black community seems powerless to resist the larger society's deviancy views of the Black woman. The African American woman's image reflects quadruple elements of distortion: the African American community's stance toward acceptance of White America's standards and definitions; America's convoluted view of African Americans in particular and women in general (the idea of male supremacy); the skewing of values based on economic class; and negative characteristics based on religious belief and sexual preference.

Gender bias together with racism operates against the African American woman in the real world and in fiction. The double reinforcement of social science research and the literary depiction of reality leads the African American community, particularly inadequately functioning men, to place the blame for their problems upon the woman instead of upon White society.[52] Abena Busia reminds us that language "is not innocent . . . language is ideologically and culturally bound, and it both expresses and conceals our realities."[53] Thus, language is where we must begin. Space does not permit the decoding of language here, but we must start, as Gates suggests, by utilizing language more precisely in order to rid ourselves of the dangers of careless usage and problematic terms. "Bitch," "broad," "hussy," "whore" are a few terms that come to mind, for which there is no equivalent male counter-term.

Focusing Our Image: Teaching Our Literature

Those of us engaged in teaching African American literature know too well the problems encountered. On the one hand there are the resistant students, on the other hand is the male canon with which we must come to terms. Busia's analysis is *mots justes,* bringing as she does, an international perspective to bear on the problem. Writing of common forces that affect women in the diaspora, she lists: (1) bastions of paternalistic power in which both sacred and secular ideologies have worked to domesticate and disempower women; (2) whatever the spirit of our faiths, in their culturally and politically institutionalized forms they have been misused to articulate us as inferior to the men of similar standing; (3) poverty renders women as the most silent in this global village.[54] Nancy Conklin and her colleagues, who produced the Southern Black women's project, suggest a good way to begin reorienting and focussing our image. They begin by examining a list of terms used to describe or used when discussing African American women or the African American experience. They list black, minority, colored, mulatto, girl, broad, mammy, Aunt Jemimah, high yellow, nappy hair, creole, woman of color/colored woman.[55] To those I add good hair, feminine, beautiful, sexy. The pedagogical objectives Conklin and her colleagues articulate are useful for teaching generally, but are especially significant for teaching women's literature. Their stated objectives are:

> to establish an open and comfortable classroom atmosphere where students feel the support of the professor and their classmates to be open and honest, where discussion can take place in personal as well as in political and cultural terms; to refocus students intellectually and emotionally from a view that African American women are marginal, exotic, and unimportant in American culture, toward the perspective in which they are viewed as important, legitimate and central to the national experience that all Americans should study, just as they study "great white men"; and to help students overcome the artificial barriers between personal experience and academic subject matter.[56]

The image of the African American woman has been rendered through the eyes of men. But men can describe only those aspects of women's lives that intersect with their own. Thus, much of the female experience has been a missing image. As the literature of women is pointing out, the experience of menstruation, pregnancy, childbirth, motherhood, menopause, abortion, rape and assault, female love and friendship must be articulated by women themselves. While it might be useful to refer to male depictions of the female experience for background discussion, central to any course are the texts by African American women.[57]

In the classroom, I seek to address a central fallacy in the pedagogy of higher education, and that is the notion that the individual is the agent of knowing, therefore the focus of teaching and learning. Learning is a communal act. Literature forces a continual cycle of discussion, disagreement, and consensus over what has been said, and what it all means or does not means. This creative conflict, if you will, is the essence of scholarship, and it is the central aim of my course.

Writing this chapter forced me to examine the space I occupy in the academy, and to question how it is that I survive. I came to Emory University from historically Black Fisk University, where a sense of ownership and pride in the institution were overriding factors in my being there. My family's decision to move provoked a crisis of sorts in my career and intellectual life, for I loved Fisk. As chair of the English Department, I knew that I was respected by my peers and valued by the students. Why, then, would I come to Emory? As it turned out, Emory was the only school in the area to offer me employment. Unwilling to be unemployed, I accepted the position with clear reservations. First it was a move from faculty to administration; I was not at all sure I wanted to be an administrator. It was also a move from center to margin, if you will. For although assistant dean is an administrative post, it is the bottom of top administration.

My first few months on the job were challenging, but I survived and will continue to do so because my spirit is nurtured by a strong and loving family. As a graduate of an historically Black institution, I have a firm grasp on and special appreciation for my heritage. I survived Boston University, Simmons College, and the University of Mississippi because I graduated from Fisk first. The Fisk experience taught me that I could go anywhere and achieve anything.

On days when my spirit is tired, my space threatened, my survival is never uncertain. I can always go home. And home is where my spirit is rekindled, my space is mine, and ownership of space is crucial to survival. How I survived is best expressed by my dedication page from a forthcoming book that reads: "For all the stars and black lights— those ultraviolet, infrared, radiant beings whose fluorescent essence reflects the black experience yesterday and today. Shine on." The title poem from that book follows.

Lodestar
in a galaxy of stars
spangling across a midnight sky
you are my guiding light
polar axis—*mc squared*
my one to the first power.
you brought me from
the bowels of muddy deep
river country, south of hell.
you pointed up the freedom
train's conductor stealing
through dark trees

along starlit streams.
you just kept on shining
high up there—Holy
shine on me
shine on me
ancient sagacious eye of God
shine on me.[58]

Notes

1. C. F. Epstein, *Woman's Place: Options and Limits in Professional Careers* (Berkeley: U of California Press, 1970).

2. J. Bernard, "Change and Stability in Sex-role and Behavior," *Journal of Social Issues* 32: 3 (1976): 207–23.

3. G. Strasser and W. Titus, "Pooling of Unshared Information in Group Decision Making: Biased Information Sampling During Discussion," *Journal of Personality and Social Psychology* 48 (1987): 1467–78.

4. Carrie Jane Singleton, "Race and Gender in Feminist Theory," *Sage* 6 (Summer 1989): 12–17.

5. bell hooks, "Black Women and Feminism," *Talking Back* (Boston: South End Press, 1989), 177.

6. Cheryl A. Wall, ed., *Changing Our Own Words* (New Brunswick, N.J.: Rutgers UP, 1989), 1.

7. Nikki Giovanni, *Images of Blacks in American Culture,* ed. Jessie Smith (New York: Greenwood Press, 1988), Foreword.

8. Stuart Gilman, "Black Bodies, White Bodies," *"Race" Writing and Difference,* ed. Henry Louis Gates, Jr. (Chicago: U of Chicago Press, 1986), 231–49.

9. *Ibid.,* 231.

10. *Ibid.,* 232.

11. *Ibid.,* 237.

12. Charles Darwin, *The Descent of Man and Selection in Relation to Sex* (New York: Appleton, 1897).

13. Gilman, 237.

14. Harold Fromm, "The Hegmonic Form of Othering: Or, the Academic's Burden," *Critical Inquiry* 13 (Autumn 1986), 197–200.

15. Gilman, 237.

16. Henry Louis Gates, Jr., *Black Literature and Literary Theory* (New York: Metheun, 1984), 341.

17. *Ibid.,* 343.

18. Ray Browne and Marshall Fishwick, eds., *Icons of America* (Bowling Green, Ohio: Popular Press, 1978), 20–25.

19. Parker Palmer, "Community, Conflict, and Ways of Knowing," *Change* (September/October 1978), 20–25.

20. *Ibid.,* 22.

21. Browne, 292.

22. *Ibid.,* 297.

23. Abena Busia, "Words Whipped Over Voids: A Context for Black Women's Rebellious Voices in the Novel of the African Diaspora," *Studies in Black American Literature,* Joe Weixlmann and Houston Baker, eds. (Greenwood, Fla.: Penkeville Publishers, 1988), 1–43.

24. Daryl Dance, "Each One Reach One and Teach One," *Black Issues in Higher Education* (April 26, 1990): 25.

25. Sandra Govan, "Each One Reach One and Teach One," *Black Issues in Higher Education* (April 26, 1990): 26.

26. *Emory College Catalogue,* 48.

27. Nancee Lyons, "Each One Reach One and Teach One," *Black Issues in Higher Education* (April 26, 1990): 26.

28. Term borrowed from Busia.

29. Harold Bloom, et al., *Deconstruction and Criticism* (New York: Seabury Press, 1979).

30. G. Gaff, "Deconstruction as Dogma, Or 'Come Back to the Raft Ag'in, Strether Honey!' " *Georgia Review* (Summer 1980): 404–416+.

31. Gloria Hull, Patricia Bell Scott, and Barbara Smith, *All the Women are White, All the Blacks are Men, But Some of Us Are Brave* (Old Westbury, NY: Feminist Press, 1982), Introduction.

32. Richard Wright, *Lawd Today* (New York: Taylor, 1963), 224.

33. Alice Dunbar Nelson, "Negro Literature for Negro Pupils," *The Black Man and the American Dream,* ed. June Sochen (Chicago: Quadrangle, 1971), 98.

34. Odette Martin, "Curriculum and Response: A Study of the Images of the Black Woman in Black Fiction," dissertation, University of Chicago, 1980. I borrow freely from Martin's work to construct a systematic approach to teaching African American women's literature.

35. E. Franklin Frazier, *The Negro Family in the United States* (Chicago: University of Chicago Press, 1939), 183.

36. Daniel P. Moynihan, "The Negro Family: The Case for National Action," *Black Matriarchy: Myth or Reality,* eds., John Bracey, Jr., August Meir, and Elliot Rudwick (Belmont, CA: Wadsworth, 1971), 150.

37. Martin, 17.

38. William Grier and Price M. Cobbs, *Black Rage* (New York: Basic Books, 1968), 38.

39. *Ibid.,* 39.

40. *Ibid.,* 42.

41. Hortense Powdermaker, *After Freedom: A Cultural Study in the Deep South* (New York: Viking, 1939).

42. William Grier and Price M. Cobbs, *The Jesus Bag* (New York: McGraw Hill, 1971).

43. Martin, 43.

44. Melville Herskovitz, *The Myth of the Negro Past* (New York: Harper, 1941), 190.

45. Joyce Ladner, *Tomorrow's Tomorrow* (Garden City, New York: Doubleday, 1971).

46. Jacqueline Jackson, "Black Women in Racist Society," *Racism and Mental Health*, eds. Charles Willie, ed al. (Pittsburgh: University of Pittsburgh Press, 1973).

47. Andrew Billingsley, *Black Families in White America* (New York: Simon and Schuster, 1968, 1988).

48. Robert Staples, *The Black Woman in America* (Chicago: Nelson-Hall, 1973).

49. Jackson, 55.

50. W. E. B. DuBois, "The Damnation of Women," *Darkwater: Voices from Within the Veil* (Millwood, NY: Kraus-Thomson, 1921, 1975).

51. Catherine Starks, *Black Portraiture in American Fiction* (New York: Basic, 1971), 111.

52. Jackson, 54.

53. Busia, 6.

54. *Ibid.*, 1.

55. Nancy Conklin, Brenda McCallum, and Marcia Wade, eds. *The Culture of Southern Black Women: Approaches and Materials* (Tuscaloosa, AL: University of Alabama Press, 1983), 8.

56. Conklin, et al., 8.

57. Texts by African American women, too numerous to list here, are readily available in book stores and libraries. See the bibliography for a list of critical works and anthologies.

58. Nagueyalti Warren, *Lodestar and Other Black Lights: Selected Poems* (forthcoming), 1.

8

Teaching Theory, Talking Community

Joy James

[P]eople of color have always theorized—but in forms quite different from the Western form of abstract logic . . . our theorizing (and
I intentionally use the verb rather than the noun) is often in narrative
forms, in the stories we create . . . [in] dynamic rather than fixed
ideas. . . . How else have we managed to survive with such spirit-
edness the assault on our bodies, social institutions, countries, our
very humanity? And women, at least the women I grew up around,
continuously speculated about the nature of life through pithy language that unmasked the power relations of their world. . . . My
folk, in other words, have always been a race for theory—though
more in the form of the hieroglyph, a written figure which is both
sensual and abstract, both beautiful and communicative.

Barbara Christian, "The Race for Theory"[1]

The Erasure of Africana Women in Academic Theory

Contemporary African American theorists such as Barbara Christian, who writes that theory not rooted in practice is elitist, think
within an African and community-centered tradition in which the
creativity of a people in the race for theory sustains humanity. However, teaching theory as nonelitist, and intending the liberation and
development of humanity, specifically African communities, contra-
dicts much of academic theory,[2] which is Eurocentric.

All philosophy and theory, Eurocentric or Afracentric, is political.
Academic "disciplines," when sexualized and racialized, tend to reproduce themselves in hierarchically segregated forms. To confront segregation means recognizing that current academic or educational stan-

dards have never worked, and were never intended to work, for us as a people. Our tenuous presence in (White) universities and colleges speaks to the fact that individuals, but not the community, may attain some success in an educational process centered on the marginalization of all but the "European" (socially constructed as White, propertied heterosexuals).

In academia many philosophy or theory courses may emphasize logic and memorizing the history of "Western" philosophy, rather than the activity of philosophizing or theorizing. When the logic of propositions is the primary object of study, how one argues becomes more important than for what one argues. The exercise of reason may take place within an illogical context. Catechizing academic canons obscures the absurdity of their claims to universal supremacy and the massive flaws in legacies, such as Platonic and Aristotelian "universal" principles derived from the hierarchical splintering of humanity; and/or the European Enlightenment's deification of scientific rationalism.

Some thinkers canonized in academia have argued that theory and philosophy are open to the "everyday" person and intend the good of humanity. However, few identify African people as both equal partners in that humanity and important theorists in its behalf. Fewer still connect the 'life of the mind' to the understanding that "Black people have to a disproportionate extent supplied the labor which has made possible the cultivation of philosophical inquiry."[3] We have also disproportionately cultivated the philosophies that provide nonabstract meanings of freedom and justice: surviving genocidal oppression allows insights into (in)humanity and (in)justice that transcend the abstractions of academic philosophy and theory. The root knowledge of African living thinkers, of democratic power and philosophy, is not often practiced inside ivory towers where provincial thinking, itself almost a universal in academia, reflects rather than critiques Eurocentrism.

"Eurocentrism" is not synonymous with European. In a society and culture where the White European represents both the ideal and universal manifestation of civilization, unsurprisingly, "Black" as well as "White" people adopt or adapt this icon as worldview. My schooling in White-dominated institutions has painfully impressed on me the depth of indoctrination and the difficulty of deprogramming myself from "truths" formulated under the tutelage of institutional bigotry which relegated "Blackness" and "femaleness" to savage superstition, invisibility or exotica and "Whiteness" and "maleness" to a paragon and the sublime.

Samir Amin defines Eurocentrism as:

> a culturalist phenomenon in the sense that it assumes the existence
> of irreducibly distinct cultural invariants that shape the historical
> paths of different peoples. Eurocentrism is therefore anti-universal-
> ist, since it is not interested in seeking possible general laws of human
> evolution. But it does present itself as universalist, for it claims that
> imitation of the Western model by all peoples is the only solution
> to the challenges of our time.[4]

White supremacy rationalizes Eurocentrism's anti-universalist stance.
It has shaped and misshapened European philosophy, with destructive
effects on the material lives of the majority of the world's people and
the spiritual and intellectual lives of all. Cornel West's description of
White supremacy applies to the Eurocentric, academic mindset:

> the idea of white supremacy emerges partly because of the powers
> within the structure of modern discourse—powers to produce and
> prohibit, develop and delimit, forms of rationality, scientificity, and
> objectivity which set perimeters and draw boundaries for the intelli-
> gibility, availability, and legitimacy of certain ideas.[5]

Adhering to the tastes of White supremacy, "white solipsism"[6] mas-
querades as philosophy within the myth of European "racial," therefore intellectual, superiority. As legitimizing a world order of domination becomes an intellectual mandate, Eurocentrism, like the carnival
house of mirrors, projects what it distorts. Its solipsistic reflections
racialize (and sexualize) theory, "whitening" thinkers indispensable
to its canons: the Egyptian philosophers, Aesop, Jesus of Nazareth,
Augustine. Given the broad paintbrush of White supremacy, it is a
tragicomedy that historical African or Semitic figures are depicted in
illustrated academic texts as physically "White," some with blond hair,
or taught paradoxically as if they had no ethnicity or race (in which
case their racial identities are assumed to be "White"). With or without
illustrations falsifying historical identities, students receive theory with
the bias that philosophy is the product of the minds of "great" White
men, and in Women's Studies of "great" White women, respectively
beneficent patriarchs or matriarches. (In African American studies the
prioritizing of African American men as theorists produces its own
distortions.)

With the European centered as "universal" or normative, all else, by
default, becomes marginal. When Eurocentric bias is seen as incidental

rather than endemic to academic thinking, "indiscretions" are thought to be containable if cauterized to allow the work to retain its status.[7] Consequently critiques of (hetero)sexism, racism, and classism failing to analyze individual writers as representatives of a collective consciousness reinforce Eurocentrism's hegemony as a metaparadigm, albeit as a flawed one.

Philosophical traditions, such as those of service to ancestors and community, challenge the authoritarian, authoritative voice of this metaparadigm. Living thinkers[8] operate, outside the worldview of "scientific" materialism and "objective" rationalism, within paradigms which hold the nonduality and interpenetration of reality—the sacred and secular, the political and spiritual, the individual and community. Presenting community as the foundation of reality and knowledge, these paradigms reject the elitism of academic thinking. They are consequently heresies; academia discredits indigenous cosmologies, and their concepts of nonlinear time, nonduality and commitments to community, as exotic aberrations and primitive thought. Since academia recognizes neither the intellectual nor moral authority of the (African) communities it dissects, and African communities do not determine how African people are to be "studied," our misrepresentation seems the rule.[9] Dismissing the centrality of African ancestral and living thinkers creates a catastrophic loss of realities and commitments present in traditional African cosmology.

The designation of academia, with its biases, as *the* legitimate intellectual realm for philosophy and theory deflects attention from traditional cosmologies and living thinkers. Theorizing within a tradition for liberated communities presents a worldview centered in spirituality, community survival, and human development. The devaluation of community and African thinking overlooks the universal aspects of the philosophy and theorizing of African "traditionalists," particularly women. Academic thinking promotes not only obscurantism but also the erasure of Africana women from theory.

Playing by its house rules, academia can set standards which no African American woman can meet *as an African American woman.* If it is assumed that we only speak as "Black women"—not as *women*—or "Black people"—not as *human beings*—our stories and theorizing are considered irrelevant or not applicable to women or people in general; they are reduced to descriptions of a part rather than analyses of a whole (humanity). When teaching about our lives as Africana women is viewed as a descent to the particular (*everything* African) from the "universal norm" (*anything* European), biology becomes destiny, with European biology as manifest destiny. Receiving recognition as "theorists" or "intellectuals" because of the "Westernization" and masculinization of our thinking (and lives) as Africana women still leave us "unqualified" as *Africana* women. Acknowledging "theory" only from those in transmutation in an Eurocentric form, reduces theory to technique. If it is only legitimized when communicated in "academese," then we must be trained out of traditional, communal communication to do theory.

If style or technical language determines much of what is recognized as theory, voguing is subjectless "objective" writing which claims to be without desires or interests.[10] Although desire and interest are not obliterated by proclamation, under the apotheosis of academic thinking, rationalism as "theory" vanquishes desire. Its technocratic jargon and writing, which "explore" or "probe" the lives of Africana women, lend themselves, like all colonial interventions and invasions, to misrepresentation and falsification. The objectification of African American women through the "expert" voice of "trained" speakers, including the voices of African American women academics who attempt to "re-articulate" knowledge,[11] is often a distorting interference. Since academese as an alien language is not designed to respectfully or adequately communicate African experiences,[12] using it we may appropriate and disrespect our own voices and people.

Appropriation requires abstractions. When we are stripped, or strip ourselves, of our context in community, caricatures incompatible with theory or philosophy deepen our intellectual alienation. The categorization of Black women in bipolar stereotypes—the "Mammy-Sapphire" swing of suffering or angry victims, without the ashé or power as ancestors and living thinkers,[13] is the prerequisite for relocation to some ghetto in an academic mind. Ghettoized in our own minds, and those of others, prevents a serious encounter with Africana women and blocks meeting ourselves as theorists. By demanding recognition for a community that theorizes, we can turn our extreme location into an advantage. The vantage point to being out on a ledge of institutional alienation is the ken of the view. Out there one can see the ways in which time, space, and people are strung up and strung out. Artificial timelines manipulate space and thought. In academic theory time is European time; space is that occupied by Europeans; great thinkers are their mythologized ancestors.

I find that people who routinely accept that European-Whites competently critique and teach African (American) thought may find it incongruous (or racial heresy) to accept that Africans-Blacks competently analyze and teach, and therefore contribute to, European (American) thought. The complaints of White European American students who rebelliously argue when assigned the writings of people of color that they "thought this was suppose to be a course on 'theory or women's studies' " are logical in this context. Their grievances are based on unmet expectations set by the false advertising of departments and programs which reduce theory to Eurocentric thought and Women's Studies to White women's studies. Attempting to bring more realism to our program, I jettison the Eurocentric paradigm in teaching my section of "Feminist Theory," renaming the course "Womanist/Feminist theory" and teaching Native American, Africana, Latina, Asian and European (American) women thinkers. My language has also changed. I more often say "Theory" without the qualifiers "Womanist" or "Black Feminist" when referring to the work of African American women theorists. (I take a cue from White men who do not title their works "*White Masculinist* Theory"; White women who do not preface their writings with "*White* Feminist Theory;" and, African American men who do not identify their publications as "Afrocentric *Masculinist* Theory."[14])

Attempts to recognize African contributions to understandings of philosophy and cosmology have focused on integration in spaces dominated by Europeans. Perhaps the most overworked decoy in academe's intellectual apartheid is curriculum "integration." Integration and "inclusivity" as new forms of segregation can act as a subterfuge for racist, (hetero)sexist and classist education. Curriculum integration, an easy home remedy to a racist canon, lends itself to the creation of more sophisticatedly segregated academic departments, programs, and courses. "Special interest" or "diversity" courses simultaneously integrate and segregate. They fail to transform disciplines which view racism as a problem of excess or indiscretion in the hegemony and not as the cornerstone of the hegemony itself. Disciplines seek to ameliorate exclusion through integration rather than struggle for new meanings and philosophies; the panacea becomes paradigmatic reform rather than a revolution in paradigms. Not the African community but academe determines the meaning, intent, and degree of "integration" of "Whites Only" disciplines; under these conditions, the reproduction of segregation is unsurprising.

In reform, the axis of the universe remains the same. Although academia bestows degrees and grants tenure, it does not necessarily produce philosophers and theorists. Eurocentric-academic theory is hardly an honorable participant in the race for theory. The purveyors of philosophy and theory retain their prerogatives to introduce anonymous, interchangeable satellites as mirrors for their own reflections: Black women are viewed as cosmetic aides to those holding firmly to their place at the center of the mirror. What does it mean that "academic theory" presents African American women thinkers as generic satellites in White star-studded galaxies? What would it mean to revolutionize the teaching of theory in academe in order to present African American women thinkers as builders of the shared universe, within African cosmology?

Making Our Presence Known

Before I can even teach theory, given its current biological construction in academia, I am continuously challenged to "prove" that I am qualified. Comparing my work experiences with those of other African American women academics, I notice that despite our having been hired through a highly competitive process, we seem to be asked more routinely, almost reflexively, if we have Ph.Ds. We could attribute this, and have, to our 'diminutive' height, youngish appearance or casual attire. Yet I notice that White women about our height, unsuited, and under 60, seem not to be interrogated as frequently about their qualifications. Continuously asked my "qualifications" as a "theorist" I cited to the inquisitive or inquisition: my *training*—a degree in political philosophy; *my research*—a dissertation on a European theorist; or my *employment*—teaching theory courses in academe. These are prerequisites for institutional membership but not measurements of competency. I accept that nothing will qualify me to students and faculty who do not struggle with their racism, fear, and hostility towards African people, philosophy, and theorizing centered on liberation. For me, teaching theory courses on the praxis of African American women permits me to claim that I think. Connecting my teaching to community organizing allows me to say I theorize. Service in African liberation qualifies me.

These qualifications make me a suspicious character if not "unqualified" for academe. A hydra for teachers and students who do not set them, criteria established without our input are shrouds. The issue is not whether there should be standards and qualifications; there always are. The issue is who sets and will set them, and for whose benefit they function. The reward of transgressing conventional academic standards is reestablishing connections to community wisdom and practice.

The specter of failing to meet institutional standards and "qualifications" inhibits the search for new models of knowledge and teaching.

In teaching, I try to learn and share more about the history of social thought. Teaching about the origins of the "academy," "philosophy" and "theory" as predating the "Greek ancestors" of "Western civilization" broadens the scope of both the time and space in which theory takes place; it expands academia's concept of who theorizes. Changing the concept of time or the timeline changes the context for philosophy and theory.[15] Philosophy extends beyond the appearance of Europeans (and their designated ancestors) in history; so theory extends beyond the spaces they occupy or rule. To restrict our discussions of the contributions of African cosmology and philosophy to the "contemporary" period implies that we have no "ancient" or "modern" history in philosophizing. Without a history philosophy is not indigenous to us as a people; and "contemporary" theorizing becomes disconnected from its tradition. That is why we must reinsert ourselves in time and history on the continuum, and confront academic disciplines attempting to erase us from that line. The ways in which I approach theory are changing.

Extending time to find other origins of theory, I encounter more comprehensive spaces and thoughts. Hypaetia, the (Egyptian or Greek) woman philosopher, sits with the "Ancient" philosophers of academic masculinist theory. The Kongo women kings theorize in a unique cosmology coexisting with the space occupied by Locke, and Rousseau and other philosophs of the European Enlightenment. Angela Davis and African revolutionary theorizing coexist with the European (American) liberalism of Rawls, Arendt, and Bentham in contemporary political theory. In "essential feminist writings," Ida B. Wells is taught alongside Mary Wollstonecraft and Susan B. Anthony; Virginia Woolf and Mary Daly are placed beside Assata Shakur and Audre Lorde.

The ways in which I teach theory are changing. Cultivating respectfulness in myself and seeking it in my students, I ask my classes: "Who are you? Do you know your personal and political relationship to the knowledge studied?" I find that autobiographical theorizing discourages appropriation and objectification, while encouraging students to identify themselves as potential theorists and embark in self-reflections that include critiques of racist, classist and (hetero)sexist assumptions (a "backlash" usually follows any sustained critique of entrenched, dominant biases). I urge students to carefully consider the claim by revolutionary African American women who write that the roles of living thinkers are open to all and that they are not "exceptional" (those who participate in a legacy follow rather than deviate from the normative).

Students encounter the women's images and voices through video and audio tapes that supplement readings for discussions on women's contributions to and roles in liberation struggles. These images, along with exploring our relationships and responsibilities to writers, stories, and theories, pull us off the sidelines as "spectators" and consumers of Africana "performance" towards our own roles as actors. Contending with my own "consumerism," I find that progressive Africana activists give me more than subject matter for courses; they also provide instruction in philosophy and democratic pedagogy. I am pushed most as a teacher-student when wrestling with the implications of philosophy and theorizing in the autobiographies of revolutionary African American women. More than any other type of writing, this form prods me to confront my personal and political responsibilities to ancestors, youth, and future generations. Attempting to share what I learn, the internal obstacles appear. They emerge out of my physical and sometimes intellectual alienation from work for community liberation and the philosophers and theorists of the community. They coexist with the everpresent external obstacles of indifference and hostility towards Black liberation theorizing. Despite the internal and external obstacles, I begin to fear less being dismissively ignored by academics and fear more my own ignorance about and faltering ties to our ancestors' loving, radical traditions. Although it grates the academic norm, responsibility means that legitimacy and authority come from the humanity of my communities.[16] If respect and recognition mean communicating our wisdom and humanity in struggle, regardless, then pedagogy will be the transport.

Talking Theory: Activism in Pedagogy

Pedagogy rooted in ethical concerns and an epistemology based on a four part process of experience, reflection, judgment, and action,[17] organize my courses. Readings stimulate and challenge students to expand their experiential base. They then enter their reflections in journals, essay papers and compare their insights in small student work groups. Judging dominant norms, students design activities or projects to demystify and challenge economic and racial-sexual oppression, and evaluate their own ideologies. Through organizing, they obtain a greater experimental base to reflect on philosophy and theorizing, cosmologies, freedom and liberation struggles. The last step in this epistemological framework is action. Ethical action expands experiences, stimulates self-reflections, and judging. A pedagogy that denies the validity of personal experiences, that make no space for self-reflection, that discourages judgment, and severs action from insight confuses fragmented thinking with knowledge. Guided by ethical concerns to think and organize to resist oppression, we walk closer to the place where humanist political thinkers stand. There, hopefully with a less distant and more substantial awareness of their theorizing, we begin to comprehend and critique.

To respectfully teach about theorizing by African American women activists requires such a pedagogy based on ethics and active commitment to community liberation. So, I reject the concept of education as value-neutral and use "extracurricular" activities as a lab component (for instance, the hands-on experience of "applied" knowledge or "labs" to supplement "book" knowledge is indispensable in disciplines such as chemistry or architecture). These activities, encouraging students to take an active rather than passive role in their self-development, advance critical analyses of: child abuse; sexual violence; adultism; racism; (hetero)sexism; and classism.

For example, in my senior seminar on "Women and the State," students wrote papers and organized educational forums for the campus and local community on relevant topics. Their educationals in the campus center, held on Tuesday afternoons in March during Women's History Month , were: "Women and Militarization," "Women and Occupation," and "Women Political Prisoners." "Women and Militarization" occurred around the time of the U.S. bombing of Iraq. Over 100 people attended this educational, which students organized as a tribunal or mock trial in which African American, Caribbean and Native American and European American women activists and teachers testified on U.S. crimes against humanity, specifically violence resulting from racism and sexism in U.S. domestic and foreign policies. The students performed-educated as poets, defense and prosecution lawyers, judge, and witnesses. They staged guerilla theatre to disrupt their mock trial: dressed in mourning garb, the "ghosts" of several women murdered by their male companions in domestic violence interrupted the proceedings, bitterly denouncing the court for ignoring their desperate petitions, as living women, to stop their batterers.

Although the majority of students in the "Women and the State" seminar stated that they found organizing their forum and attending and critiquing the others as one of their most difficult and most rewarding educational experiences, interrelating doing and knowing for ethical-political action is not a popular practice in academe. White students have told me that they resent not the request to engage in activities outside the classroom (they do for other classes), but the request to act against racism, believing it unjust to require, as proper and necessary, that students (staff and faculty) confront adultism, classism, racism, and (hetero)sexism in their courses and themselves. (Other more liberal advocates of multiculturalism have argued that critiques of texts are the only *responsible action* in academic classes.)

I argue for activism as an indispensable component in learning. Action promotes consciousness of one's own political practice; such self-consciousness is a prerequisite to literacy. "Interest" in the lives of Black women and democratic struggles is superficial and the "knowledge" acquired specious if one remains illiterate in the language of community and commitment spoken by the women activists. Activism promotes literacy. It is usually the greatest and most difficult learning experience, particularly if it is connected to communities and issues broader than the parameters of academic life.

Theory and philosophy "born in struggle" carry extremely difficult lessons. Activism concretizing ethical ideals in action, allows us to better comprehend a form of thinking unfamiliar in abstract academic thought—theorizing under fire or under conditions of confrontation or repression. Thinking to stay alive and be free is the heart of liberation praxis. For half a millenium, Indigenous and African peoples in the Americas and Africa have theorized for their individual lives and the life of the community. Theorizing as a life and death endeavor rather than leisured, idle speculation, embodies revolutionary praxis. As faculty we may find ourselves in positions where living by our beliefs and theory carries the hazards of not receiving grants, promotion or tenure; students may lose scholarships and higher grades. We rarely though find ourselves in positions where living by our ideals carries the possibility that we may die for them. We generally never have to risk our lives to claim our ideals and freedom, as have radical thinkers and activists such as: Harriet Tubman; Anne Moody; Assata Shakur; Martin Luther King, Jr.; Malcolm X; and, Fred Hampton.[18]

Several years ago, while a visiting scholar at a midwestern university, I was able to learn more about how risk-taking and radical organizing test ideas, ideologies and commitments. During my semester tenure, the Ku Klux Klan based in its national headquarters in

Indiana decided to march and stage a rally in the local campus town. The general response against the march and rally centered on individual comments of fear and anger. There was little collective, organized response until one night, as part of a woman's film festival, a small number of students viewed William Greaves' video, "A Passion for Justice," on the life of Ida B. Wells. An African American woman senior facilitated the discussion session that followed the video during which students shared how they were impressed by Ida B. Wells' courageous and influential activism, which began at such a young age, their age. They were silent when asked about the relationship between their feelings of inspiration for the story of Miss Wells' resistance and their feelings of anger and fear about the upcoming Klan march. Exploring these issues later that night in their dorm rooms, students began strategy sessions: they decided to allow their admiration for Miss Wells to lead them to organize a counter-educational critiquing racism, homophobia, sexism, and antisemitism in response to the impending KKK march.

African American women students led the organizing and formed a coalition with European Americans, European Jewish Americans and gay and lesbian activists. Some of these African American women students had experienced the most violent racial/sexual assaults on campus. At an early organizing meeting, one African American senior spoke of being dragged off a catwalk into bushes as her White male assailant yelled "nigger bitch" while repeatedly punching her. As she struggled away she noticed White student spectators who made no effort to assist or intervene. The woman student stated that the university's investigation and handling of the attack were equally unresponsive.

Faculty criticisms and complaints about White dominated universities did not translate into support for the student initiated organizing. Most African American faculty and administrators, like their White counterparts, were reluctant to publicly support a student "speak-out" against racist, sexist, and homophobic violence critical of the university. University employees mirrored the divisions among African American students in which more cautious or conservative students dismissed student organizers as "radical" and ridiculed them for "over-reacting." Political differences among African American students, faculty and administration were exacerbated during the KKK organizing.

Fear of criticizing the administration or faculty, along with homophobia, sexism and caste elitism allowed faculty and more conservative African American students to distance themselves from student activists. Yet students and youth face the greatest dangers from racial-sexual violence on campus and in society. Alongside community women and men, only two European American women and I as faculty actively organized with students educating against, in the wake of the Klan rally, increasing racist/antisemitic verbal abuse and physical violence on campus. The Klan rally highlighted faculty ambivalence and refusal to support student organizing and the university administration's unwillingness to publicly take an uncompromised stance against and responsible action for diminishing racist, antisemitic, homophobic, and sexual violence on campus.

It seemed that we faculty and administrators believed our class and caste status in academe granted us immunity from the violence assaulting many African American youth, women, and gay and lesbian students. My own inabilities, with others, to always speak and talk to community in the midst of organizing conflicts, were compounded by my impatience and frustration with the political rhetoric and passivity of nonactivists. The confusion and strains impressed on me the precarious balance of teaching and talking for justice and my own uncertainty and anger, with others, about the terrain of struggle and community.

Community

Individual changes in classroom teaching to deconstruct racist-heterosexist curricula and build community are marginal if not supported by the department or program and other instructors. Often the struggles for more accuracy and accountability in education are labeled and depoliticized as personal (personnel) whims of faculty rather than responsible action. I have found that personalizing my confrontations with eurocentric thinkers or academic careerists is a form of depoliticization that contributes to my own isolation and ineffectualness. Supporting progressive curricula and pedagogies demands political change. Yet, my experiences show that few are willing to engage in the type of activism and restructuring necessary to supplant tokenism.

I share Toni Morrison's observations in "Rootedness: The Ancestor As Foundation," applying her thoughts on writing to teaching, another art form:

> If anything I do in the way of writing . . . isn't about the village or the community or about you, then it is not about anything. I am not interested in indulging myself in some private, closed exercise of my imagination that fulfills only the obligation of my personal dreams—

which is to say, yes, the work must be political. It must have that as its thrust. That's a pejorative term in critical circles now: if a work of art has any political influence in it, somehow it's tainted. My feeling is just the opposite: if it has none, it is tainted.[19]

Academics and students, if not always content, seem comparatively "safe" from the political-economic conditions destroying African communities and villages. Educational status and economic "stability" grant us space to move about the world as if our survival were guaranteed, despite the increasing impoverishment and death of Africans worldwide.[20] Privilege may reduce our primary preoccupation in academia to struggles for accreditation and legitimacy from the intellectual representatives of the "new" old world order.

I am paid to, and so I pay my bills and taxes to the military, by teaching "theory" in a White university's White Women's Studies program in a White suburb called "Amherst." On my better days, I think freely about a people loving and theorizing for liberation. I try to think in the traditions in which philosophy and theory are the tools of initiates and "slaves"[21] to the community, rather than the techniques of academic employees; this is problematic in places where people talk and write about life and death in and to abstraction. Although at times afraid to forget and to always remember my indebtedness to the militant Black praxis that forced open the doors of White academia, I am grateful to the call to be in a tradition of midwifery to philosophizing and theorizing, a tradition that intends community and respect for African ancestors, the living, and future born.

Notes

1. Barbara Christian, "The Race for Theory," reprinted in *Making Face, Making Soul; Haciendo Caras,* edited by Gloria Anzaldua, (San Francisco: Aunt Lute Foundation, 1990), 336.

2. Native American writer Lee Maracle notes the circular logic of academic theory: "Theory: If it can't be shown, it can't be understood. Theory is a proposition, proven by demonstratable argument. Argument: Evidence, proof. Evidence: demonstratable testimony, demonstration. . . . Argument is defined as evidence; proof or evidence is defined by demonstration or proof; and theory is a proposition proven by demonstratable evidence. None of these words exist outside of their inter-connectedness. Each is defined by the other." Lee Maracle, *Oratory: Coming to Theory.* North Vancouver, B.C. Gallerie Women Artists' Monographs, Issue 1 (September 1990), 3.

3. European American feminist Elizabeth Spelman cites this quote from a journal

issue on African Americans and philosophy in her work *Inessential Woman: Problems of Exclusion in Feminist Thought.* (Boston: Beacon Press, 1988).

4. Amin continues: "Eurocentrism is a specifically modern phenomenon, the roots of which go back only to the Renaissance, a phenomenon that did not flourish until the nineteenth century. In this sense, it constitutes one dimension of the culture and ideology of the modern capitalist world." Samir Amin, *Eurocentrism* (New York: Monthly Review Press, 1989), vii.

5. Cornel West, "A Genealogy of Modern Racism," *Prophesy Deliverance* (Philadelphia: Westminster Press, 1982).

6. The phrase "White solipsism" comes from White lesbian feminist Adrienne Rich's article "Disloyal to Civilization: Feminism, Racism, Gynephobia," *On Lies, Secrets, and Silence* (New York: Norton, 1979). Solipsism is the belief that only one's self is knowable or constitutes the world.

7. Racist, classist, and (hetero)sexist thinking routinely garner the title of "philosophy" or universally true—even when Eurocentric studies decree a new universal truth that there is no "universal truth." Although Europeans and European thought were not and are not the center of the universe, "civilization," or "theory," what tends to accompany "de-centering" the European, as Barbara Christian notes in "The Race for Theory," is the claim that there is no center. That traditional African cosmology, or Native American cosmology, might contain a center is rarely raised in academic theory. The relativist claim of "no center," backed by the hegemony of White supremacy, is like the claims of being "colorblind" or "raceless" in a racist system. It is blindness by convenience to deny domination and struggles for equality.

8. See Chapter 3, "African Philosophy, Theory, and 'Living Thinkers' " in this anthology.

9. Generally in Women's Studies, White women choose the Black feminist/womanist scholars. Recently, I found myself in the odd position of comforting a White woman on her difficulty in securing a position as a professor in African American women's literature. All her interviews had been with European Americans who controlled the hiring process. White women decided which Black woman they would hire for their "Black Women's Studies" line, based on their definition of Black feminism; since they decided on me, I'm working. I try to define and shape a program that respects rather than objectifies African people. The WORCC proposal in the appendix is one such attempt. However, the Center for Teaching committee rejected it, reportedly as "controversial," and "something you would do anyway" without institutional support.

10. Patricia Hill Collins describes the ideology of this worldview where "research methods generally require a distancing of the researcher as a 'subject' with full human subjectivity and objectifying the "object" of study . . . the absence of emotions from the research process . . . ethics and values [as] inappropriate in the research process . . . adversarial debates . . . [as] the preferred method of ascertaining truth. . . ." See: Patricia Collins, "Learning from the Outsider Within: The Sociological Significance of Black Feminist Thought," *Social Problems* 33:6 and *Black Feminist Thought* (Boston: Unwin Hyman, 1990, reprint Routledge).

11. Patricia Hill Collins uncritically argues for such "rearticulation" in "Learning from

the Outsider Within: The Sociological Significance of Black Feminist Thought," *Social Problems* 33:6 and *Black Feminist Thought.*

12. "When alien voices attempt to convey the African center, everything is lost in translation." K. Kia Bunseki Fu Kiau in a talk at the Caribbean Cultural Center in New York, January 1991, spoke of four different levels of language: level 1 of everyday life, level 2 of the esoteric or philosophical traditions of a people, and level 3 of those who mediate and translate between both levels. The fourth level came with colonization and conquest. Level 4, alien language, is where Europeans interrogated African people on level 1, the non-initiated. Foreigners believed they had encountered a whole people and their cosmology or lack of cosmology by speaking only with those on the level of everyday life.

13. For examples of ashé or power of African women see: *Gelede: Art and Female Power Among the Yoruba,* edited by Henry and Margaret Drewal (Bloomington: Indiana University Press), 74.

14. Eurocentric masculinist theory centers on White men while Eurocentric feminist theory (responding to the "gender," not race/class/heterosexual bias of masculinist Eurocentrism) focuses on White women. This cohabitation reflects obedience to academic houserules: Eurocentric feminist theory courses are also taught within a White canon of "essential writings." The increasing role of Europeanamerican women in teaching Africanamerican women writers may merely signal increasing appropriation. Without a paradigmatic shift from Eurocentrism, appropriation features colorized reruns: the paradigm of White middle class women's victimization in blackface. Without an African centered paradigm from which to teach writings by women of color critiquing racist feminism, the center remains "White," and the works remain criticism of the prevailing hegemony not theorizing from African philosophy.

15. Academia's presentation of time and consequently the history of thought promotes the delusion that philosophy (and civilization) began with "the Greeks" rather than the African scholars who preceded and taught them, and the African civilizations which predate Athens. Voids in timelines manufacture artificial "origins" which, legitimizing European rule, deny the African ancestral lineage in European philosophy. "Ancient" becomes the 'sui generis' thinking of "Europeanized" Greeks; "Medieval" the European Christian Church, with a de-Africanized Augustine; "Modern" European Enlightenment philosophs; and "Contemporary" European (American) writers and thinkers." "Ancient," "Medieval," "Modern," and "Contemporary" as categories for time also become categories of space and "race," denoting geography and ethnicity. Theorists assigned in each category are invariably "White" men in masculinist theory (where Hannah Arendt qualifies as the "exceptional ("White") woman) and "White" women in feminist theory.

16. Bernice Johnson Reagon argues this about the work of Martin Luther King, Jr., see "Nobody Knows the Trouble I See"; or, "By and By I'm Gonna Lay Down My Heavy Load," *Journal for American History* (Vol. 78, No. 1, June 1991).

17. Theologian Bernard Lonergan discusses in *INSIGHT: An Understanding of Human Knowing* (New York: Harper and Row, 1957) an epistemology similar to the African (Afrocentric) ethical paradigm in which knowledge exists for the sake of communal good and individual human liberation (which are not presented as oppositional). Experience, reflection, judgment, and action are part of the process

by which people (knowingly or unknowingly) learn. Action is indispensable to the learning process: you know how to ride a bicycle or drive a car not from merely reading books about bicycles or cars, but from riding or driving one as well (building furthers your knowledge). One knows how to live, learn and teach without patriarchal, White supremacist, or classist elitist assumptions by doing activities that confront and diminish racism, sexism, heterosexism, and classism.

18. Prior to his assassination by the FBI and Chicago police in 1971, Fred Hampton prophesied: "I'm going to die for the people because I live for the people." Quoted in "A Nation of Law? (1968–71)," *Eyes on the Prize-Part II* which documents Hampton's political work for the African American community, the FBI's disruption of the Black liberation movement and its eventual assassination of Fred Hampton and Mark Clark. This segment of *Eyes on the Prize, Part II* also covers the Attica uprising for prisoners' human rights and its violent repression by the New York State government.

19. Morrison, 344–45.

20. The U.S. dominates international financial institutions such as the World Bank and International Monetary Fund (IMF). These institutions have underdeveloped Africa, Latin America and the Caribbean so that we as a people are poorer in the 1990s than we were in the 1960s. According to UNICEF's 1988 report, *State of the World's Children,* the "Third World" is in debt to the U.S. and Western European nations/financial institutions for over $1000 billion (U.S. currency). People in the most impoverished countries in the world pay to the West more in interest and capital than they receive in new aid and loans: each year African, Caribbean, and Latin American nations transfer $20+ billion to historical colonizers. UNICEF estimates that over half a million young children died in 1988 because of these economic policies in which 14% of the world's population—U.S. and other "Western" elites—consumes 70% of its resources. While IMF austerity programs decimate lives and autonomy of regions, U.S./Western European based multinational or transnational corporations exacerbate dislocation, labor and sexual exploitation of women and children—the "docile" labor supply. In this economic crisis of contemporary colonialism, modern day vampirism of the Black World enriches foreign and native elites. At "home" the situation is not very different.

In the U.S. "austerity programs" against the poor take on a new dimension as the World Bank and IMF implement "development" projects for what remains of indigenous people's lands. African American people are poorer today than when we were a generation ago: the "poverty draft" provides "equal opportunity employment" in military "service" or prison industries. Here, two out of three adults in poverty are women; with women of color twice as likely to be poor than White women. Here, an estimated 33 million people live below the whimsically set "poverty line." Millions live on the line and over one million do not even "register" because they are homeless. Ten percent of the U.S. people own 83% of the wealth and resources while twenty million are jobless. In some cities, up to 80% of the 16–19 year old African American youth have "dropped out" of the labor force; 70–80% are driven out of high schools. The National Urban League's 14th annual "State of Black America" (1988) report quantifies the results of the dominant U.S. philosophy and theory in practice: from 1984–1986, the life expectancy for Whites increased (from 75.3 years to 75.4), while the life expectancy for African Americans decreased (from 69.7 to 69.4 years); an African American infant is twice as more likely to die in her/his first year than a White infant.

21. According to Bunseki Fukia, in Kongo philosophy the Nganga—the initiated elders and teachers—are "slaves" to the community (lecture, Caribbean Cultural Center, New York City, February 1991).

Survival

9

The Revolution Within: Transforming Ourselves

Patricia Coleman-Burns

When a determined core of militant students took over the Helen
Newberry Joy student services building on the campus of Detroit's
Wayne State University in April of 1989, I unhesitatingly supported
them, and knew I would until the end. The identified leaders were "our"
students, enrolled that semester in Black Studies[1] classes, and, more specifically, in my classes. There was, though, a "bottom line" which I hoped
we would never reach. I hoped I would never have to choose between my
own principles and political beliefs and those of the students.

I had long recognized students' growing disenchantment with the
"older" generations as well as their emerging feelings that they had
been betrayed by the older radicals and moderates/conservatives (my
peers and their parents' generation) of the Black Liberation Movement.
It was Black Studies that had been the first introduction for many of
these students to the contributions and accurate historical perspectives
of people of African descent within the United States and in Africa
prior to the period of enslavement.[2] I understood their dismay with
parents, schools and others within the African American community
whom they felt had denied and continued to deny them their African
history. Many of the issues that emerged in the "study-in" which
led to the student activism were present in my youth. These issues
represent(ed) the phenomena of the progressive movements of the
1950s, 1960s, and 1970s, and contemporary movements poised on the
horizon of the twenty-first century. They also represent(ed) the crisis
in values, vision, relationships, and cultural and spiritual integrity.

Pedagogy of Transformation: Analyzing Racism

One day at the end of a class on Black social and political thought,
a young African American student came in to the classroom to speak

to me. He was very curious as to why the class tended to run over. He remarked that in most of his classes the students tear out of the classroom. He wanted to know what it was that we were doing that captivated the students' attention and was intrigued that they consistently hung back at the end of the period and emerged from the room engaged in interesting discussions. At first I was taken aback. In my nineteen years of teaching I had come to see the runovers as normal. I had forgotten that many classroom sessions are quite boring to students. I had to ask myself, as I had on other occasions, what was different about Black Studies and what, if anything, was unique about my method of teaching.

First and foremost, the subject of Africana Studies is people of African descent and their experiences in the United States, Africa, and throughout the diaspora. They are viewed not as a pitiful people stripped of their humanity and without hope, but as a people who struggle to define their humanity and shape their destiny against those who would dehumanize them. In a society in which racism is so pervasive and fundamental to its inception and history, it is exciting for students, Black or White, to see African Americans as human beings acting on their own behalf. African Americans have played an integral part in the development of this nation, materially and intellectually. Often in academic works they are treated as passive objects being acted upon. Africana Studies makes the experiences, perspectives and worldviews of people of African descent central; subjects of and actors in their own story.

Africana Studies challenges traditional scholarly practices and "historiographical process"[3] in the academy. It grapples with the troublesome issues of cultural, class, and racial myopism in a culturally and racially diverse society, questioning the silencing and exclusion of the voices of the different, the "non-hegemonic," "the othered."[4] This history of African Americans and other people of color is shaped by the cultural definitions and limitations of the larger society. A study of the history of North America is inseparable from race, class, and gender. There is a growing body of scholars who are challenging the Eurocentric, male-chauvinist perspective in understanding African, Asian, Mexican, and Native American histories. The thrust towards other-centered perspectives has great scholarly potential. There is a historical basis for projecting that African American people in general, and Black women in particular, provide a pivotal, centered perspective.

Inevitably in the classroom one of the topics of discussion is the purpose of education. Without fail, the majority identify the purpose as obtaining a degree in order to get a better job. When we review the history of education, I point out that the notion of educating a labor force is a very recent goal, linked to Henry Ford in the 1940s, introduced with the shift of the United States from a primarily agricultural to an industrial-based economy. Prior to that time the purpose of education, specifically for the upper and ruling classes, was to train the next generation to govern. In class the example we start with of a "ruling" class is the ancient Egyptians (Kemetians) and the Egyptian Mysteries Systems which were designed to pass on the great mysteries of the universe from generation to generation.[5]

My goal is to train students, the next generation, to run this nation. While everyone needs to be able to provide for her/himself and their dependents, I encourage them to want more than just a job. Those who have made it through the halls of higher education comprise the next generation of the African American intelligentsia.[6] I encourage students to see the possibilities of their making fundamental decisions for the direction of this nation, and to use their knowledge, training, creativity, and skills in the interest of the oppressed people of the United States rather than in furthering exploitation of people. I encourage them to be fundamental actors in the creation of a pedagogy of transformation[7] to liberate, transform, and revolutionize people. The classroom is the first step in their own transformation and, perhaps, intellectual and spiritual liberation.

We discuss racism, a concept and ideology nearly all students are able to understand, though we have to struggle a little to get over the tendency to make the term synonymous with racial prejudice and bigotry. Blacks, particularly elected officials, can be agents of racism. However, racism is an historical and political ideology, particularly in countries which engaged in the enslavement of Africans. In these countries this ideology is systemic and systematic and is based on White supremacy and power. Key to understanding this ideology is understanding the historic oppression and dehumanization of people of African descent and the creation of an underclass or a second-class hierarchy below that of Whites and those new immigrants aspiring to become "White." Some particular forms the ideology of racism has taken are the slave codes and Jim Crow laws in the United States, and apartheid in South Africa. The more sinister form is internalized racism.

External racism created within the African American community a subservient attitude which, according to Martin Luther King, Jr., reflected an acceptance of the "place" assigned to the African American.[8] What is so devastating about racism is what it does to oppressed people. In academe, senior faculty and administrators of color are often the hardest and most uncompromising when it comes to the promotion and tenure of junior faculty of color. They are often the first to expose the negative about a colleague of color. African American academicians will often excuse their collusion with White administrators and faculty by explaining that they are doing the person of color a favor in identifying weaknesses before Whites do. This, they explain, gives them credibility and proves that Black faculty are able to go beyond thinking of color. If the person of color in question can measure up to the (sometimes impossible) standards and expectations placed on them by their own, surely, the argument follows, they'll be able to meet the standards of the White academy. This attitude is used against students of color as well.

No White faculty or administrator is held solely responsible for the success or failure of any White faculty or student. There is a difference between challenging a student or junior colleague to achieve his/her own level of excellence and setting up false, discriminatory and rigid standards of excellence to which few people (Black or White) can measure up. We see this attitude in the community in the sense that some African Americans will never go to a Black physician, or lawyer, just as some African American women will never believe in an Anita Hill or a Desiree Washington. African American academics often act as if they have a limited number of markers which they must conserve, and unless they cast their vote for the "successful" student or candidate of color they'll lose their credibility and authority. Internalized oppression is a no-win situation. This slave mentality protects the interests of the slave master (in this case, White privilege of the academy) and usurps the power of people of color involved presently and in the future.

My own coming to maturity and political evolution as a young Black woman in the 1970s paralleled the evolution of the Movement through its various stages of development from antiracism and anti-imperialism and to antisexism and anti-cultural hegemony. Clearly racism had been fundamental to the development of many antagonistic contradictions in the United States since its inception. All Whites, even the poorest, were legally and in practice deemed racially superior to all Blacks. The racism of White women in the Women's Liberation Movement and in society made it difficult for Black women to achieve the gender-based solidarity with White women comparable to the racial solidarity which African Americans were able to accomplish. The strength of the Black Liberation Movement of the 1950s, 1960s, and 1970s was its ability to polarize, sharpen, and then unify a view of the world under one philosophy. The Movement addressed the contradictions of racism and oppression and raised political acuity. Whether we were poor or rich, educated or illiterate, high yellow or black as a starless night, the common wisdom of the African American community was clear that we were "Black and Proud" and that we wanted "freedom" and we wanted it "now." Recognizing our Blackness was not enough. Where there is no vision, the people perish. Questions of identity, freedom, and new reality had to be defined.

Issues other than race were viewed by Movement people as raising peripheral and marginal questions that some believed would diffuse, undermine, and divide the larger struggle. The Movement for unity became illusive. Being Black was not inherently revolutionary, and wanting freedom without a clear sense of purpose and human transformation was not fundamental change. During the 1970s other concerns, other voices unleashed by this growing awareness around race were coming to the fore.

Women began to challenge the domination of males in the leadership and decision-making aspects of the movement. The working and poorer classes began to question the preponderance of middle-class and educated Blacks, who tended to focus on affirmative action, integration, and equality between Blacks and Whites. These new forces were voicing their concerns for fundamentals. They were more concerned with jobs, health care, housing, education, and human dignity than with integration. Issues of gender and class began to vie with race for attention.

Malcolm X's popularity, King's shift to concerns of the working class and poor, and later Marxist class analyses reflect the Movement's willingness to embrace some class questions. The contention of C. L. R. James, James Boggs and the League of Revolutionary Black Workers that Blacks were the most progressive social force among and within the working class demonstrated the necessity and correctness of bringing the issue of class to the Black Liberation Movement. Bringing the issues of class, sexism, and human transformation into the contemporary classroom is also necessary and correct, particularly for African American students.

To help students understand the interconnectedness of their reality and that of "uneducated" brothers and sisters, I draw upon historical and current examples. We discuss how David Walker, author of *Walker's Appeal . . . to the Colored Citizens of the World But in Particular and very Expressly to those of the United States of America*, (1829) called for solidarity between free and enslaved Africans within the United States, and between Africans in the United States and the world. The question of solidarity is then brought to the present. I often use myself as an example of how degrees, including the Ph.D., mean nothing to those bent on oppressing African Americans (even though education is supposed to be a prerequisite to equality and higher status). I tell of being treated on many occasions the same as persons who did not have my level of formal education. In this racist society most African Americans are treated with the same amount of disrespect.

I turn to newspapers which are replete with stories of rich and famous African Americans who found this to be true. One such story is of a young athlete who was driving his Mercedes Benz and was pulled over by the police, because of the stereotypical belief that the only Black men with such wealth are drug pushers. Another story is of Isiah Thomas of the Detroit Pistons who wears disguises in order to go shopping without being constantly asked for autographs. The price he pays, he says in a local newspaper, is that he gets treated like every other Black person in Detroit, which is in a dehumanizing way (for instance, followed around in department stores as if Black people only come in to a store to shoplift). I remind my students in their pursuit of a good job through obtaining a degree not to forget their interconnectedness with all African Americans and their responsibility and need to work to change the whole society for all.

Gender Politics and the Study-In

To go beyond understanding racism as an instrument of White supremacy and oppression to understanding one's own complicity in its existence is difficult. To discuss classism and sexism alongside racism is even more difficult. Most students do not have a consciousness of these aspects of internalized oppression, dehumanization, and objectification. The gender question has tended to be especially problematic.

Gender was the first issue around which I thought I might split with students involved in the study-in. In an early meeting called by the students to discuss strategies for fighting against what they believed was the administration's attempt to "dismantle" the Center For Black Studies, the student leadership, which was predominantly male, outlined its platform. The decision was to focus only on issues of racism. The movement would not be divided or watered down by other issues. Homosexuality and feminism were ridiculed. As troublesome as this pronouncement was to me, even more disturbing was the exhibiting of many backward, sexist behaviors and attitudes in the actual study-in.

Every day for twelve days, on an average of fourteen hours a day, two other female professors and I were present at Helen Newberry Joy student services building where the students occupied a portion of the facility they affectionately called "home." I feared a myriad of potentially dangerous "worse-case" scenarios, such as a violent reaction by the administration and the campus police to the students' presence, or the abuse of alcohol or other drugs. I was anxious about what contradictions the gender question would uncover. Without a clear principle of respect for women, the possibility of male chauvinism, misogyny, and sexual abuse was my foremost fear. Such a backward perspective could endanger the psychological or physical well-being of the female protesters while compromising the legitimacy of the struggle. There were already examples of chauvinism and patriarchal domination being exposed.

At first the "men" took care of security, while the "girls" handled the food. The dominant spokesperson and strategists were males. My female colleagues and I were allowed to sit in on the leadership and planning meetings of the student organizers, and we used the opportunity for consciousness raising. I saw my role (and I believe my colleagues did as well) as "elder." It was the students' struggle. I wanted to insure their safety and to challenge the community and others in the academy to do the same. I felt faculty, staff and the community should support the students' struggle, because of their right to be heard and because they were "our children." We didn't have to agree with their tactics, nor all of their analyses. Particularly, I felt I had a responsibility to mediate the struggle between the students and their identified "enemy" without (the administration and campus police), as well as the "enemy within" (themselves).

So my colleagues and I, along with my husband and prominent people from Detroit's African American community set up a vigil around the students. School children, state legislators, a senator, a congressperson, ministers, representatives of the mayor, union representatives, church groups, ministers, city and state officials, and media personalities also participated. People from the community were allowed to come into the occupied building to bring food and necessities, but mainly to bring wisdom and spiritual and mental sustenance. We constantly discussed a code of ethics that would guide the students' behavior. The "elders" and the student leaders knew that as long as the students maintained a principled struggle the community would support them. Key to this was the treatment of the young women. There were several parents of young men who came to check on their sons, but the greatest concerns were articulated by the relatives of the female protesters. Were the young women being respected? Where did the students sleep? Were the arrangements coed? The consistent presence of female professors was a source of strength for students and their parents. The elders spent a lot of time in front of the building talking to parents and community people to reassure them that all was well inside, communicating what the needs of the students were, and bringing messages of support to the students. We were committed to dealing with very sensitive issues of personal and human relationships, while leaving the "political" and "strategic" issues to the student leadership.

By the end of the first week of the twelve day study-in the "sisters" (still not referred to as "women") demanded that some of the more blatant forms of sexism be dismantled and many took on the responsibility for "security." Other young women began to fight for their inclusion in the leadership and took responsibility for managing the personal well-being of those inside. All and all the students were exemplary in their conduct. The parents and community maintained their support and celebrated the student's victory with them on the twelfth day.

The student study-in in April, 1989, which demanded the creation of Africana Studies as a department, was exactly the kind of push the university needed to understand the needs and desires of the students and the African American and progressive communities of Detroit and some of its suburbs. The study-in also exposed several contradictions within the students and within the discipline of Africana Studies (also known as Black Studies, Afro-American Studies, and so on) and revealed a new awareness and interest in African and African American history, paralleling a trend within the African American youth. Many of the students who had no knowledge of Black history were inspired by the struggle to learn more.

Often the first stage of new awareness is anger at those who have denied them their history: parents, faculty, educational institutions, community, and adults in general. Many of the students in the study-in were inspired to bold, militant, often adventuristic activity by those peers who had a little more knowledge than they. They were additionally inspired by selective interpretations and superficial readings of certain heroes who had been reduced to slogans, phrases, and isolated concepts, exemplified by rap, medallions, African garb. Malcolm X became the new hero of these students. But it was the Malcolm of "by any means necessary," rather than of self-revolution through self-transformation. Often these students were apolitical, ahistorical and anti-intellectual, as well as cultural and historical revisionists/reductionists. As a result they often substituted "militancy" for political astuteness and integrity. Subsequently, because those who seemed the most knowledgeable were also the most vocal and dogmatic, the leadership of the movement fell to those with versions of nationalism or political agendas unrepresentative of the majority of student activists, who were often intimidated into following those with "greater political experience."

In the period following the study-in, the young women became more visible and vocal. Although the women had felt dehumanized, they often did not have the language, awareness, or consciousness to express what they felt and to move towards change. After the study-in female and male students who had been part of the struggle and those who had been on its periphery came to the classes I taught, on female/male relationships and on the Black woman, to continue the consciousness-raising that had begun within the twelve days.

In teaching classes on gender and relationships I often see the reluctance of students to take the oppression of women seriously. When a male student makes a particularly ludicrous male chauvinist statement, too often the women laugh inappropriately. The subject matter of the courses, however, makes it difficult to evade the issues. In discussions which are often poignant in their challenge to African American males and females to go beyond a culture of oppression to a culture of self-determination, many students respond defensively. The intensity and concentration around gender issues create the circumstances whereby the contradictions of sexism and misogyny are brought to the fore. It is often in these classes that consciousness is obtained.

Other voices within the collective voice have always existed. They existed in the Black Liberation Movement and in the Wayne State study-in. They went against the grain, the status quo. Today these voices have moved from the margin to the center of struggle, attempting various and new forms of solidarity. The concept of "all the women are white, all the Blacks are men, but some of us are brave"[9] focuses on the unique effort, particularly by African American women in the United States, to make the struggle for freedom and liberation an holistic process of transformation against gender, class, and racial oppression. European cultural hegemony and Western White supremacy have not ended. The challenge to racism evident in the Women's Movement and in Women's Studies comes from a new awareness and ideology among women of color[10] (including African American, Latina, Arabic, Native American, Asian women) resulting in solidarity around a common analysis and a unified goal.

Contradictions Within Community

Topics such as the Black all-male academies, the Clarence Thomas confirmation hearings, and the rape trial of Mike Tyson create opportunities in the classroom to discuss the contradictions of racism and sexism as they affect the race-gender code of America. Analyses of these topics provide a basis for understanding the concept of the "enemy within" first through examples external to the students.

There is a tendency to view the historical revolutionary character of the Black community and the Black woman in terms of a slave or a victim mentality. In addition there is a tendency to deny the existence of male chauvinism in the Black community, and to evade the need to challenge Black men and Black women to develop themselves in order to move the community and whole society forward. Slavery is seen as having no dialectical features other than its dehumanizing ones. Blacks blame slavery, and racism, for every contradiction in the Black community, including the destruction of the family and destroyed female/male relationships. This is a linear, static and narrow view of history. After all, a people who can endure such brutalization, who can undergo such dismemberment, and still thrive and take the initiative in achieving freedom are more than the sum of their brutalization. Seen in this perspective, the history of the lives of African Americans has been one of the great human experiences, and one of the great triumphs of the human spirit in modern times, in fact, in the history of the world.

The African American community has been one group of citizens (who came to the United States by choice or in chains) which has consistently and constantly challenged North American society. African Americans exposed the hypocrisy of concepts of inalienable rights, life, liberty, and the pursuit of happiness in the presence of institutional racism and enslavement, the most dehumanizing systems in the history of humankind. The United States supported the idea of democracy and equality while simultaneously supporting enslavement and racism. The legacy of Black people, which has been transmitted through the ages, has been an unshakable humanity in the face of brutality. African

Americans learned within their families the difference between right and wrong, even when most Whites, blinded by racism, did not.

The African American heritage is replete with experiences of Black men and women transforming, supporting, and leading their families and communities out of dehumanization. During slavery, when White society purposely attempted to break up the Black family, Black women's resistance kept families together and helped them survive. From slavery to the sixties, the family has been the primary reason for the survival of African Americans in the United States, and has been the fundamental place where the principles of struggle and resistance are learned. The African American family is in danger, as are relationships between Black females and Black males. Part of that danger is the result of the African American community blaming White society for problems which are rooted in the Black community. For example, the African American community allows Black men to get away with brutalizing women and children, absolving them of responsibility and creating macho images for them instead. Many Black women have accepted the prevailing view of male superiority, denying the need to reject the ahistorical assumption of the dominance of Black women.

Black women during slavery were oppressed as were Black men. Black women not only worked in the fields beside Black men, afterwards they went home to do the domestic chores. As Angela Davis points out in her 1971 article on the role of Black women in the community of slaves, she was performing "the only labor of the slave community, which could not be directly and immediately claimed by the oppressor."[11] Therefore, the Black woman in chains could help to lay the foundation for some degree of autonomy for herself and her family. She was therefore essential to the survival of the community. Her experience has also exposed her to the contradictions of surviving. She recognized that her humanity and that of her family was impossible to separate from the reality of the total society. The domestic life of Black women kept alive a profound revolutionary consciousness of resistance, thus encouraging those around her to keep their eyes on freedom.[12]

African American Culture and Community:
The Enemy "Outside" and "Within"

My course, entitled "Black Social and Political Thought: Theory and Practice," is designed to examine several key African American ideological perspectives that interpret events, and project change and transformation of the collective peoples and of society. This examination often involves application of theory to current issues and events within the African American community and larger society. In early lectures we discuss the institutionalized and systemic nature of racism and its manifestations in the academy, the media, and society. We talk about racism in textbooks of higher education which distort and diminish the importance of the Ancient Egyptians (Kemetians) as part of the continent of Africa. We also analyze the negative press coverage on African Americans which can be seen daily in local papers. For example, when some University of Michigan students after the annual football game with Ohio State University were shown on TV trashing Ann Arbor, the commentators lightheartedly described the behavior of Whites as "boys will be boys." When similar scenes unfolded in Detroit for example, after the Tigers won the World Series, across the nation the media described Detroiters as "rioting." Later it was found that most of the troublemakers were not from Detroit, but its suburbs, and were White, not Black. The media seldom portray Black families and their members as loving and caring. When a young African American male is caught on the wrong side of the law, no images of him or his family as human beings are projected. With a young White male the viewing audience is subjected to several interviews with teary-eyed parents, relatives, and friends who are totally baffled that this could happen to such a child. The media often attributes the behavior of African American youth to "something gone very wrong," and for African American youths for something to go wrong is seen as the norm.

Students in the study-in and young people in my church and community groups have lamented that too often Africana Studies courses are the only places where external contradictions in our society are addressed. When discussions of internal contradictions emerge they are often offered as asides or as reminders, and sometimes out of the frustration of some students as overstated negative expressions of the character and morality, or lack thereof, within the Black community. On one occasion we had, in a prior class meeting, discussed the physical deterioration of the houses and neighborhoods of Black communities from the perspective of the external enemy. We discussed the costs in terms of finances, morale, and services in large urban areas, the aging and depreciation in worth, value, and quality of property, and the subsequent blaming/faulting of the African American community for the demise of these cities. For example, African Americans have been able to move into certain neighborhoods only after years of redlining excluded them, and by that time the property and city are "old" and deteriorating. When one Black male student began to focus on the internal contradictions within the African American community in exaggerated and degrading terms, labeling Blacks "lazy" and "ignorant," there was a tremendous outcry against this characterization. Interestingly enough, several of the other students had similarly pointed out some of the age-old values within the Black community which had been lost, such as pride in the appearance of the neighborhood and oneself. However, once this young man raised negative characterizations of the African American community in such a derogatory manner, discussion of these internal contradictions was impossible.

One very chilly and damp day in October, 1990 I entered my classroom quite disturbed. The seventeen-year-old daughter of one of my colleagues in Africana Studies had been shot in the head and killed in a house of unknown "activities" on a first date. Discussions about the sexism and misogyny in the lyrics of the Black rap group 2 Live Crew, and the seeming acceptance of crack in the Black communities, as well as the murder of my colleague's daughter, led me to force the issue of internal contradictions. As I began to express my outrage against the savage and senseless killing of this young woman, all of my frustration as a mother, as an African American woman, as a teacher, spewed forth. What guidelines could we offer our children to help them identify those whose values, behavior, and judgments would endanger them? During my youth and teen years, my parents warned us against certain behavior and against certain acquaintances which would compromise and endanger us. Membership and attendance in church was one standard for determining the potential moral character of our classmates and their families. While we were also taught to not judge or look down upon people, there was a standard of behavior whereby we could assess the character of those around us. Economic standing and social background were not predeterminants of character.

When I asked myself what standards and guidelines we can offer to our young people today, I realized that the old ones were not enough. Our young people are being killed randomly, anywhere, seemingly by anybody, and without reasons. The reasons or causes advanced are the onslaught of illicit drugs, gang wars, and the resolution of conflict through murder. Each of these are factors within the African American community. "Black on Black" crime and murders, the plague and destruction of drugs which lead to preying on the community and one's own family, the general disrespect for life, come from within the community. Therefore, the logical solution would be an all-out struggle against the enemy within.

Tied to the discussion of the young woman's murder by another Black youth or youths was a discussion within the class on the syllabus of political tendencies within the African American community. The lecture focused on how political tendencies help clarify, identify, and locate ideologies within political thought. Particularly, the lecture identified "counterrevolutionary" tendencies within the Black community which stifled forward, progressive movement towards changing the status quo and towards social and spiritual transformation, and against which the community must struggle. I identified pimps, prostitutes, drug pushers, murderers, agent provocateurs as representatives of counterrevolutionary tendency, often people we knew, members of our own families, friends and acquaintances. The external enemy of "racism" or White people was as well more readily identified and struggled against. If a White person were to kill a Black person or discriminate against African Americans in public and private facilities (which had happened within a thirty-day period in Detroit) we are ready as a community to voice our outrage, organize, march, and protest against this treatment (which had actually been done). On the other hand, we are reluctant to struggle against similar and as destructive, internal, identifiable enemies because they are Black. We are more comfortable placing the blame on something or someone else, outside ourselves. The dialectic of the enemy within and without is crucial in understanding the process of revolutionary transformation. The concept of purification through scapegoating is instructive in explaining the resistance to change in our behavior and thinking, and the desire to keep things the way they are and have always been.[13]

There was strong resistance within the class against various political tendencies and ideologies. Students who had before articulated a Marxist, working-class ideology adamantly voiced their disagreement with the analysis I was making regarding the enemy within. Students who consider themselves nationalists, including those who are members of the Nation of Islam and who are equally concerned about the killings within the African American community voiced their resistance and disdain for what I was advancing. "You're blaming the victim" they decried. "It's racism." "It's White folks putting drugs in our communities." As the temperatures and tempers began to rise I realized that, as is often true when one has a painful revelation, I faced one of the fundamental issues that we, the African American community, have consistently been reluctant to confront, that is, our own complicity and role in our continuing oppression. As several of the students tried to convince me to remove the characterization of "pimps, prostitutes, drug pushers, etc." from the definition of "counterrevolution" and escalated their insistence that "racism" was the blame and that the term "counterrevolution" should be reserved for the KKK and David Dukes, I equally insisted that as scholars and potential intelligentsia we were required to be dialectical. I firmly reiterated the social scientists, revolutionaries, and Black thinkers who had urged this holistic analysis, for instance, David Walker, Maria Stewart, Anna Julia Cooper, Frantz Fanon, Amilcar Cabral, Malcolm X, National Organization For An American Revolution (NOAR). I had come full circle to understanding the concept. Phrases and concepts leapt forward in my mind, such as those from Amilcar Cabral: "Struggle of the people, by the people, for the people."[14] Cabral discusses a two-front revolutionary struggle of the people of Guinea-Bissau against the Portuguese colonialists:

> So at each moment of this great struggle we are waging, we must focus on two phases: one, against the colonialist capitalist ruling classes in Portugal and imperialism; the other, against all the internal forces, whether material or spiritual (meaning ideas from the mind), which might arise against our people's progress on the path of liberty, independence and justice. These demand courageous struggle against imperialist agents. But in addition permanent and determined struggle against those who, even if they are militants, responsible workers or leaders of the Party, do anything which could prejudice our people's march to total conquest of their dignity, their liberty and their progress.[15]

Similarly, Malcolm X urged the African American community to struggle against a "slave mentality" while struggling against racism. The challenge coming out of the Black Liberation Movement was for African Americans to transform themselves and all human relationships, while changing the existing oppressive and racist institutions.[16]

One student was so emotionally involved in this debate that she, usually a very respectful and helpful student to me as a faculty person and elder Black, began to shout, refusing to check her outburst when I brought the class back to order. She rambled on about how she could not see her brother as the enemy and how this was a life-and-death question, and how she loved her brother and loving him required forgiving him. Soon after the debate subsided with great resignation, she dramatically (attempting invisibility yet achieving great conspicuousness) rose and stormed out of the room, slamming the door. I was disturbed all weekend, several times trying to reach her unsuccessfully. When she returned I called her aside to express my concern and to apologize for upsetting her. Before I could explain, she quickly apologized explaining her embarrassment and revealing how she had come face to face with a part of herself she never before had realized was within her. I surmised that her unconditional love for her brother, and her realization that one of the enemies had a face quite familiar to her, was a revelation as significant for her as it had been for me. I realized that to focus only on the enemy outside was to focus on institutional racism only and was also a way of not addressing the enemies of classism and capitalism within the community.

Reflections and Future Directions

What guidelines do we give to our youth whereby they can ascertain who can be trusted among their elders? Young people feel they are prisoners, captives in a world they do not control, in which they have no say, no rights and no power. They say, "Nobody asked me if I wanted to come here." "We are forced to go to school and the teachers lie to us. And then my parents tell me I have to respect the teachers and not talk back." "My parents treat me like a baby. They tell me if I don't follow their stupid rules I have to leave. Don't I have any rights?"

Students' new political awareness is often accompanied by backward, counterrevolutionary ideas. Most obvious is the ethnic chauvinism, misogyny, homophobia, and anti-intellectualism rampant in youth culture. In music, film, and on TV, we see the attitude that youths know what is best for themselves and their peers. This is accompanied by distrust, disrespect, and dismissal of adults.

A new awareness of the role and responsibility of elders in preparing the next generation of youth to take over the leadership and stewardship of the earth is needed. Elders must not be intimidated by the arrogance and guilt-tripping of young people. Instead they must go beyond a victim mentality and romanticizing to transform and create a new, more humane culture. This new kind of leadership requires a revolution within.

Many elders understand how the notion of unlimited rights for individuals has led to a breakdown in the morality and ethics of the whole society. In redirecting the concept of rights, adults have a responsibility to clarify exactly what young people are to expect from their elders. Young people have a right to be fed, housed, loved, nurtured, and educated in terms of passing on knowledge from one generation to the next, rather than passing on bigotry, hatred, racism, sexism, and polluted waters, streams and air.

Adult African American men and women have the awesome responsibility of being caretakers of future generations regardless of the odds. Values must be provided and projected. Our children must be protected from harm and abuse; nurtured, stimulated, valued; connected to a history, culture, and tradition. They must be shown, through example, a vision of what they can become. Elders have a responsibility to protect against racism, sexism, and classism in life and in school, to fight against carcinogens and pollutants, oil spills, wars, and other destruction; to be political, social, and environmental activists; to insure our children are not homeless; to protect them from drugs and murder; to love and nurture, not physically, mentally or sexually abuse them or to allow abuse. Elders must pass on to the next generation the progressive values, traditions, morals of the best of our ancestry and society. Elders must introduce the next generation to a spiritual as well as material side. Each adult has a responsibility to introduce our young people to our God, step back and give them the space to develop a sense of their own spirit.

We have to be clear that to be political, to determine our own destinies and to govern ourselves is true liberation and respect. I know of only one way to show my concern for my family. I cannot guarantee their survival, let alone their creativity through material things, not even through spending time with them, which money is supposed to buy. I can only show my concern and my love for my child and my family in the 1990s and the twenty-first century by being political, by actively working towards the transformation of our society, its ideology, and ourselves into new human beings.

In the United States we must revolutionize the culture, the institutions, and especially ourselves. I am convinced that the individual and material pursuit of happiness at the expense of the collective good and the environment is wrong. The basic philosophy and ideology which has guided our nation since its inception is dehumanizing. African Americans all too often find it very easy to simply point to racism. There is a reluctance to tackle the fundamental principles of United States society. We want to be a part of the unlimited wealth and materialism, and yet not be exploited. Today, to be a caring Black man or woman, is to be political; to be political is to take up the legacy of the history of the African American struggle, and to create the vision and the struggle to transform our entire society. We should have no illusions, however, that change will come without a fundamental transformation of ourselves. It is not only the culture and institutions that need revolution. We the people need a revolution within.

These are the choices before us. The future is before us, and the future is up to us. Which side of the struggle will you be on? It is not a question of which "ism" is more oppressive, nor of whether to hear the new voices which are emerging and coming to the center. Which struggle comes first or is more important is not what we should be struggling around. We must look at the whole picture, and see how we have become part of the problem. We have accepted wholesale the values and the principles of individualism and materialism, and of a Eurocentric, Western, hegemonic, White society, which has become dehumanizing to all of us, regardless of race, gender, or class. The existing social, economic, and political order is insufficient in resolving the contradictions of the day. The challenge before us is to not be part of the problem, but creators of the solution.

Notes

1. October, 1989, as a result of the study-in, an agreement was reached between the students and the university, and the Center for Black Studies was transformed into the Department of Africana Studies.

2. This was not true for the student spokesperson and some of the other students who would come forth to give leadership and direction to the study-in movement. Many of these leaders had come to political awareness outside of the academic classroom and had clearly defined political and social philosophies and ideologies, as well as objectives and goals.

3. Ann duCille, "'Othered' Matters: Reconceptualizing Dominance and Difference in the History of Sexuality in America," *Journal of the History of Sexuality*, Vol. 1, no. 1 (July 1990): 103–105.

4. duCille, 105.

5. Maulana Karenga, *Introduction to Black Studies* (Los Angeles: University of Sankore Press, 1989), 172–173.

6. Patricia Coleman-Burns, "African American Women—Education For What?" *Sex Roles*, Vol. 21, no. 1/2 (July 1989).

7. See Paulo Freire, *Pedagogy of the Oppressed* (New York: The Seabury Press, 1970) for a full exploration of the educating of the oppressed for his/her own liberation.

8. Martin Luther King, Jr., "Facing the Challenge of a New Age." An address delivered in December, 1956 in Montgomery, Alabama. Reprinted in *Phylon*, vol. XVIII (First Quarter, 1957): 27.

9. Gloria T. Hull, Patricia Scott and Barbara Smith, eds. *All the Women are White, All the Blacks are Men, But Some of Us Are Brave* (Old Westbury: The Feminist Press, 1982).

10. There is a very significant article on the usage of "People of Color" as a "new language formation" by William Safire, "People of Color," *New York Times Magazine*, November 20, 1988.

11. Angela Davis, "Reflections on the Black Woman's Role in the Community of Slaves," *Black Scholar*, vol. 3, no. 4 (December 1971); reprint 12, no. 6 (November/December 1981):7.

12. *Ibid.*

13. Kenneth Burke, *The Philosophy of Literary Form* (Los Angeles: The University of California Press, 1973), 202–203.

14. Amilcar Cabral, *Unite and Struggle: Speeches and Writings of Amilcar Cabral*, trans. by Michael Wolfers (New York: Monthly Review Press, 1979), 75–79.

15. *Ibid.*, 79.

16. National Organization for An American Revolution, *Change Yourself to Change the World* (Philadelphia: Box 3281, Philadelphia, PA 19121, 1979).

10

African American Women Teachers Speak About Child Abuse

Dianne Smith

Introduction

The narratives of womanist writers are active arteries through which Afra-American (Black) women produce and reproduce memories and speech to resist and survive in a male-dominated (overwhelmingly White male-dominated), oppressive world. Our discourse of resistance has been a forum for self-recognition and self-emancipation that we have brought forth to our being in this space. For example, Linda Brent (also known as Harriett Jacobs) wrote from within the cage of slavery, and she was able to illuminate her condition as a person enslaved by a White male slaveowner, as well as to redefine herself as a compassionate woman soliciting assistance from Northern White women to become an active participant in the emancipation of her Black sisters still held in bondage. Linda Brent wrote the following words in one passage of her text:

> O, what days and nights of fear and sorrow that man caused me! Reader, it is not to awaken sympathy myself that I am telling you truthfully what I suffered in slavery. I do it to kindle a flame of compassion in your hearts for my sisters who are still in bondage, suffering as I once suffered.[1]

Maya Angelou's work is one of many that exhibits a multifaceted self emerging from the bosoms of familial women, or wisdom women. Her poetry and autobiographical texts demonstrate the trials, repressions, and survival which we as Black women know. And Billie Holliday's narrative relates her life as a singer in the 1930s through the 1950s. Through voice, she positions her experiences in a historical context, thereby defining unities, relationships, and serial events; the themes of racism and sexual exploitation are evident during each era of life.

These women's powerful autobiographical words, or stories, have a place in our minds, and their words resonate throughout our history. For they have become an important impetus for many Black women in constructing a sense of reality and self; as well as identifying that which can be. However, while Linda Brent, Maya Angelou, and Billie Holliday—as three examples—have been able to document their resistance to sexual and economic exploitation and solicit emancipatory support, most Afra-American women have not had access to such space; in essence, our voices have been silenced. Therefore, I am claiming a space for myself and six Afra-American women teachers living and teaching in a Southern rural county. And in this space, text, or forum, I will speak about my experiences as an educator, researcher, and survivor of child sexual abuse. In addition, I will present the voices of the six women as they speak about their experiences, in their school space, in reporting their suspicions about children who live in and/or experience violence in their environments (that is, home or other familiar surroundings).

I do not intend to become a ventriloquist[2] for their voices. However, Henry Giroux writes that "Teacher voice points to the need for educators to unite in a collective voice as part of a wider social movement dedicated to restructuring the ideological material conditions that work both within and outside schooling."[3] Thus, by weaving my voice together with the voices of the six women, I will create a collective voice as a movement toward restructuring received assumptions. In addition, I believe that my interpretations of their stories will bring forth the recognition that Black women, once given an arena, do engage in discourses of dangerous memories. Or, Black women do make the familiar strange!

The Women

I was born and raised in a small South Carolina town during the early 1950s. I am the second of twelve children—one of my siblings died of Sudden Infant Death Syndrome and the second during birth. I bring a legacy of first-generation education to my family—I have my Doctor of Philosophy degree in Education—and I am a professor of curriculum theory for an urban university in Missouri. I am a survivor of child sexual abuse and unlike most women who confess such an invasion of one's life, I can peacefully say that the perpetrator was not my father. Rather he was a White man. Sisterfriend, I know that you are thinking: Why, after so many years, engage such revelation in a text written for millions to read? Well, I now feel powerful enough to do so, for I have found and claim my voice; therefore, it is a form of talking back[4] that is very much needed for me and other Afra-American women living and surviving in our macro-micro world. In addition, I believe that other women living and surviving in this space will gain from my text.

This revelation of self-empowerment and self-love has caused me to produce a counterdiscourse to resistance and survival in a patriarchal, oppressive culture. That is to say that, while womanist writers have produced and reproduced countermemories and counterdiscourses to resist and survive, I do not believe that Black women teachers have been empowered to use voice as a form of resistance within the patriarchal environs of the schools. Thus, as a critical womanist researcher, I am weaving a counterdiscourse of resistance into the academic space by acknowledging the words of living, oppressed women within an institution of a White, patriarchal culture. In essence, I will identify six Black women teachers in order to understand the silencing and self-empowerment of these women in schools, relative to their reporting practices of suspected child abuse. More specifically, by presenting the voices of these Black women teachers who can or cannot speak about child abuse, I seek to understand the desires and fears which give structure and shape to silences[5] in reporting child abuse to authorities.

In order to understand how these Black women have socially constructed the "norms of social interaction and rules of behavior"[6] in reporting child abuse, I find it necessary to get inside their world and see the world of child abuse through their eyes. In so doing, I journeyed to my home county in South Carolina; and I invited these women teachers to share with me their lived experiences and knowledge, through storytelling or narrative, regarding their reporting practices of child abuse.

These women range in age from twenty-eight years to sixty-plus years; and their years of teaching total more than 119, include grades 1–12 and children labeled handicapped. I interviewed each woman individually in their homes, schools, and one in a Black Baptist church. For the sake of confidentiality, each woman's name has been changed. I will do my best to provide a very brief sketch of each woman, according to my social interactions with each one, and their place in their school space.

Ann is in her mid-thirties and has taught elementary school for thirteen years in the same school. Our conversation took place in her home. We were seated around her kitchen table; and during our conversation she spoke very openly about the racist practices of her principal. The second woman is Tenar who is in her late forties and has taught elementary, junior high, and students labeled with learning disabilities. She is considering retiring, for she is quickly approaching thirty years in the system. Tenar would like to pursue another career after her retirement. Her story was told to me in her home, and she was "nervous" as we began our conversation. The third woman is Plinar, who is in her mid-fifties, and has taught primary grade students for more than twenty years in a local school. Plinar is committed to her church duties and views the church as a source of her strength. We talked in her classroom while her students were studying art. The fourth woman is Beth. She is in her mid-sixties, has taught in the county schools for more than forty years, and serves as a home-bound instructor for the county system. Due to a family-owned business in the county, Beth has more visibility than the other five women interviewed. Beth's story was told to me in my home church. The fifth woman is Nancy, around twenty-eight years of age. She teaches deaf students, and recently completed her Masters degree in special education. Her spouse is a minister and she also has a certain amount of visibility in the community. Our conversation took place in her living room. The sixth woman is Sherry, around thirty-nine years of age. Sherry is a fifth-grade teacher and she has worked in the same school building for over fifteen years. She is active in the county and state Baptist association and her story was told to me in her classroom. As I reflect, each woman has a strong commitment to her church and church-related activities. All of the women are married, all but one has children, and each woman has a Masters in Education.

I will use these Black women's stories to illuminate their desires and fears regarding child abuse reporting practices in terms of personal history and institutional power, that is, to explicate their construction of consciousness and knowledge within the patriarchal, socio-political power of schools regarding child abuse. For when schools exercise power, they create and cause to emerge new forms of knowledge and accumulate new bodies of information, for knowledge and power interact one with the other.[7]

School Space: Black Women Thinking, Knowing and Speaking

Child abuse is defined by the United States government as the following:

> Child abuse and neglect means the physical or mental injury, sexual abuse, negligent treatment, or maltreatment of a child under the age of eighteen by a person who is responsible for the child's welfare under circumstances which indicate that the child's health or welfare is harmed or threatened thereby.[8]

In 1985 the United States reported a total of 1.7 million cases of suspected child abuse; and each year two to five thousand children die as a result of abuse and neglect. The American Association for Protecting Children issued the *Highlights of Official Aggregate Child Neglect and Abuse Reporting 1987*, which reported that an estimated 2,178,000 children suffered child abuse and neglect. The rate of reporting is 34.0 children per thousand and an estimated 1,404,000 families were reported in 1987. Overall reporting levels have increased 225 percent between 1976 and 1982.[9]

According to Robert Shoop, Lynn Firestone, and Patricia Levin, the initial stage in the protection of children from abuse is the reporting system; and because of teachers' close and ongoing contact with young children, they are increasingly seen as key factors in detecting and reporting child abuse. The public assumes that schools are the social institutions that touch the lives of children and families on a daily basis, and due to compulsory education laws it becomes difficult to hide abuse, because teachers see the children regularly. Schools and teachers are in a unique position to combat the problem of child abuse and neglect; therefore, teachers are held responsible for reporting suspected and/or known cases of abuse.

While all fifty states have laws or regulations (developed by White men) that require teachers to report their assumptions, it is postulated that reports cover only one to ten percent of the high rate of abused school-age children.[10] Patricia Levin's research concluded that teachers are fearful of reporting their suspicions for the following reasons:

(a) the inability to recognize the signs and symptoms
(b) lack of administrative support
(c) interfering with parental discipline and/or family autonomy
(d) possible court appearances and/or lawsuits
(e) parental threats
(f) separation of children from parents[11]

I do not deny the value of this research, for I do believe that teachers experience feelings of fear. As a teacher of Head Start children, I remember the feelings of fear one day as I observed a five-year-old girl exhibit signs of sexual molestation. I talked to my assistant about my suspicions; however, I did not report this to my supervisor as regulated. Needless to say my suspicions were confirmed one morning, as I was told that the girl's mother had killed her lover because she found him sexually molesting the child with a soda pop bottle. And I continue to live with guilt for the disruption of the child's life and the mother's life, due to my fear and silence.

As I engage this text, I recognize that my fear and silence were twofold. That is, I believed that my silence would keep those painful memories of my own sexual victimization as a six-year-old from awakening. If I were mute then it would all go away. Secondly, my silence was created by the fear of a possible court appearance, the uncertainty of my suspicions, and the possible separation of the child and her mother. I also feared that the bureaucrats of the organization would not support my efforts. Hence, my experiences of fear and silence regarding reporting suspected child abuse confirm Patricia Levin's conclusions.

However, while I have shown that there is a sense of fear which generates silence, it becomes important for me, as a critical womanist researcher, to justify and mobilize this fear.[12] By this I mean to raise the idea that patriarchal power relations, intensified by the issue of race, have taught us women to doubt our own control over our material and symbolic worlds, which may lead to fear and silence. In so doing, I will unmask the existing beliefs which presuppose that fear is the primary factor in the failure of teachers' reporting to authorities. Accordingly, I will present a theoretical analysis of the ways in which White, male patriarchy and racism cause these women to socially construct their terrain and lived experiences in schools relative to reporting suspected child abuse. To accomplish this task, I will develop an alternative discourse, or a counterdiscourse that speaks to White, male patriarchy and racism as underlying currents of fear that silence antichild abuse discourse. And by braiding together the strands of womanist theory, feminist theory and critical educational theory, I will weave the subjective *practice* of the Black women teachers with *theory*, to show ways in which the narratives of these women are inscribed in patriarchal relations, intensified by the issue of race.

To do this, I will present the following four arguments:

(a) primary fear expressed is the fear of reprisal from men;

(b) Black women teachers are caught in the institution of White male supremacy;

(c) the lack of in-service child abuse training is a representation of institutional power created to perpetuate the inequality that exists within our society; and

(d) the creation of contradictory situations within school space is extensive.

An Alternative Discourse: Argument A: Teachers Fear Reprisals from Men

Levin, Shoop, and Firestone suggest that one reason teachers fail to report suspected child abuse is due to fear of parental threats or reprisals. However, the narratives of Nancy and Beth posit that there is fear of reprisal from men who live in the households. For Nancy said to me that she "was worrying about what was going to happen to me if I said . . . I knew she had an older brother and there was a male figure in the house. I felt that [he] would hurt me." And Beth names the fear of reprisal from a grandfather that she suspected, according to the granddaughter's story, was sexually abusing his granddaughter. She said, "I didn't follow it up. Her grandfather was very mean. And I sort of was afraid to question him; he was mean to his wife . . . he beat her up." I, too, was afraid to talk about my suspicions of the little girl who was being molested. I felt that the male perpetrator would seek me out and "beat me up." Each of us women names the fear of violence from men as a legitimation for our fear and silence.

It is important for me to place this idea in context. To do this, I am compelled to quote a rather lengthy passage from a text written by child sexual abuse feminist researchers, Cathy Waldby, Atosha Clancy, Jan Emetchi, and Caroline Summerfield:

> Patriarchy is the world view that seeks to create and maintain male control over females—it is the system of male supremacy. In contemporary society men as a class dominate women as a class. This dominance is maintained by men's organization of control over the structural systems that constitute the society we exist in, for example, the health, legal, welfare, educational, economic, judicial, religious, and familial systems. In addition, the way these systems function is primarily determined by patriarchal beliefs and values. Male hegemony is based on the assumption that men's perception of reality is

the only one. Women are viewed as adjunct, secondary, an object for male manipulation. The mechanics of male supremacy are buffeted by the cross-currents of social class, racial oppression and cultural difference, which also inform our power relationships.[13]

Also Delores Williams defines patriarchy as:

the power of white men and white women: a familial-social ideological, political system in which white men and white women—by force, direct pressure, or through ritual, tradition, law and language, customs, etiquette, education, and division of labor, determine what part black women shall or shall not play, and in which the black female is everywhere subsumed under the white female and white male.[14]

By using these definitions of patriarchy, I am able to place Nancy's, Beth's and my naming of fear of violence in context with male control over females. For I remember many a day, as a girl, watching men physically violate the bodies of the women in my life. I was not born at the time, but I have been told about the death of a paternal aunt due to a violent beating by her lover. I recall, vividly, the shooting death of a first cousin by her spouse and fearing the same thing would happen to me because my ex-spouse and I were experiencing marital problems; and I painfully recollect the huge hand of a former lover as he slapped me across my face, and I felt the cold tile floor meet my body due to the blow.

Abbey Lincoln writes that "the black mother, housewife, and all-around girl Thursday is called upon to suffer both physically and emotionally every humiliation a woman can suffer."[15] And White male violence against Black women includes more than three hundred years of beatings, mutilations, and rape or sexual coercion; as Angela Davis suggests, male violence (White and Black) against Black women is a constant threat in this society. Pearl Cleage postulates that:

In America, thousands of women a day are raped and/or tortured and abused by men in as many ways as you can think of, and probably a whole lot more you haven't thought of, and don't want to, including beating, shooting, scalding, stabbing, slapping, shaking and starving. Men beat and torment women because they *can*. They are usually bigger and physically stronger and they've structured a culture that condones absolutely the possession and control of women by any means necessary.[16]

Male violence is a form of patriarchy that seeks to create and maintain male control over females—it is the system of male supremacy; therefore, the threat of male violence is a subtle way of muting the voices of women teachers regarding child abuse.

Argument B: Black Women Teachers Are Caught in the Institution of White Male Supremacy

Delores Williams theorizes that the White-controlled public school system retards the "intellectual, emotional, spiritual, economic and physical growth of black women."[17] Thus, a woman finds that the tools of male supremacy are buffeted by the crosscurrents of social class, racial oppression, and cultural difference, which also inform our power relationships, as suggested by Cathy Waldby, Atosha Clancy, Jan Emetchi, and Caroline Summerfield. This becomes evident in the narratives of Beth, Ann, Plinar, and Nancy regarding support from their White principals.

I asked each woman why she did not report her suspicions to the principal or assistant principal. Beth said that "you couldn't interfere with that, at that time;" Nancy's response to me was, "No. No. No. Not at the time . . . no way!" And Plinar indicated to me that "based on my past experience with his reporting I felt that it would not get any further than him. . . . And it would just be another bit of gossip to him." She also informed me that she had suspected a White male teacher of engaging in sexual activity with White male and female students in his class. Plinar's narrative shows that she reported her suspicions to the principal:

> I watched for evidence and when I finally came to the conclusion that this was going on it was like perpetual motion pulled me from where I was into the principal's office. I told him. He asked if there was a pattern and I told him yes . . . he gave the impression he was going to check on it which he didn't. I think he became totally blind to it because he didn't.

These women do engage in counterdiscourses and actions of resistance; however, as I have noted, currents of racial oppression, social class, and cultural difference inform power relationships that exist in a White-controlled public system. However, they doubt their own control over their material and symbolic worlds, which may lead to fear, silence, and powerlessness. Sherry reported her suspicions of physical abuse of a female student. She said to me during our conversation: "There wasn't anything I could do regarding that because these people are very, very careful and you can't. Well I reported it, the people in the office knew about it."

Although Beth, Plinar, and Nancy acknowledge the lack of support from their principals, they do not name racism as an issue to be considered. Ann does name racism as a driving force for the absence of support from her principal. Her narrative follows:

> He has the feeling that Black teachers cannot perform as well as White teachers, And over the years it has really shown. I had an incident with him a year and a half ago . . . he has never apologized and the first day of school he came up and gave me a big bear hug. And I thought to myself, "I ought to kick this man between his legs." He has never apologized to me for what he put me through.

Ann names racism as a divisive force in their relationship, however, she does not explicitly decipher the undercurrents of the "big bear hug." Therefore, as a critical womanist researcher, uniting my voice with the women's voices, I am compelled to name this White male principal's "big bear hug" as a form of racism that has nourished itself by encouraging sexual coercion. According to Angela Davis, such assaults are "ideologically sanctioned by politicians, historians, novelists, and other public figures who systematically represent black women as promiscuous and immoral. . . . While black women and their sisters of color have been targets, white women have suffered as well."[18]

Gloria Hull and Barbara Smith state that:

> The political [economic, social, and class] position of Black women in America has been in a single word, embattled. The extremity of our oppression has been determined by our very biological identity. The horrors we have faced historically and continue to face as Black women in a white-male-dominated society have implications for every aspect of our lives, including what white men have termed "the life of the mind."[19]

Gloria Hull's and Barbara Smith's assumption regarding our oppression and the horrors we have faced historically and continue to face as Black women in a White-male-dominated society yokes the voice of Tenar, as she and I talk about the possibility of appearing in court to testify about her suspicions that a female student was being sexually abused by her male foster parent. I asked Tenar what kind of burden would have been placed on her shoulders had the case gone to court. She nervously laughed and said, "Oh, gosh! Not a burden, but it would have been scary because I wouldn't have known what to say in court. None other than what the child had told me, and that was it."

While Tenar's voice, on the surface, validates the received knowledge that teachers fail to report suspected child abuse due to the fear of court appearances, I will flush out a hidden assumption. That is, the American judicial system is a viable spoke in the wheel of White-controlled institutions, and as Delores Williams suggests, such institutions impede the intellectual, emotional, and spiritual growth of Black women. Vivian Gordon writes:

> This control usually emerges from an internalized system of privilege and hierarchy based upon race and male gender which justifies consolidations and coalitions which block out others. . . . There is the ability to maintain control through local, state, and federal military.[20]

Gordon's discourse continues with the assertion that Black women are born into an oppressive culture, from which there appears no escape or liberation.

Emily Driver offers a perspective regarding the failure of women to talk about child sexual abuse. She posits that a common reaction to allegations of child sexual assault is disbelief, followed by denial. Such denial has been maintained by the macro society, and by academics and theorists who have sought to study the phenomenon objectively and without passion. Emily Driver believes that "professional and academic myths are sometimes juxtaposed with stereotypes created by the lay community."[21] That is, one assumption in traditional Western mythology of child sexual abuse is that children and women lie. Sherry names this as a possible reason for teachers' failure to report their suspicions: "I talked to the principal about it . . . didn't anything come of it so I don't know really if the child was telling the truth or not. I have known children to do that purposely because they want to get back at parents."

This thought becomes evident in my own experiences as a survivor and teacher. First, I did not tell my mother and father about the molestation of myself, because I was afraid that they would not believe me. Who would believe a six-year-old girl's story: that my grandmother encouraged me to allow the victimization to occur in that man's living room, as she cooked his nightly supper. Second, as a teacher, I contemplated the same thought as Tenar regarding testifying in court. Tenar said, "I wouldn't have known what to say in court . . . other than what the child had told me, and that was it." I, too, felt that I would not know what to say in court. I feared that an examination of me in a courtroom would render me naked, and nobody would be available to cover me up.

Tenar's fear of being called gullible because she relied on the child's story of being sexually molested, and her fear that the child is lying, have particular implications for allegations of sexual abuse made by children and adult women. And according to Emily Driver's interpretation, the myth alleges that the child's accusations of sexual abuse are based upon sexual fantasies rather than on reality; and that children project hysterical personality traits, or they are delusional and paranoid.[22] This implies that adult women who "claim" to be survivors of incest or sexual assault are fantasizing about childhood experiences, or they are delusional. In essence, this becomes a mechanism by which women's voices are muted and discounted as dementia.

Argument C: In-service Child Abuse Training, or its Absence: Representations of Institutional Power

According to Shoop, Firestone, and Levin, teachers are fearful to report their suspicions of child abuse due to their inability to recognize signs and symptoms of child abuse. My position is that teachers are aware of these indicators. For example, while Sherry's and Plinar's schools had not planned a formal session on child abuse for teachers, both women are familiar with signs which might imply abuse. Sherry informed me that "Some people think that you just beat a child, that's abuse. But to me, when you don't provide an adequate home and surroundings and the necessities and everything for a child, to me that is abuse." She referred to a girl: "She would come in crying sometimes or something like that. She showed me what had been done to her. There wasn't anything I could do regarding that . . . well, I reported it." And Plinar is more specific in her interpretation of possible signs of abuse: "If we saw a child who was very withdrawn; came to school dirty all of the time; didn't socialize well with other children; who would want to withdraw if you touched that child; or if you saw that child playing with his private parts; if that child used unacceptable language; to investigate that."

Their voices indicate that they are aware of and name signs and symptoms; in addition, they are aware of their legal responsibilities as agents of the state. Thus, there appears to be an apparent contradiction regarding the received assumption of teacher knowledge and action in this area. While their voices refute the assumed reality of teacher knowledge, an important question becomes evident: if teachers are held accountable for reporting suspected child abuse, why do schools fail to provide in-service training on the subject?

Kathleen Weiler suggests that schools are matrices of institutional, personal, and social forces caught up in deeply contradictory tensions; and Henry Giroux and Stanley Aronowitz theorize that "schools are relatively autonomous institutions that not only provide spaces for oppositional behavior and teaching but also represent a source of contradictions that sometimes make them dysfunctional."[23] That is, while schools are sites with visions of education as empowerment and transformation, they are also institutions of domination and repression.

This idea becomes mobilized in Michelle Fine's discourse as she examines "what doesn't get talked about in schools and how 'undesirable' talk is subverted, appropriated, and exported. . . . In the odd study of *what's not said* in public schools, one must be curious about whom silencing protects."[24] Specifically, silencing constitutes a process of expelling from written, oral, and nonverbal expression, critique and possibility. Michelle Fine posits that silencing is a process by which contradictory ideologies and experiences are buried or discredited, and that the fear of naming imbues silence. That is, "Naming gives license to critical conversation about social and economic arrangements, particularly inequitable distributions of power and resources and naming may be dangerous to beliefs often promoted in public schools."[25]

I project Fine's theory of silencing and not naming to argue that child abuse is an "undesirable" subject in our society. Sherry identified a female student who exhibited signs of abuse and Sherry indicated that she reported her suspicions; however, she said that there wasn't anything that she could do about it. My past experiences indicate an unwillingness to discuss or claim my victimization or my suspicions, or create an antichild abuse discourse. Emily Driver has named the reason for an antichild abuse discourse:

> The occurrence of [child abuse] may not be overtly denied, but it may be minimized at a more subtle level even when it is admitted to have taken place. [Child abuse] denial seems to have three purposes:

> to silence the survivor, to protect the attacker; and to comfort the community member or professional worker with the idea that she or he is totally removed from the experience of the people involved, and free of any responsibility or collusion; thereby to reinforce the illusion that [child abuse] is an isolated aberration rather than a fundamental pattern of societal abuse.[26]

Consequently, not naming child abuse becomes normal and subsumed in the lack of in-service child abuse training. Or, not naming is the silencing of antichild abuse discourses, by failing to insure that teachers know how to recognize abused children, or know how to proceed in suspected cases, which is representative of institutional power, or patriarchy. In-service training would give legitimacy to naming child abuse, create a legitimate discourse in schools, and raise critical conversations about social arrangements.

While I have argued that a lack of in-service child abuse training is a representation of institutional power, or patriarchy, which silences the antichild abuse voices, I must recognize that some institutions do provide in-service child abuse training. For example, Ann's, Tenar's, and Nancy's schools did provide teacher in-service training on the topic. Tenar said that "last school term we had a workshop in (place). And it was informative"; and Nancy indicated to me that "during the beginning of the school year, we had an in-service with some of the teachers from (place) who came over and talked to us some about abuse and neglect of children in the classroom."

However, Ann suggests that her school's in-service session was implemented due to an incident in her county: "They had an incident within the county itself and so they thought they had better have an in-service on it. They had a speaker to come in from the state department to tell us about the laws and that was all within the same year." My point for this acknowledgement is that this becomes a reactionary procedure. And I connect such reactionary actions to the excellence-in-education (or age of accountability) movement in the 1980s. The excellence-in-education movement became a fiery force due to the status quo's fear of losing world power and domestic power.

Christine Shea posits that

> since the early 1980s, public policy experts have become increasingly concerned that the performance of the American economy has not kept pace with other leading world powers. . . . The resulting portrait has generated the fuel for the latest series of school reform activities

and has catalogued renewed discussion in educational policy circles concerning the role and structure of educational institutions in the future American economy.[27]

Hence, the mainstream school reform rhetoric spewed at us more teacher preparation, coursework, smaller class size, more tests, longer school days, corporate-America-style management or leadership, and so on. Such eruption flowed with reactionary procedures from which we have inherited an abundance of cold, unusable ashes.

I suggest that this ideology becomes embedded in Ann's discourse as she describes the child abuse session in her district:

> When we had a school in-service the principal told us to make sure that we had an understanding. He gave us some sheets that had the laws on it and he told us that we should familiarize ourselves with it. He said that because now we're in the age of accountability; and we're going to be held responsible. Even if we're not responsible, we're going to be held responsible.

That is to say that when in-service child abuse training is provided, it is due to the age of accountability and this is a representation of institutional power. And this institutional power has trivialized such training for teachers.

Stanley Aronowitz and Henry Giroux write that the discourse claiming that public education is in a crisis informs the idea that schools have failed to take the issues of excellence and creativity seriously, and in so doing have undermined the economic and academic possibilities that could be conferred upon both students and the larger society.[28] Therefore, as intimated by Tony Wagner, "recent education reform efforts have accelerated the trend toward making education an assembly-line process with standardized tests, homogenized students, and quantifiable products."[29] These reform efforts smother the intelligence, judgment and subjective experience that teachers bring to the classrooms. And as Aronowitz and Giroux theorize, "the call for excellence and improved student creativity have been accompanied by policy suggestions that further erode the power teachers have over the conditions of their work."[30]

The call for excellence has placed additional control over teachers' work in schools. Michael Apple defines this as intensification. He suggests that intensification is long hours spent on technical tasks such as record-keeping, testing, and grading. He notes that intensification has many forms, "from the trivial to the more complex—ranging from being allowed no time at all even to go to the bathroom, have a cup of coffee or relax, to having a total absence of time to keep up with one's field."[31] Apple expands this definition to suggest that:

> while patriarchal relations of authority which paradoxically "gave" teachers some measure of freedom were not totally replaced by more efficient forms of organizing and controlling their day-to-day activity, they legitimated both new forms of control and greater state intervention using industrial and technical models and brought about a new generation of more sophisticated attempts at overcoming teacher resistance.[32]

Michael Apple's theory of patriarchal relations and authority becomes apparent in the voices of Ann and Tenar. I hear Ann's voice suggesting that teachers' desires to talk about child abuse become silenced, or trivialized, as school authorities include child abuse in-service due to "the age of accountability." Thus, teachers are not empowered to become desiring subjects who think, act, and dismantle those social forms that reproduce control and oppression, nor do they have the capacities to critically construct the notion that patriarchy, intensified by race, creates their space (or terrain) and being.

Tenar names accountability as a means of controlling that which is discussed in schools and that which is not discussed. She talks about the integration of testing and competency-based instruction within the curriculum: "The paperwork is terrible. You don't have that much time for teaching them. Test scores! Test scores! That's all they think about now. Teaching how to pass the test. Maybe that is good, and maybe it's not." In addition, Tenar's narrative mirrors Aronowitz and Giroux's theory that policy changes in the name of excellence have eroded the power teachers have over the conditions of their work. Tenar's and Ann's stories suggest that the patriarchal beliefs of education reformers, through intensification, mute their desires and/or attempts to create an antichild abuse discourse. Thus, these women's school space is constructed for them as a result of patriarchy and racism.

Argument D: School Space and Contradictory Situations

Each woman feels a personal and public obligation to report her suspicions to authorities, and they have nurtured the emotional and physical needs of the children whom they suspect are being abused. Sherry said to me: "I got a point across to her that this was a place she could come and there was somebody there that cared for her, I think it would make her feel better." While there have been instances when each woman suspected an abusive situation and reported her suspicions, there were other times, however, when she did not report her suspicions. These actions are inconsistent, and as contradictions are revealed, new ways of thinking became obvious.

According to Peter McLaren, schools are sites of both domination and liberation, and the critical educator endorses theories which recognize the problems of society as more than simply isolated events of individuals or deficiencies in the social structure. He posits that

> rather, these problems are part of the interactive context between individual and society. The individual both creates and is created by the social universe of which he/she is a part: men and women are essentially unfree and inhabit a world rife with contradictions and asymmetries of power and privilege.[33]

That is, as Kathleen Weiler postulates, while women teachers have access to power of judgment (for instance, marking papers, disciplining students) and the weight of the institution (the institution backs her as one of its agents), she is at the same time fixed according to race and gender, and thus, she participates in complex, conflictual relationships. For "women know who they are through a double process—the male experience is taken as the norm, and women are either insignificant or incomplete. Women know themselves through male hegemonic vision of reality, in which acting subjects are men or something other than women."[34]

It is implied that the Black women's contradictory situations limit their power or desire to talk about or report their suspicions of child abuse to the authorities. Due to patriarchal power relations, we have been taught to doubt our own control over our symbolic and material worlds—which leads to failure to report suspected child abuse. Kathleen Weiler posits that recognition of conflict, oppression, and power does not mean acceptance. It does mean creating consciousness so that they can be addressed and transformed. Critical educational theory rests on a critical view of society, arguing that society is both exploitative and oppressive, but it is also capable of being changed.

As a critical womanist researcher listening to and presenting voices of these Black women teachers (and my own voice) who speak, or cannot speak, about child abuse, I have woven a counterhegemonic discourse of resistance into the academic realm. To this end, I have acknowledged the words of living, oppressed women within an institution of White, male patriarchal culture, while creating a language that dares to make the familiar strange. Our voices have become a form of resistance and opposition. Our voices resist and oppose the existing assumptions as we know them to be: for talking back is no mere gesture of empty words; it is the expression of our movement from object to desiring subject—the transformed, liberated voice—within our school space.

I have presented a language of critique regarding teacher voice and reporting suspected child abuse; and I have argued that patriarchal power relations, intensified by the issue of race, have taught us to doubt our own control over our material and symbolic worlds—which may lead to fear and silence. Now, it is important for me to create a language of possibility: conceptualize a frame of reference for transformation, or that which can be.

Conclusion: A View of Utopia

I have tried to create a liberating, transforming text that imbues passion within human beings. Throughout this space I have sought to take my reader to another dimension in researching and talking about child abuse and teacher reporting. At this juncture, I will continue the notion of alternativity by not providing traditional recipes or steps for teachers to follow as we are confronted with suspected child abuse in public school space; for a discourse of possibility goes beyond the traditional how-to's. Giroux and Aronowitz theorize that a discourse of possibility informs language that acknowledges and legitimates a political project whose fundamental purpose is to seek hope and emancipation. They suggest that:

> Moreover, as an expression of specific forms of knowledge, values, and skills, it would take as its object the task of educating human beings to become active and critical citizens, capable of intellectual skills and willing to exercise the forms of civic courage needed to struggle for a self-determined, thoughtful and meaningful life.[35]

Subsequently, my goal is to advocate a political project that is committed to the notion of hope and emancipation which is linked to self and social empowerment. By this I mean to empower us teachers to be silent no more about suspicions, and to claim control over our lives and our ways of knowing and acting, to claim utopia. Instead of being silent, thereby denying the existence of child abuse in our society, we must take risks for transformation. More specifically, as women teachers, we must name those structures that indirectly cause us to doubt our power and control over our lives and our beliefs.

I suggest that teachers form reading groups and support groups; develop newsletters; seek university courses that engage the issues of race, class, and gender, and plan social events. For example, Michele Russell engaged Black women in a survey course that studied the role of the teacher, and in order to make the process conscious and the content significant, she included storytelling, or testifying, to give political value and meaning to the daily lives of these women. During one class meeting, they studied the blues as a coded language of resistance.

Teachers could form critical reading groups that speak to how power and knowledge are socially constructed and legitimated through the education process. Mary Helen Washington suggests a study of Black women writers as a means of tracing the themes of racist and sexist oppression that occur in these writings. Such readings would illuminate struggles of women but also highlight self-empowerment and redefinition and liberation. A support group would bring about the nurturance and communality that Black women need to survive and succeed. Women would be able to share unique lived experiences and common lived experiences, create a language of critique, and move to a language of that which is possible.

A discourse of possibility empowers us to see visions and dream dreams; to generate new understandings and new meanings; to engage in risk-taking; and to seek utopia. For fear and silence threaten our existence, and child abuse threatens the lives which we create, nurture, and love. We can create and live in a world which is not yet, where dreams become a reality; a just and compassionate community within which a discourse of possibility becomes a guiding principle for a new social order; and a world in which boys and girls live lives of happiness, laughter, and visions of a future.

Notes

1. Linda Brent, *Incidents in the Life of a Slave Girl*, 1861 (New York: Harcourt, Brace, Jovanovich, 1973.), 26.

2. Michelle Fine presented the idea that a researcher cannot assume the role of speaking so that the voice heard appears to come from one source other than the speaker (March 12, 1990, Miami University, Oxford, Ohio).

3. Henry Giroux, *Schooling and the Struggle for Public Life* (Minneapolis: University of Minnesota, 1988), 45.

4. bell hooks, *Talking Back, Thinking Feminist, Thinking Black* (Boston: South End Press, 1989.)

5. Michelle Fine, "Sexuality, Schooling and the Adolescent Females: The Missing Discourse of Desire," *Harvard Educational Review* 58 (1988): 30.

6. Sondra Farganis, *Social Reconstruction of the Feminine Character* (Totowa, N.J.: Rowan and Littlefield, 1987), 28.

7. Michel Foucault, *Power and Knowledge* (New York: Panetheon Books, 1977).

8. *Child Abuse and Prevention and Treatment Act of 1973*, as quoted in Richard Gelles, "The Social Construction of Child Abuse," *American Journal of Orthopsychiatry* 45 (1975): 363–361.

9. American Association for Protecting Children, *Highlights of Official Aggregate Child Neglect and Abuse Reporting* 1987 (The American Humane Association, 1989).

10. See Robert Shoop and Lynn Firestone, "Mandatory Reporting of Suspected Child Abuse: Do Teachers Obey the Law?" *West's Educational Law Reporter* 46 (1988); and Patricia Levin, "Teachers' Perceptions, Attitudes, and Reporting of Child Abuse and Neglect," *Child Welfare* 62 (1983).

11. Patricia Levin, "Teachers' Perceptions, Attitudes, and Reporting of Child Abuse and Neglect," *Child Welfare* 62 (1983).

12. See Paulo Freire, *The Politics of Education: Culture, Power, and Liberation* (South Hadley, Mass.: Bergin and Garvey, 1985) for his discourse regarding justifying and mobilizing fear.

13. Cathy Waldby, Atosha Clancy, Jan Emetchi, and Caroline Summerfield, "Theoretical Perspectives on Father-Daughter Incest," in Emily Driver and Audrey Droisen (eds.), *Child Sexual Abuse: A Feminist Reader* (New York: New York University Press), 97.

14. Williams, "The Color of Feminism," *The Journal of Religious Thought* 43 (1986): 48.

15. Abbey Lincoln, "Who Will Revere the Black Woman?" in Toni Cade (ed.), *The Black Woman: An Anthology* (New York: Mentor Books, 1970), 82.

16. Pearl Cleage, *Mad At Miles: A Blackwoman's Guide to Truth* (Southfield, Michigan: The Cleage Group, 1990), 28–29.

17. Delores Williams, 49.

18. Angela Davis, "Rape, Racism and The Capitalist Setting" in *The Black Scholar* Nov/Dec 1981 p39–45 reprinted from Vol 9 April 1978

19. Gloria Hull and Barbara Smith "The Politics of Black Womens' Studies" in Charlotte Bunche and Sandra Pollack, editors *Learning Our Way: Essays in Feminist Education* (NY: The Crossing Press 1983) p 20. The interpolation is my thought

20. Vivian Gordon, *Black Women, Feminism, Liberation: Which Way?* (Chicago: Third World Press, 1987) p 17

21. Emily Driver, "Introduction," in Emily Driver and Audrey Droisen (eds.), *Child Sexual Abuse: A Feminist Reader* (New York: New York University, 1986). 27.

22. *Ibid.*, 27–28.

23. Stanley Aronowitz and Henry Giroux, *Education Under Seige* (South Hadley, Mass.: Bergin and Garvey, 1985), 73.

24. Michelle Fine, "Silencing in Public Schools," *Language Arts 64* (1987): 157.

25. *Ibid.*, 160–161.

26. Driver, 27.

27. Christine Shea, "Pentagon vs. Multinational Capitalism: The Political Economy of the 1980s School Reform Movement," in Christine Shea, Ernest Kahane, and Peter Sola (eds.), *The New Servants of Power* (New York: Praeger, 1990), 4.

28. Aronowitz and Giroux, 23.

29. Tony Wagner, "Educating for Excellence on an Endangered Planet," in Alex Molnar (ed.), *Social Issues and Education* (Arlington, VA: Association for Supervision and Curriculum Development, 1978), 106.

30. Aronowitz and Giroux, 23.

31. Michael Apple, *Teachers and Text* (New York: Routledge, 1986), 41–42.

32. *Ibid.*, 40.

33. Peter McLaren *Life in Schools* (New York: Longman, 1989), 166–167.

34. Kathleen Weiler, *Women Teaching for Change* (South Hadley, MA: Bergen & Garvey, 1988), 143.

35. Aronowitz and Giroux, 141.

11

Balancing the Personal and Professional
Adrianne R. Andrews

I am the other. As a member of a group whose members are often perceived of as others (African Americans) I have been plagued with feelings of ambivalence surrounding my membership in the group of others known as anthropologists. It is awkward to be an underdog member of a discipline that is often treated as an underdog in the academic context. My critique of the discipline will be brief in that I, in the amorphousness that surrounds ambivalence, have not as yet fully been able to articulate in precisely rational terms what, exactly, constitutes my discomfort with anthropology. What follows are, therefore, free-flowing thoughts on the discipline.

To my way of thinking, the prototype of anthropology (if there can be such a thing as a prototype of a discipline) originated with the idle musings of Malinowski[1] about the sexual habits of "savages" while stranded in the Trobriand Islands during World War II. Prior to that, the colonial governments that controlled various African nations used those who came to be known as anthropologists, and missionaries, to gather information about the colonized peoples in order to effectively control and assimilate them. The ultimate outcome of this intrusive, invasive behavior on the part of representatives of colonial Europe and colonizing America was the appropriation of the cultures or, perhaps more appropriately, the artifacts of the cultures (material and cognitive) of the people whose land and resources they took. There was a certain arrogance associated with the *assumption* of the right to "study" people, with the purported aim of gaining a better understanding of themselves; using the world as if it and the people inhabiting it were specimens in a laboratory. The incorporation of the useful, and the contemptuous discarding of the rest, leaving the carcass of culture for the people to try to salvage some semblance of their former selves from, was yet another outcome of the European pursuit of a human identity by using the "other" as a "mirror for man," with "man" taken literally and with Caucasian implicit. This attitude is still with us, as reflected in the following commentary offered in an exploration of the current "post-modern predicament" (the predicament of the other talking back, reappropriating what is rightfully theirs/ours?): "Anthropology is not the mindless collection of the exotic, but the *use* of cultural richness [the other's culture?] for *self-reflection* and *self-growth*"[2] (emphasis added).

The discussion which follows illustrates another dilemma inherent, in my opinion, in the discipline of anthropology—the epistemological question. (The following is extracted from my doctoral dissertation.)

The Epistemological Crisis: Data in Search of a Paradigm

"The problems of doing ethnography are many. In struggling to organize the data for this ethnography I found myself at an impasse. I read book after book on writing, overcoming writing blocks, scientific writing. Examined volume after volume on the philosophy of science. I felt as if I had data in search of a paradigm.

"Was I a functionalist? If so, how did I frame my data to fit that paradigm. I somehow felt I wasn't, because functionalists support the status quo, systems-in-equilibrium model. I know I'm not for maintenance of the status quo, although there is something to be said for systems in equilibrium. . . . Did I wish to espouse a feminist position? Yes, in certain respects and in those respects I think a great deal of what could be called feminist is inherent in what I write.

"I knew that the hypothesis, statistical, empiricist approach to data collection and analysis just did not feel right. But, if not that, what? I have been wrestling with the demon of fear of not having what I wrote/ write be taken seriously (by whom?) (by colleagues, advisers, self) if I didn't present my findings in that mold. That pat, formulaic mold of disseminating information.

"What about validity and reliability? They're supposed to 'be there,' aren't they, so that others can replicate your research? I had the dread that I was producing inferior work because I did not want to adhere to what Michael Agar refers to as 'the received view' in social (and natural) science. The received view is that dominant language of social science associated with the systematic testing of explicit hypotheses.[3] Agar explains that while there are different styles of social research there is 'but only one dominant language to talk about them'. And this dominant language has been my hang-up. The notions of hypothesis testing, predicting, probability analysis, and so on seem to me to be totally irrelevant to understanding and making sense out of human behavior. Human beings are not units or objects to be modeled and manipulated, viewed in terms of dependent and independent variables. Human beings are not objective entities (well, maybe) devoid of any qualities other than those that are measurable, quantifiable.

"And now I've discovered that Michael H. Agar, University of Maryland, feels that way, too. And if he does then there must be, are, other reputable, authentic scholars who feel that way, too! So, I am not alone in my views, my approach to understanding is not a brand of 'less than' scholarship produced by someone too inept or, calling a spade a spade, too stupid to understand and use statistical analysis. I will confess that I see statistical analysis as eloquent and elegant, exquisite in a sense and having numerous applications, but the results don't *mean* anything. They stand for mathematical relationships, but mathematical relationships are not human relationships. And human relationships, and the products of those relationships, are what concern me.

"I have had no confidence in ethnographic method, voila, no confidence in my ability to communicate my findings, my analysis to an audience of scholars. I feared the questions for which I had no real answers (just fake ones, saying what I thought was expected or what you're supposed to say, the answers you're supposed to have on the tip of your tongue):' "What's your hypothesis?" "How do you measure that?" "How large is your sample?" "Did you pretest the instrument?" "Did you use discriminant function analysis?" So goes the litany of questions that the received view generates.'[4]

"The attitude is that the method is worthless, therefore the product is worthless.

"Discovering the language of ethnography.

"Ethnography as an art and a science." (Andrews 1988, personal journal).

The above "free association" represents the quandry I found myself in when I was struggling with the issues of dissertation writing. I did not know at the time that the intellectual turmoil I was experiencing as a personal crisis was, in fact, reflective of a crisis within the discipline itself. So now anthropology and anthropologists are faced with "the process of reconstructing the edifices of anthropological theory from the bottom up, by exploring new ways to fulfill the promises on which modern anthropology was founded. . . . "[5] The "promises," however, may never be fulfilled because they were not made by the Other(s) of their own free will.

Women have also been constructed as "other" in the context of social science research. Much of the ethnographic writings of anthropologists has dealt with women as individuals in a specific cultural context. Shostak's *Nisa: The Life and Words of a !Kung Woman*[6] and Smith's *Baba of Karo: A Woman of the Muslim Hausa,* [7] originally published in 1954, are examples of ethnographic work about women which tend to create individual models or icons of womanhood. While both of these works are indisputably significant contributions to the literature, they do not speak to larger issues faced by women as a class in contemporary societies.

I have attempted to move beyond the collection of individual life stories of exotic others by women who have accompanied their husbands (who were doing the "real" research in the male sector?) into the field and have decided to find a "mirror for woman," again, with Caucasian implicit. The narratives which I present below fit into the contemporary scene. We are no longer dealing with Nisa in the bush. We are now concerned with women who must function in nonegalitarian, postindustrial and postcolonial societies. Rather than perpetuate the tradition of non-Black anthropologists seeking to understand *self* by using "others" (be they female or male) as alter egos embodied in brown, it is incumbent upon African American and African anthropologists to enable Black people to reflect upon our multifaceted selves in the mirror. The narratives which follow, by Black American women of their experiences as women in the academic profession, are intended as a step toward that end.

The "double whammy" of race and gender, being Black and female, compounded by the attainment of a high level of education, predictably creates problems on both a professional and personal level. Black women must contend with the professional pressures associated with working in an historically White, middle-and upper-middle-class, male-dominated profession, as well as attempt to balance the demands of life outside the professional domain. The vast majority of the tiny minority of Blacks (both female and male) in the academic profession come, primarily, from Black middle-class backgrounds (distinct from the middle class of White America) and have internalized American middle-class values with some modifications based on cultural and socioeconomic factors. Therefore, class should be a less significant factor in shaping the experiences of Black women in academe than race and gender. The comments of my respondents tend to support this assertion. Several, in fact, felt that they had experienced discrimination that was, in their opinion, based on gender as often as on race, but made little direct reference to class status as a significant factor in their experiences. This does not mean that this status is a nonsignificant factor in their lives but that, with rare exception, it was not raised as an issue by this particular group of African American women.

In the personal domain, Black American women with doctorates are faced with decisions to marry or not to marry, where to find a suitable mate, and, for those who have family responsibilities, how to prioritize the demands of both their professional and personal lives. On the professional level, the issues of concern to the African American women I interviewed reflect those of concern to Euro-American women as well. The findings from my larger sample illustrate that the problem of negotiating success in the context of what more than one woman referred to as "the old boy network," pay equity, earning tenure, and juggling family and professional responsibilities are concerns shared by women in the academic profession regardless of race or ethnicity. Beyond this shared set of concerns, however, are issues that are specifically related to being Black *and* female in the academic environment. What emerged out of the conversations I had with the women I interviewed was that the issues they felt were the most pressing ones facing them as Black women, were not only the impact of gender and salary discrimination based on male dominance in the profession, and struggling to get tenure, but racial discrimination and a type of role conflict and professional burnout that was compounded by the fact of race, as well. Culturally determined attitudes toward academe helped to shape responses to these pressures and to the pressures of managing family and professional demands. Discrimination based on gender has been a major issue in the academic profession. In a discussion of the impact of affirmative action on opportunities for women, and for African American women in particular, Barge[8] suggests that the legislation has not brought about equality in academe. Following Bodger,[9] she asserts that women are less likely to be hired than men, and when they are hired often fill nontenured positions. Further, women receive lower salaries than men. In reference to male domination of the profession and the "old boy network," Jessie, a never-married woman in her early forties, said that the biggest problem she saw for herself as a Black woman in the academic profession was:

> getting a job. If you're talking about Black women or minority groups it would be competing against White males . . . and White women. It is still the old stigma, you must be the best of the best [to get a job and] . . . to maintain it.

Jessie went on to say that:

In Departments we are treated as "dog's bodies." As if we're just slaves to the whole system. It's not racial. Have you ever been to a departmental cocktail party? Have you ever noticed that even though women are academics, they can hold their heads high and say that I published this, and that, that the men exclude them, still, and they have to end up with the wives? I think that's unfair. The old boy network!

Helene, a senior academician with many years of experience in the profession also saw the fact that most of the disciplines in the academic world are run by men, "even today," as problematic.

And even in the profession that we usually think of as belonging to women, such as English and languages and so on, that stops with the fact that women are predominant in those fields, that stops . . . look at the percent on the faculty. That is not true of the higher echelons. The higher you get the more all departments are just dominated by men. So, it comes down to competition. If there were just lots of jobs open for just everybody then you wouldn't have to feel that women are still very much discriminated against. But there aren't as many jobs so when it comes down to it, I think women are not favored, they're still victims of masculine, what would you call it, dominance.

Denise, a thirty-seven-year-old divorced woman, asserted that:

With increasing numbers of women, I don't feel the sense of alienation that I think I would [otherwise]. I think men . . . God help us, men still have a hard time dealing with women as peers, colleagues. The sexual factor always sort of gets into it and writes you off as totally asexual, or they put you on a pedestal, deal with you as a sex object. But they do have hard times dealing with us as people.

The issue of sexism of the sort described by Denise is compounded by race. Franklin and Pillow[10] suggest that much of the manifestation of sexism which we see in present-day interaction between women and men is a function of the internalization, or lack of internalization, of the "Prince Charming" ideal. Behavior based on this culturally held ideal is premised on the

philosophical belief that being a responsible, mature male means the assumption of a protective, condescending, providing and generally patriarchal role regarding one's female mate and women in general.[11]

Denise's observations of male to female interaction in the academic arena support the above definition of behavior based on the internalization of, and the ability to act upon the ideals contained in the definition of, the Prince Charming ideal. She also notes a difference in the way this ideal is enacted based on race and how this racial difference in enactment impacts on the professional lives of Black women:

> Many men, I think this is true more for Black men than White men and I hope I'm wrong, they make objects out of us. And just as many White men do it, too. But I just know some of the men I've been exposed to in my experience . . . the Black men . . . they can't be your friend. They either view you sexually or not at all. And you're not a real person to them.
>
> And, so what I'm saying with increasing numbers of women . . . I just want collegial relations. And that's the way I deal with it. But if women were not increasing in higher education and it was still primarily male, I could be in serious trouble.

Lee, a divorcee of eighteen years, had a slightly different view of what she saw as happening to women, not only African American women but women in general, in terms of hiring and tenure in the context of a system structured to operate in the interest of males first:

> The women that are coming in now are coming in with these high-powered men and it looks like that's the only way women can make it in academics. They hire the man and the man says you have to take my wife or find a place for my wife.

The issue of gender inequality is of real concern to African American women academics. The women I interviewed, as evidenced by the above comments, are directly affected by sexism in the workplace in a variety of covert and overt ways. Salary discrimination was also seen as based on gender, in conjunction with race in some cases. Jessie stated that while she felt that women of color did earn less money that all others in the profession, "It's with all women, though. A fight." When I asked Helene what her views were of salary equity in academe, she responded:

> Well, it's one thing about higher education . . . the salaries are fixed according to rank. And if there's a union anywhere around, even the . . . AAUP [Association of American University Professionals], which is not a union but which does sort of supervise that sort of

thing, so there's not that kind of equality at the higher levels. It's not like businesses and other professions. Now, there is a point for discrimination . . . since salaries are conditioned by rank there might be a little influence . . . suppose you had a woman and a man coming up for tenure for changing in rank. I have a feeling that there would still, in higher education, be some tendency to take the man. That relates to salary.

Elena, a woman with a young son who is unmarried by choice, said that she felt salary discrepancies existed to a lesser degree now than in the past.

What happens is that there are more men in those areas of academic life that pay more. For example, professional schools of business, law, and medicine tend to pay as much as twice as much as is paid to people who are in [other areas].

On the other hand, there were women who responded that they did not see any discrimination in salary based on their gender or race. Sometimes this was dependent upon intangible factors such as having "a cool department."

And we cannot discuss the academic profession without discussing tenure. The achievement of tenure, the recognition by professional peers of one's scholarly ability and achievement, is the goal of all academics who strive for success in their respective fields. Hazel had some definite views on what tenure means for Black women in terms of salary as well as some other insights on academia and our educational system in general.

And I think tenure is another, one way, to keep me from earning a decent salary. So people get all caught up in $35,000, $25,000, whatever it is, that's no money! You've spent x number of years educating yourself. You never recover the cost of your education when you go into education, you've got to go out in the corporate world to do it. You're writing little piddly books, little piddly articles. And what for? Our educational system has never been worse. Most people can't read. So, I'm very cynical about it.

You can be fifty and still be an assistant professor if you're a Black woman . . . so, now, they're all wondering why they don't have minorities. And the only reason they're concerned about why they don't have any minorities is because they're not going to have any students because of the baby crunch, there's a dearth of students

who are going to be coming in in the next ten or fifteen years . . .
so, they might have to take a chimpanzee in the . . . future.

Hazel commented further that tenure rules keep changing and that
women with family responsibilities are at a tremendous disadvantage
in a university system which was designed by and in the interests of
White males. She also saw cultural values and attitudes as impacting
on the motivation toward tenure as a career goal and the process of
attaining it. Hazel described that process as:

> fiercely competitive. Blacks are not necessarily competitive in the
> same way that Whites are. You know, by the time you're thirty
> you've got to have sixty or one hundred articles, getting grants. And
> when you come into it late, they keep changing the rules for tenure
> and it gets harder and harder to join them.

Paulette, a tenured professor, reflected upon her position in a state
university in which, she felt, the pressure to publish and earn tenure
or perish was less intense for members of the faculty than it may have
been at other types of institutions.

> I'm in an unusual situation. I haven't had any problems in tenure,
> promotion or any of those things. But it's probably because of the
> department and the college that I'm in. And it's comfortable in a
> state institution where it's not a "publish/perish" kind of place . . .
> it's typical of places like this. We grant only up to the Master's
> degree, a teaching institution. That's not to say that in promotion
> those things are not considered, but it's not death if you are not
> published in seventy-nine refereed journals! So, your comfort level
> in a place like this is a whole lot different than other places that are
> highly concerned about research and publishing. Teaching is primary
> here. And service to the university.

As with other women interviewed, Paulette thought the real problems dealt with women's access to higher administrative positions in
the university system. At her institution this was what she saw as
problematic. Additionally, she felt that women were more capable of
handling administrative positions than men in many instances simply
because women routinely juggled many responsibilities simultaneously
and therefore were conditioned to handle the multiple-task situations
in administration.

Women are not being put into the higher administrative posts. I don't want one but I would like to see that in higher education, i.e., women as vice-presidents. We don't have any here and I think that this is reflective of higher education, generally. For women generally in higher education those avenues need to be open. Women are totally capable of doing administrative jobs. Most women that I know juggled about three or four different things during graduate school and they didn't have any problems doing it, so! They're more organized and have more notion of what's going on than a lot of men. They are, men generally, the majority seem to have blinders on. They can't do but one thing at a time. They can juggle some few things, but women do that all the time. So, higher education needs to begin to take advantage of those kinds of abilities.

Veronica, who teaches at the same institution as Paulette, an institution with a large African American student population, voiced similar views relative to being in a more relaxed environment where matters of tenure were concerned.

You know I was just thinking today that my situation has been very relaxed because I'm at this place and not somewhere else. I'm not at Northwestern or Michigan, I don't have to publish or perish, I don't have White colleagues breathing down my neck. I don't have White students complaining about me. . . . I teach students who look like me . . . .

You know, the look on their faces is really kind of cute. Half the time, it usually alternates between bemusement, like "Look at her up there, just struttin' and talkin'," and genuine pride. Obviously, there are some looks of total confusion and boredom! There's that, too.

Racial prejudice is a fact of American life. I was interested in determining if the African American women I interviewed felt any ramifications of overt or covert racism in their professional lives and, if so, how they handled it in conjunction with sexism. When I asked Denise, who is a divorcee in her late thirties with one child and who had been at her present institution for about a year, what her views on this issue were she responded:

I had some of it initially. But, it was both race and class . . . people said I shouldn't be here 'cause I was Black and a female . . . you can't separate that out. You put both of them together you got a problem, but you just go out and prove yourself. When I came to this place for the first time, I knew that was the case and I set out just to prove 'em wrong. Which I've done. So I'm not concerned with that any more. But you know what their standards are and you just deal with it yourself.

Affirmative action has not curtailed racial prejudice either, and while some women (minorities) have emerged as high achievers, ". . . [B]lack women in higher education are isolated, under utilized, and often demoralized. . . . Compared with nonminority women and minority men, minority women are the least well-represented group among tenured academics."[12]

Role conflict is the terminology often used to describe the impact on women of juggling career and family. It is a very real problem for women with such dual responsibilities. In reference to the most pressing issues facing [Black] women in academe, Hazel said:

> I would say in essence, role overload is the biggest problem. Being a mother and housewife and so on. And you've got to be on the one hand feminine and on the other, a competitor . . . get research grants and things of this sort. So, we just have too many pulls and tensions on our personality."

"Burnout" is another term used to describe the consequences of the above-mentioned role conflict often experienced by Black women in academe and other professions. The statements made by Veronica, a thirty-four-year-old, never-married woman who teaches at a state university, illustrated the type of strain that results from being pulled in so many directions at once.

> But that's the real demand or pressure that's been placed—that's on me, and that's controllable. It's the demands that the students make on me because they can't connect and a lot of them have a need to connect, too tough! That's happenin'. So . . . so the pressure has been, again, more, something from within, you know, trying to just be prepared, do a good job, and so the—it's gotten to the point— I've backed off, I've disengaged from my students and I think that may have been the result of a little burnout because when I first went there I used to teach real large classes, I used to teach a lot of classes, students would come and talk to Black faculty about their personal problems. I was the advisor for the [Black students' association] for five years, and that's more mother than advisor.
>
> It becomes a problem when they start making demands on time

and that's when it really got to be burnout, I think, when they started making demands on time that I wanted to give to something else. You know? That became a real issue. . . . so what I found was that I had to, I've disengaged. I advised last year, I'm not doing that next year. And I've really found that I don't want to be advisor, I don't want that. [emphasis added]

Another aspect of being a Black woman functioning in college and university settings is the impact of the emotional drain created by the needs of African American students in an environment that is often-times hostile to them. The Black woman professor is often called upon to serve as mentor, mother, and counselor in addition to educator in these settings. The consequences of these multifaceted role expectations by students are compounded by the existence of similar demands placed upon Black women by colleagues and administrators in the institutions in which we hold positions. If we consider the fact that Black women often also have these same expectations to meet at home it is abundantly clear that in many cases something has to give.

Following Naisbitt,[13] Barge asserts:

> Highly educated, motivated women . . . continue to face the dilemma of trying to balance career and family responsibilities while simultaneously creating and implementing strategies to resolve conflicts arising from their multiple roles. Stress results not only from efforts to balance opposing roles but also from the prevailing promotion system which creates career mobility barriers for women.[14]

This work further supports the notion that the strains inherent in managing the multiple roles required of academic women, and other professional women, with family responsibilities can often be over-whelming. In relating the story of earning her doctorate, Hazel described the determined way in which she managed to get by on four hours of sleep each night in order to attain her goal. She "wore a groove in the table" where she studied, every night from 10:00 P.M. (after the children were in bed) to 2:00 A.M.:

> Most women have family responsibilities, and when Black women have family responsibilities they're even more difficult for us than for the White woman because for us many of us are the first, second generation at best. In university life . . . I could go to a Black university and get over big. But, then you wonder what for?

Hazel's case illustrates the extra determination and willpower required of many African American women in all professions. Of course, due to cultural conditioning and traditional expectations about women held by both men and women, all of us have a double load to carry. Additionally, a far higher percentage of African American women enter graduate school with family responsibilities, both as single parents or in intact marriages, than Euro-American women. This reality requires an extraordinary amount of dedication and motivation in order to succeed. Hazel's story is uniquely her own while at the same time representative of many, if not most, Black women's experience.

Marsha, a married woman in her mid-thirties with two young children, felt an inordinate amount of stress and role overload in her attempt to juggle family and career demands. As a relatively recent recipient of a doctorate, she was struggling to do well in her first teaching position and fulfill the demands of parenting, finding a competent and reliable child caregiver, maintaining the house, preparing meals and all of the domestic responsibilities that fall to a woman married to a man whom she euphemistically described as "less than cooperative."

> I've got to have a faster turnover in terms of conducting research and getting it out. That for me is a matter of having the time to do that. And that is a matter of organization. I've got to get my life more structured ... although I think it's about as structured as it's gonna get, to be honest. I need more. I need assistance. I can't do everything on the home front. I can't be everything to everybody. I need a little more time to myself. And I need assistance at home. I need another adult there. A grandma figure, or another Mommy figure, an auntie. It could be a man, too. I need support, you know, to get through a day-to-day life. It can't be just me doing this *balancing act* for everyone. But I just can't, even if I could just physically get through it, I don't have the mental energy left afterwards to put out extra on top of my job. [I suggested she might want live-in help.]
>
> I'm thinking of that. I was thinking originally of an older person, someone with an income, and I'm told that there are community centers, [the city] has some kind of center that helps link up with that. I'm going to call the babysitter who said she knew of a couple of organizations that help with that. That was my first choice, I could even save more money and so on. But at this point it's gonna cost me, for the next year or two years, half my salary. Half my monthly salary. I don't have a Yuppie salary. I have an academic salary. When you're earning $60[,000] or $80,000, OK, bring in the

au pair girl. But when you're earning what the *au pair* earns yourself, shoot! It's the different bag of beans!

And if I look for someone it'd preferably be a non-American cuz I have to have some food we can eat! She can be a Black American, Haitian, or Jamaican or something like that. I need someone who's dependable and doesn't have a whole lot of distractions. But they have to be able to cook, OK? [emphasis mine]

In a follow-up interview, I learned that Marsha has since abandoned the effort to be all to all, and is currently a full-time homemaker, which is what she intends to remain until her two children are considerably older and self-reliant. Marsha's story was paralleled by that of a woman who was not Black, who also reprioritized the demands in her life, decided the hassle was not worth it, and abandoned academe rather than wear herself to a frazzle. For many African American women this strategy is not an option. Most of the women I talked with who had children were divorced and therefore, felt it imperative to maintain their employed status.

For African American women, values held toward higher education and academe are, in large part, culturally determined. These values will obviously influence decisions and priorities in both the personal and professional realms. Black women have historically, and in a cultural context, been advised, encouraged, socialized, and pressured to pursue higher education in order (1) "not have to depend on a man" and (2) not have to work for Whites as domestic servants. Hazel addressed some issues that had particular relevance for Black women in the academic profession that were culturally determined. She saw the perks in academe as very intangible, whereas life for Blacks is very concrete.

It depends on which bus you're trying to get on, where you're trying to live. So, this is kind of a vaporous kind of an atmosphere here [in academe]. It's not real. And as soon as you leave the office you've got to deal with something else. So, we don't have the journal clubs and things where we can sit and ponder over a couple of sentences from Kant and something of that sort. So, it's hard for me to get too excited about it.

Jessie, cited previously, expressed similar views which point to the significance of cultural factors in shaping Black women's experiences in academe, and the value and meanings placed on those experiences.

but, I want to live my life. I do not want to sit in cloistered halls . . . writing academic papers for the rest of my life. That isn't a life. What are you going to do, get to be sixty-five years old . . . have nothing to show for it but a bunch of publications . . . you say "I wrote this, I wrote that." Give me a break! [A: Maybe we like to think we're making a contribution to society.] *Everybody* makes a contribution to society, even the Blackstone Rangers [an urban street gang] make a contribution to society! And the El Rukns [another street gang] are *certainly* making a contribution [laughing] and that is the way I feel about it. I have enjoyed my education, it's given me a lot of benefits and I've never been without anything I didn't need. I could want it but I don't *need* it.

Overall, the African American women whose views are presented in this paper express a wide array of perspectives on the situation of Black women in academe. While the views are diverse, there are common threads that run throughout them. The perceived impact of being, first of all, a woman and, secondly, a Black woman, in what has traditionally been a White male-dominated arena ran throughout the interviews. While race was seen as a factor that had some bearing on their position in the institutional hierarchy, gender issues emerged as an important theme.

Given the candid comments presented in this paper, how do Black women in academe balance the personal and the professional. First of all, I believe that we don't. We juggle at best and throw the ball down at worst. Perhaps the dichotomy is a false one. The two, the personal and the professional, seem to be so intertwined that balancing is not the issue. A more accurate description may be untangling the personal and the professional if, indeed, Black women would want to do that.

There was, however, an underlying tone of frustration with the inordinate pressures, created by the felt demand to be everything to everyone, with which Black women seem to be faced. This frustration can be sensed in the comments of Marsha, for instance, as she described feeling pulled in different directions by the demands of child care, an uncooperative spouse, and strained finances. Hazel also described a frenzied lifestyle during the time she was earning her doctorate, again with the concerns of childrearing (which she gave priority) and an uncooperative husband complicating matters. Veronica, an unmarried woman with no children, also described the burnout she felt because of student demands.

In contrast to these expressions of stress, other women, such as Paulette, appear to be unperturbed by the demands of academe. Her nonchalant attitude toward marriage was also her attitude toward the profession. She had felt no pressure to fight the "publish-or-perish" battle even though she did earn tenure. Hazel also reflected this more casual attitude (perhaps disenchanted is a better term) when she described the process as "fiercely competitive," and felt it was hard for her to get excited about it. Jessie's comments seem to sum up a generally held attitude toward the situation.

> I want to live my life. I do not want to sit in cloistered halls . . . writing academic papers for the rest of my life. That isn't life.

Black women seem to be willing to play the game, and play to win. Yet when the personal costs outweigh the professional gain in what many consider "the White man's game," Black women, if these voices are at all representative, rearrange their priorities, back off from the stressors and, in a few cases, simply take their ball and jacks and go home!

Notes

1. Bronislaw Malinowski, *The Sexual Life of Savages in Northwestern Melanesia* (New York: Halycon House, 1932).

2. George E. Marcus and Michael M. J. Fischer, *Anthropology as Cultural Critique* (Chicago: University of Chicago Press, 1986): ix–x.

3. Michael Agar, *Speaking of Ethnography* (Beverly Hills: Sage Publications, 1986) 11.

4. *Ibid.*

5. Marcus and Fischer, *Anthropology*, ix.

6. Marjorie Shostak, *Nisa: The Life and Words of a !Kung Woman* (Cambridge, Mass.: Harvard University Press, 1981).

7. Mary F. Smith, *Baba of Karo: A Woman of the Muslim Hausa* (New York: Praeger, 1964).

8. Frances C. Barge, "Nursing Education Administrators: Blocked Women," *Nursing Clinics of North America* 21 (1986).

9. C. Bodger, "Sixth Annual Salary Survey," *Working Woman* 85 (1985): 69.

10. Clyde W. Franklin, II and Walter Pillow, "The Black Male's Acceptance of the Prince Charming Ideal," *The Black Family: Essays and Studies*, ed. Robert Staples (Belmont, CA: Wadsworth Publishing, 1986).

11. *Ibid.*, 70–71.

12. R.J. Menges and W. H. Exum, "Barriers to the Progress of Women and Minority Faculty," *Journal of Higher Education* 54 (1983): 123–144, in Barge, *op. cit.*, 189.

13. J. Naisbitt, *Megatrends* (New York: Warner Books, Inc., 1982) 261–268.

14. Barge, *op. cit.*, 186.

12

Place but not Importance: The Race for Inclusion in Academe

Ruth Farmer

Introduction

A driving instructor once told me that a car will go wherever the driver is looking. Concentrate on the curb, and that is where the vehicle will go. For centuries, women and men of color, as well as White women, have concentrated on the culture of White males as a central point of discourse, often coveting its position in the world. The knowledge that it has been a warrior culture, one of domination and destruction for the most part, has not lessened the obsession to be included within it. Domination and destruction are reflected in educational systems which exclude from curricula contributions, theories, and cultures of those who are not White and/or male. Scholarship on women and men of color, and White women, when included, may be warped in ways which reflect gender and racial biases. In other words, a warrior mentality of invasion, pillage, and enslavement can be seen in curriculum design.

Remedial measures, via curriculum integration or mainstreaming projects, attempt to compensate for omissions and distortions. Syllabi are slightly modified, to add books by or about people of color (and White women, where necessary). Often these books are optional reading covered at the end of the semester if there is time, thus giving them place but not importance. This race for inclusion, a frantic scramble to proffer people of color associate (peripheral) membership to the mainstream, that is, White male culture, is a palliative administered where more radical changes are necessary and indeed demanded by concerned students, faculty and administrators. The race to include materials by people of color is a poor response to the pressing need for

196

overall societal change. It does not challenge the status quo at all, for it simply adds a few courses with the words race, ethnicity, diversity, multiculturalism, and so on, in their titles, or allows the teaching of the same old courses with different titles, or the addition of one book by a person of color. (I must acknowledge, however, that such relatively innocuous actions have caused a great deal of conflict in many quarters.) What is most important in terms of empowering people of color (which is *purportedly* one of the goals of inclusion), what traditionally White colleges and universities are finding extremely difficult to achieve, is enrolling students of color who would benefit from culturally and racially inclusive courses, along with their White classmates; and employing professors of color to teach the courses, and administrators of color to help change the atmosphere in which learning takes place.

The race for inclusion assumes that the educational mainstream is viable as it is. Adding courses from "others" is not done to improve the quality of education but to keep the political lid on. Integration of the curriculum is opposed by those who believe it threatens educational excellence. "Excellence," in their minds, is a euphemism for a preponderance of White values, perspectives, and ideals, that is, White supremacy. The mainstream is based on the necrophilic philosophies of patriarchy and White supremacy, both of which require the worship of dead White men, the marginalization of scholarship that threatens the fantasy that White men are greater than anyone else, and the killing of creativity by forcing these ideals as normative. Racism, sexism, and other systems of discrimination have tainted what good there is in the mainstream. It is exclusion, therefore, which shapes it, not excellence. As educator Johnnella Butler has written:

> The mainstream is very sick, and rightfully near death. We must be about ultimately replacing it through transformation. We have got to provide a curriculum that seeks to *tell the truth* and that, in turn, releases the full material and spiritual potential of human beings to learn not static content, but to comprehend content in relation to the everyday world *and* in relation to the plural character of the world and of human life.[1]

To many people (mostly, but not exclusively Whites), transformation of curricula is the brainchild of fanatics. Scholarship by and about people of color is viewed as a dangerous tainting of educational quality. When students, faculty, or scholars ask for a reformation of the canon as opposed to simply addition of texts, these requests are often viewed as charity work rather than enrichment of a lopsided, narrow system which has miseducated and undereducated people of all races for centuries.

The everyday world is more than elite White males. Yet in the United States and many Westernized countries, the experiences and judgments of elite White males shape everybody else's daily realities. Expanding reading lists has not and will not change this. What has resulted is that faculty and administrators become bogged down in discussions of which books reflect true history or valuable scholarship, and essential discussions which could lead to structural changes within academe do not take place. This necessary dialogue is avoided under the guise that it is too political for the educational forum. Problems shaped by racism, sexism, class oppression, heterosexism, and other forms of domination will only be solved through analysis of power dynamics and a commitment to altering power bases.

I pose this question: Is change something that is the goal of too few people with too little power?

White males, in addition to being overwhelmingly represented in texts and on faculties, hold the majority of upper echelon administrative positions, that is, when those positions are not held by White females. I question whether diversity, inclusion, or even transformation can occur with such monolithic input. Inclusion of texts by and about people of color is vital to improving educational quality. However, resources and insights from qualified people of color are not being utilized when formulating educational goals (including when deciding which texts and topics are to be taught) because there are so few people of color, particularly women of color, in decision-making positions. Despite curriculum integration projects, the contributions of people of color are still viewed as mere tributaries to the great oceans of White scholarship and organization.

Absence Speaks Louder Than Words

The number of women of color in universities and colleges with high-ranking administrative positions is dismally low. In a comprehensive profile of college presidents, resulting from questionnaires to the chief executive officers of 2,822 regionally accredited higher education institutions, the American Council on Education (ACE) found that the typical college president is White, male, married, and 53 years old.

Seventy-five percent, or 2,105, responded to ACE's questionnaires. Ninety-three percent of the responding presidents were White males. The presidents who identified themselves as minorities included one hundred Blacks, thirty-seven "Hispanics," eight Asians and three American Indians. Two hundred of the respondents or 9.5 percent were women.[2]

Data collected by ACE's Office of Women in Higher Education (OWHE) indicate that 328 women were chief executive officers of colleges and universities in December, 1989, making up 11 percent of all presidents of approximately three thousand educational institutions accredited by six regional associations. Forty-three or one percent of chief executive officers are women of color: twenty African Americans; sixteen "Hispanics", most of whom head colleges in Puerto Rico; two Asian Americans; and five American Indians, heads of so-called tribal colleges.[3] Interestingly, ACE's profile indicates that a higher proportion of women and minority presidents of educational institutions hold Ph.D.s than do White male presidents, confirming the contention that women and "minorities" must be better qualified than White men in order to hold comparable positions.[4]

Though the possession of a doctorate, specifically a Ph.D., is supposed to lead to upward mobility within academe, its attainment offers little protection to African American women from the detrimental effects of racial/sexual biases on professional mobility. In his article, "Women of Color in Academic Administration: Trends, Progress, and Barriers," Reginald Wilson, senior scholar of ACE, comments on findings which show that in academic administration, "sex and race measurably affect the upward mobility of women of color independent of degree attained or field of study."[5] Women of color do hold faculty and administrative positions; however, they are usually directors of remedial programs, affirmative action offices, and ethnic studies programs, positions which are not considered mainstream administration and, consequently, rarely lead to deanships, vice-presidencies, or presidential positions no matter how talented the person happens to be.[6]

Wilson points out that both the church and the academy, the two institutions most identified with preserving the nation's ethical and democratic values, are the most resistant to democracy and diversity in their leadership.[7] This is significant, in that White males within both institutions have for centuries fought with "outsiders," that is, the rest of the world, over what constitutes worthy canon. This Exalted Canon is either religious or educational, but it is always White and male. Allowing people other than Whites or males to experience, share or (re)define the canon is still considered blasphemy. In the church and in the academy, the sanctity of the canon, the fear of "confusing the issues," even the fear of God have all been used to exclude people, by virtue of the perceived inferiority of their race or gender.

Contrary to what we would like to believe, neither democracy nor diversity exists in most institutions within this country. Historically it is only when members of excluded groups chip away at the reasoning for their exclusion that canons and rules have been changed. Educational institutions are especially resistant to inclusion by people of color within their hallowed walls, as Reginald Wilson notes below.

> Despite higher education institutions' protestations that they eagerly seek minority students and staff, the history of American higher education reveals to the contrary that minorities and women were forced into the elite universities by the courts, by Congress, by presidential executive orders, and by citizen and student demonstrations, by people of color in the cities and on the campuses. The universities were reluctantly forced to open their doors, and they resisted every step of the way, as they continue to resist up to today.[8]

Educational canon and power structure reflect a belief in the supremacy of Whites and males and, for this reason, the majority of those who direct educational institutions (Whites and males) find absolutely nothing amiss with things as they are. Students and scholars, constantly reminded of that to which they must aspire, are forced to pay homage to the canon's gatekeepers, representatives and surrogates, and to duplicate as closely as possible the postures and thought processes of the mainstream. When searches for additional staff or faculty are made, centuries-old stereotypes against "others" prevail. Search committees unconsciously and consciously seek to duplicate what was there before the vacancy or to create a reasonable proximity of themselves. On predominantly White campuses, those people will be Whites and are often males. People of color may approximate the White male model but still remain side shows or entertaining exotica.

There is strong, often violent, resistance to any attempts to include people of other races in policy and decision-making processes. In a world which is rapidly changing politically, the oppression of people of color in general and women of color in particular has remained intransigent. Despite the fact that the United States and the global community are comprised of many cultures and races, the inappropriate and educationally bankrupt one-race university remains an acceptable model. Diversity in curriculum and staffing is a political issue because it has been made one. If educational excellence is truly a goal of academe, then the demand for diversity would not be needed, for diversity would already be present, because a broad, diverse view is tantamount to a good education, as Johnnetta B. Cole, President of Spelman College, points out below.

> An enormously destructive myth exists—that excellence in education is impossible if there is diversity. I am convinced that excellence in education is *only possible* if there is diversity among the students, faculty, and staff who make up an academic community. . . . We must include all of us in the curriculum of our colleges and universities or we threaten true excellence. Either we learn to deal with diversity or we will be "unified" in our destruction.[9]

In his paper on affirmative action and Blacks in the university, Kellis Parker notes that hiring a few token Black faculty and administrators does not automatically lead to change since these tokens are not in sufficient numbers nor have sufficient power to effect change.

> The hiring of one [Black] is as bad as the hiring of none because neither position changes the symbol of Black exclusion. . . . Unless the one Black faculty member is hung from the flag pole so that everyone can see that there is a Black presence at the university, she will have a difficult time trying to be a symbol of the institution's paradigm shift. . . . Tokens are incapable of changing the ethos of all-white institutions. It is this ethos that white people have nurtured and developed for centuries that dominates the process of thought at universities.[10]

Having only Whites at the helm conveys the idea that only Whites can direct progress, can direct movement into the twenty-first century. Hiring one or two Blacks will not change this notion.

> Hiring one Black person probably signals change for a short time, but in time that signal comes to be a beacon of the institution's acceptance of the idea that Blacks have no role to play in fashioning progress. Only when the hiring of Blacks . . . happens randomly and often enough is the message of a new idea of progress conveyed.[11]

According to Parker, ideas are either subject to speech acts and other forms of expression, or they are subject to signs and symbols other than speech acts.

[R]acial integration has been given preferential treatment in the expressive realm while racial segregation has been given preferential treatment in the symbolic realm. Thus one finds institutions that have none or only one Black faculty member, a handful of Black administrators spread in insignificant ways throughout the university, and a few Black students. . . . [T]heir failure to move beyond their token numbers broadcasts their symbolic preference for racial segregation.[12]

Faculty and administrators are located somewhat differently within academic hierarchy; however, people of color, whether faculty or administrators, are commodified in ways that their White counterparts are not. This especially occurs when, through either internal or external pressures, educational institutions are forced to "diversify" their personnel. What often results is the positioning of faculty and administrators so that they have visibility (thus improving the institution's public image) but very little autonomy or power (and power remains concentrated with the White race). Under these circumstances, people of color, like the scholarship of people of color, are given place but not importance.

Students of color in predominantly white institutions cannot help but interpret the dearth of faculty and administrators of color as a sign that their alma mater is not a potential employer. University administrators who claim they cannot find qualified "minority" candidates to fill faculty and administrative positions defame whole races and, by not hiring even their own graduates, are defaming their own institutions which have graduated these supposedly unqualified people.

Everyone is placed at a disadvantage when an institution lacks faculty and administrators of color: Programs and curricula are developed in the vacuum of exclusively White thought. Students are robbed of the experience of having role models, support, and mentoring from people of diverse backgrounds. In addition, the few faculty and administrators of color who are on campus are required *de facto* and *de jure* to overextend themselves to accommodate the university's segregationist policies.

Between a Rock and a Hard Place

CENSORSHIP
Are my words too much for you?
Are they too dark, too sharp,
too colored with experiences
you will never be expert in?

Have I said too much?
Am I too plain,
putting out what I have to say
as it comes to me,
not shading sex with fruit
or hiding pain with flowers.
Do I have too few sunrises,
insufficient levels of illusion,
or is it too obvious that I have a point of view
which is unexpected?
Should I not talk about racism
because it's old hat,
poverty because it's passé?
Should I go back to the European roots
that were planted in my educational garden, and
pull out sonnets
and other controlled modes of expression?
Am I too wild,
unstructured
nonlinear
mosaic
indefinable
to be read by your erudite constituency?
Am I too Black?[13]

Many African American women find that academe is not conducive to professional development or job satisfaction except with constant struggle. Yolanda T. Moses, in her study *Black Women in Academe: Issues and Strategies*, examines the climate for African American women in predominantly White colleges and universities, using results from a questionnaire done by the Project on the Status and Education of Women (PSEW) and a survey of literature concerning African American women and higher education. Some of the typical problems experienced by African American women administrators and faculty include:

(1) being constantly challenged because she is viewed as "other" and therefore inferior;
(2) a lack of professional support systems;
(3) overscrutinization by peers, superiors, and students;
(4) an unstated requirement to work harder in order to gain recognition and respect;

(5) assumptions that her job was acquired through affirmative action and, therefore, that she is unqualified for the position;

(6) being tokenized, that is, seen as a symbol of her race rather than as an individual; and

(7) being denied access to power structures normally associated with her position.[14]

Racial and sexual biases dictate that the African American woman administrator be all things to all people. If she does not allow herself to be treated in this manner, she is considered cold, unapproachable, antisocial, and not a team player. Often she is said to be incompetent if she cannot or will not juggle all the responsibilities thrust upon her. She may even feel guilty that she cannot help all who need her. Yet if she does all that is required of her as a person of color, simply because the institution refuses to hire other people of color—for example, integrating all-White committees and functions and acting as unofficial, uncompensated and often unacknowledged counselor to students of color—she will not be viable in her own job and may bring emotional stress upon herself.

African American women administrators are often in the ranks of the lower echelon and are expected to be hands-on workers, not ideas people. Creativity is squeezed in between other demands, since lower-echelon administrators are rarely granted the time or space within work environments to develop ideas. These luxuries are afforded to higher-echelon executives.

The African American woman is on display and her activities are often scrutinized and questioned: What is she doing? Is she doing what she is "supposed" to be doing? Why is she here? Is she qualified to be here? The bulk of this chapter was written during my period of employment at a traditionally White institution. I lacked the space and the time to fully conceptualize this article, except on my own time, even though it directly relates to my field.

Up until November 1991, I worked as an administrator in the Barnard Center for Research on Women (BCROW). My job title was Associate Director. I was office manager, conference coordinator, *maitre d'*, personnel manager, computer consultant, resource collection manager, employee assistance officer, budget manager, and so on. As everyone except the director worked in an open space, spatial deficits placed me at everyone's beck and call: coworkers, colleagues, and anyone else who came into the office, whether they wanted center-specific information or were looking for the bathroom. Thinking my own thoughts under those conditions was understandably difficult. Like many women, particularly African American women, my role was a domestic one. Ultimately, it was my responsibility to "take care of. . . . " Any intellectualizing on my part was lagniappe.

Being neither male nor White, professor nor student, nor the head of my department, it was often assumed that I had no role worth noting. Most visitors seemed to think that all the women working at BCROW were secretaries to the director. When people discovered I was the associate director, invariably their heretofore less than cordial attitude toward me dissolved with a murmured "ooohhh."

It is difficult to talk about being Black in a White space, even though in the United States such is usually the case. The difficulty is to speak, to name, without appearing to whine, a near impossibility, since African American women are not expected to speak at all. It is particularly difficult to be heard, since despite the reality, the myth still prevails that African American women are making great professional strides. Enmeshed within this myth is the belief that even when African American women are suffering, obstacles are faced stoically and handled with a prayer, and a smile. In other words, we always overcome. We African American women are reluctant to dispel this myth for it is one of the few positive stereotypes afforded us.

Racial and gender biases within the academe present constant challenges. The racist manner in which administrators of color are treated ranges from blatant disdain and disregard to subtle forms of exclusion. The treatment is paternalizing and maternalizing, and always includes the assumption that Whites know best.

Often the administrator of color is not given certain assignments, ostensibly so that she will not be "exploited" or "overworked." Coincidentally those assignments are usually high-visibility ones which could bring her in contact with influential people. Job-related information may not be relayed, yet the African American woman administrator is expected to function as though she is privy to this missing information. It is especially galling not to have access to information when one learns that White subordinates and students do, simply by virtue of their skin privilege. Though chaos usually reigns due to this racism, the offenders are so biased they can't see that their prejudices are hindering the growth and effectiveness of the department or institution. In order to grow professionally, it may be necessary to virtually climb over the heads of superiors to get the attention of those who are in the position of granting promotions, thus risking dismissal by one's immediate supervisor.

An African American woman is viewed through lenses colored by gender and racial biases; therefore ideas, instructions, and feedback from her may be received hostilely, in a patronizing manner, or sometimes blatantly ignored, with impunity. Typical responses to her words may be immediate challenge, dumbfounded silence, and/or a continuation of conversation as though she had not spoken at all. People may finish her sentences for her or restate her words as though she has spoken a foreign language. These silencing mechanisms are used to denigrate her, to let her know she does not belong, that she has no ideas worth hearing, much less using. If she is not a higher-echelon administrator, she can effectively be shut down (and up) simply by excluding her from the realm of information and policy-making, for instance, by not inviting her to meetings, even though the agenda is within her area of responsibility and expertise. In these meetings from which she has been excluded, credit can be taken for suggestions she has made, thus giving the impression that she is not contributing to the maintenance and growth of her department. Sometimes a superior may ask the administrator of color to stand in (at the last minute) at a meeting which the administrator had no idea was taking place, even though the meeting is directly within her realm of responsibility. In this instance, she goes to the meeting ill-prepared, and therefore appears incompetent.

Another professional assault is not being introduced as an administrator at meetings (while others are introduced by title) It is then assumed that she is there to take notes or do the xeroxing rather than to participate in the decision-making process.

Yet, the African American administrator's name is utilized in publicity in order to lend authenticity to claims of diversity or to render a stamp of approval which implies that the organization is nonracist. University catalogs may show pictures of her (and the two other Blacks on campus) and quote dubious statistics about percentages of Blacks on campus (a 50% increase in staff doesn't tell the truth: the number went from 2 to 3). Typically, whenever there is a "Black" issue on campus, African Americans are brought forth. The likelihood of an African American's presence and input being actively sought is far greater if an event deals with issues of race or if a guest speaker is an African American. We are very popular during February, Black History Month.

Of course, it is assumed that the African American woman's interests lie solely in the topics of racism, multiculturalism, and cultural diversity. And she is expected to know all Black people of note. When a

White person turns to you during a reception or meeting and asks, "Do you know So-and-So?" you can rest assured that Mr. or Ms. So-and-So is Black.

Often African American women are only included in policy discussions as afterthoughts, after the agenda has been set and all the "important people" (Whites and possibly men of color) have been invited. Even though Asians, Blacks, Latinas, and Native Americans have different agendas, needs, viewpoints, and experiences, it is believed that any woman of color will serve just as well to talk about the needs of the rest of the millions of women of color on the planet.

Any African American woman who rebels against these assumptions in any fashion, either assertively or aggressively, is seen as a Sapphire. And since all women are expected to be nice, this can be a real career killer.

A lower-echelon administrator works under precarious economic conditions, lacking organized employment protection which unionized employees sometimes have. Due to the lack of leverage, lower-echelon administrators bear the brunt of cuts when financial difficulties arise; they take on extra duties without an increase in salary when others are fired, or are let go themselves. When BCROW lost a key staff position, that of resource collection manager, the duties of that job fell to me by default: the director was protected by virtue of her ability to define her role within the department, and the clerical worker was protected because of her union status. My only recourse would have been to refuse to do anything pertaining to the collection; this was not an option, since my responsibilities included supervision of staff who worked on the collection.

The termination of my position as associate director at BCROW is typical of what happens to associate and assistant directors and other similar types of administrators. In mid-October of 1991, the director of BCROW was asked to resign. I will not speculate here on the reasons for this, for they are complicated issues, too numerous to articulate in this chapter. Suffice it to say that the restructuring of BCROW (as it was being called), excluded the input of BCROW staff members, and was touted as a budgetary decision.

Rumors that my job as associate director would end circulated throughout the campus grapevine. However, for an entire week, the dean of faculty had yet to approach me about my status. I finally made an appointment to speak to him and discovered that the rumors were true; my position was to be eliminated. He assured me that he had not been ignoring me, but was merely waiting until he had settled with the director before he talked to me. This hierarchical approach to terminations is probably common, but is no less unprofessional for that. The director and I were expected to leave BCROW by November 1, which by the time the dean and I talked was less than two weeks away. A new director had been appointed weeks before (this was discovered at the time we found out we no longer had jobs) and was already formulating plans for the restructured BCROW.

The significance of this synopsis is to point out how easily people of color are frozen out of the decision-making processes which affect their professional lives. Personally, I can think of any number of alternative ways the restructuring of BCROW could have been handled. However, as a lower-level administrator in a department which was itself considered outside of the mainstream, my input was not sought, nor heeded once I offered it unasked. Barnard College administrators made a decision which is very common throughout educational institutions: rather than institute an open search for a new director, they appointed a known quantity: a Barnard alumna who had worked as an assistant professor at the college, who had been turned down for tenure, and who had friendly ties with the president of the college, herself a Barnard alumna. Written and verbal requests to the dean and the president by faculty and staff that an open search be held fell on deaf ears, as did numerous letters of concern,[15] and protest which inundated the dean's and the president's offices, written by people who had used BCROW's library, attended conferences and lectures there, or had other professional connections to BCROW. We were all presented with a *fait accompli*.

Once in office, the new (White) director proceeded to hire a recently graduated (White) Barnard alumna to fill a new position, that of administrative manager. Because of her union status, Barnard was required to give the assistant to the director (the clerical support of BCROW) a month's notice before letting her go. It was this African American woman's task to help the two White women learn the ropes of BCROW. She held a degree comparable to that of the recently hired administrative manager, and many years of relevant work experience over and above her three years as an employee of BCROW. Out of the mess and bad feelings which were created by the dismissal of the entire staff of BCROW, Barnard's administration would have looked like "good guys" if they had at least offered the position of administrative manager to this woman, for it would have been a promotion for her. Instead, the decision was to replace three people, two of whom are Black, with two Whites, people who were not hired because they were more qualified than the people already in-house, but because they were connected to the power structures of the college.

Where one's professional career within academe relies upon having direct ties to upper-echelon administration, and the possibility of acquiring qualified candidates by holding a national search to fill vacancies for upper-echelon positions are eschewed for the easy and comfortable route of appointment, people of color, particularly women of color, will find it extremely difficult to move into the ranks of higher-level administration. The professional connections needed to become a candidate for these positions are often race, class and/or gender specific. Qualified people are often not even sought after in the effort to maintain the status quo.

Beyond Survival

As a poet I read and watch, teach and learn through my poems, speaking words that sometimes only I hear, either because the words are too private or because "the powers that be," that is publishers, don't want poems from people like me—unknown, and Black, writing about issues that are no longer fashionable, like racism and power.

As an activist, I have worked with many groups trying to head off the violence-mongers who think progress means killing others or allowing people to waste away from lack of resources. Though there are many allies in this fight, I am often dismissed because I am unknown, and Black, talking about unfashionable issues like racism and power.

I have learned with difficulty that multiculturalism, diversity, and other similarly vague and innocuous terms can be discussed in so-called progressive groups, but one must never speak seriously about racism. Promoting the need for antiracism work is considered divisive. To suggest that racism is everyone's problem causes even progressive, liberal Whites to feel guilty for having power, or angry because they are made aware that their guilt alone doesn't change things. Further, confusion results at even the suggestion that Whites are dehumanized when they dehumanize others through racist acts. It is more acceptable to Whites (and to many African Americans) for African Americans to take the role of victim, rather than activist. In addition, this country is currently operating under the illusion that racism has diminished to the point where it no longer poses a serious problem for anyone. If people of color have not "made it" it is because they are not qualified or have not tried hard enough.

In the academic community, much is written about racism, race dynamics, and racial attitudes, yet little is done about these same issues personally, departmentally, or institutionally. Race is viewed abstractly. Many Whites do not even identify themselves racially, possibly because having a race is A Bad Thing. (An exception to this are neo-nazis and other similar White-supremacist groups). Pseudo-objective intellectualism in the academic community leads to disparagement of discussions of racism as it affects individuals and institutions as being too personal or too political. However, writing about racism within the context of victim studies is considered academically sound.

It would be beneficial for groups which have been historically harmed because of racism to band together and fight for structural changes which would allow people to achieve based on talent and merit. However, rather than building coalitions to eliminate or at least alleviate the professional stagnation which results from racial prejudice and elitism within academe, natural allies often fight among themselves: The stratification and hierarchical arrangement of staff, students, and faculty is a serious impediment to political work which could improve the professional climate on campuses, and broaden the prerequisites for upward mobility.

Gerda Lerner explores the dynamics of cooperation with hegemony by people who would be better off challenging it. While she is specifically referring to patriarchy in the following quote, the same dynamics occur wherever hegemony exists and in whatever form it exists.

> [C]ategories of "deviants" or "others" ... are always defined as being "different" from the hegemonic group and assumed to be inferior. It is upon this assumption of the inferiority of presumed "deviant" groups that hierarchy is instituted and maintained. Hierarchy is institutionalized in the state and its laws, in military, economic, educational, and religious institutions, in ideology and the hegemonic cultural product created by the dominant elite. The system which has historically appeared in different forms ... depends, for its continuance, on its ability to split the dominated majority ... and to mystify the process by which this is done. The function of various forms of oppression ... is to accomplish this division by offering different groups of the oppressed various

advantages over other groups and thus pit them one against the other.[16]

Divide and conquer has always worked. Because this is a patriarchal society, men of color have access to power which women of color do not. Therefore, we find that high level African American women administrators in historically Black educational institutions are in short supply because sexism impedes their professional progress.[17] While women in general do not fare very well in the academic community, White women are making remarkable progress compared to women of color. Their White skin privilege gives them access to power which women and men of color lack.[18] The advantage Whites have over darker-skinned people is maintained institutionally, such that a caste system based on skin color exists. Working-class White women, for example, have privileges which are denied to people of color, (male and female), even when people of color have higher educational and economic statuses, assets which are supposed to improve one's station in life. On predominantly White campuses, dark-skinned people are assumed to be outsiders. This is demonstrated clearly when trying to gain access to campus buildings and one's identification card is more closely examined than that of a White person's.

For the African American, despite intelligence, years of experience, or level, number, and types of degrees, in the United States the color of one's skin is one of the strongest factors determining how, where, and even if, one lives. To paraphrase Malcolm X, a Black Ph.D is still called a "nigger."

Can any African American woman thrive in a predominantly White institution, where we are either negated or studied but never experienced as people? We survive, but that is simply not enough. We must ask ourselves: Is there space for African American women on predominantly White campuses in a predominantly White country where power defines space, where power is assumed to be White, where everyone assumes African American women have no power, sometimes even the women themselves?

African American women are not doing very well professionally speaking, particularly when their status is compared to that of White men. Compared to White men, nobody is doing very well. Compared to White men, we are all becoming extinct, at least the juicy parts of us, those parts we want posterity to know about. Women and men of color and White women are being portrayed in print and visual media as weak, feeble, or barbaric, when we are portrayed at all. According to prevailing myth, the White male will save the day, the planet, the universe, write intellectually superior discourse on the experiences of everyone on the planet, and be home in time to spend quality time with his children.

The rest of us will remain his satellites.

My daily reality is shaped by the images produced on those flickering weapons called televisions, and by those printed bombs which pass as information: newspapers, books, and other printed media. People take what they read and what they see on television as truth, especially when an expert speaks. (And there are numerous experts). When African American women are not invisible, we are victims or objects. This is no different from our positions in the academy. There is no neutral approach in communicating with us. As an African American woman, I am rarely allowed a conversation which is not filtered through my shade of skin: I must have said that because I'm a Black woman. I must have written that because I'm a Black woman. I must have . . . that because I'm a Black woman.

One of my friends said that African American women in White institutions should get combat pay. I wholeheartedly agree. African American women are constantly under fire in these institutions. Even when people are allies, they have their sights trained to see if sufficient gratitude for their support is displayed. If it weren't for a sense of honor, and a sense of self—both of which are difficult but vital to maintain—African American women would not be able to survive.

Given the rarefied conditions under which an African American woman administrator works it is essential to have allies within and outside of the employment space. My friends and family have always been tremendous means of support. They have been valuable resources of common sense and reality checks. During the times when I felt as though there was something wrong with me, speaking with them has given me strength and hope.

Establishing professional connections is also an important means of support. While at Barnard, I was a member of the Columbia University Employees of Color, an organization formed to foster professional development and networks among faculty, administrators, staff, and students of color. The group grew out of concern over discriminatory hiring and work practices, as well as several racial incidents which occurred throughout the university community. The organization meets regularly to determine the needs of people of color working within the university, and it sponsors workshops, conferences, and discussions relevant to the professional and personal lives of people of color. Because the group is relatively new, it is difficult to gauge its effectiveness. However, with tenacity and direction, it could become an important force in this particular university community by building networks among people of color.

Making Space

Educational progress requires that policy decisions include input from those who feel they have a stake in the process and outcome. Otherwise, there is a constant struggle around legitimacy, quality, and mainstreaming, and little dialogue about change. Obstacles to changing power dynamics partially result from a belief that (a) only the "outside" group will benefit from change, and (b) these outsiders will take from the "insiders." This is a direct reflection of the individualistic attitude which prevails in capitalist societies. Competition is seen in every corner. If one person has something that must mean someone else is being deprived. Despite fears, Whites will benefit from the inclusion of people of color, structurally and educationally. In fact, Whites are benefiting now from the race for inclusion. There are many White professors and administrators who are capitalizing on curriculum integration by designing and teaching courses and directing curriculum integration projects. They are fast becoming the experts in the field, which is easy to do when your views are the only ones allowed audience. People of color are thus being kept out of the "mainstream" of mainstreaming. In addition, those against curriculum reform projects are garnering lots of media attention, speaking engagements, and grant money to proliferate their objections to tampering with the canon.

To facilitate the incorporation of people of color into campus life, administrative support is essential. There must be a belief that all will benefit when everyone's input is valued. In academe as in other businesses, competition, or the threat of it, dictates strategies. Colleges and universities may jump on the bandwagon of inclusion simply to obtain grants, or to appear equitable in order to obtain choice faculty. An institution is not serious about supporting diversity in curricula and staffing if it is simply tokenizing people of color in order to receive foundation monies, or in order to appear antiracist without actually working toward that goal. Diversity requires a commitment to retaining people of color hired, including people of color in group research projects, establishing and maintaining clear guidelines for upward mobility, and recognizing the value of committee work and mentoring when considering candidates for promotion.

To help make a more diversified staff and faculty a reality, an institution could invest in targeted opportunities for students of color through sponsorship of undergraduate and graduate programs, with the understanding that graduates would become a part of the college community either as faculty or administrators. Over the years, many medical students have had their loans "forgiven" by working in rural or inner-city areas for a prescribed length of time. To encourage women and minorities to obtain doctorates and to increase their numbers on its faculty, the California State University system has a similar program in which up to $30,000 of loan money is "forgiven" if a graduate will consent to work five years within the system.[19] Columbia University's Minority Faculty Recruitment Program was created in 1989 to provide incentives for hiring Black, Latino, and Native American faculty. When a person of color is hired via the program, two-thirds of that professor's salary is paid in the first year and one-half is paid in the second year, giving the hiring department temporary budget relief.[20] Programs like these could be instituted to hire people of color to fill jobs which might lead to higher-echelon administrative positions.

To effect real change there must be a consistent and concerted effort to hire people based on qualifications. African American women professionals must be sought after outside of the usual old boy/old girl networks; for example, placing ads in publications which are geared toward professionals of color; or recruiting candidates from historically Black colleges and universities, and colleges and universities in the U.S.'s numerous commonwealth islands. Search committees must be made aware of their prejudices regarding African American women. Also, once hired, African American women must be given the support and respect needed to meet the demands of their jobs.

Conclusion

It has not been my intention to give a thorough analysis of the conditions of African American women administrators within academe. Rather, I have attempted to offer food for further thought for researchers and administrators who are truly concerned about the status of African American women on predominantly White university campuses. There is very little recent literature specifically concerning the status of African American women administrators. When articles are written they are usually shaped within the context of "women of color." I believe the concerns of the different groups of "women of color" are distinct, and should be dealt with in that way for analysis. Asian American women are discriminated against racially, for example, *and* they are put in the dubiously favored position of the "model minority." This places extra burdens on them and often creates animosities in relationship to other women of color. Among women of color, on an intragroup and intergroup basis, there are hostilities resulting from the internalized racism we experience. These issues have been explored by Cherríe Moraga, Gloria Anzaldua, bell hooks, Audre Lorde, and Mitsuyi Yamada to name but a few.[21]

University administrators must develop new models of administrators and determine whether their hiring standards are realistic, or simply arbitrary; whether their hiring and promotional practices garner qualified people, or simply people with whom they are comfortable.[22] In the case of BCROW, the refusal to hold an open search for the position of director, and the refusal (or lack of consideration) of promoting a qualified African American woman for the administrative manager position, is a vivid example of how administrators of traditionally White institutions retain power firmly grasped within the White race. Employees of color within academe should take a proactive role on campus, finding people of color to apply for positions and critiquing guidelines for promotions. Employees of color should also hold ongoing discussions on how divisions among people of color disempower and divide. This can best be accomplished through employee groups.

Because of the violently racist and sexist basis of this country and others like it, it is extremely difficult to gain upwardly mobile positions if one is not White or male. African American women are not whining for jobs which are not deserved or for which we are not qualified. Rather, we simply want the opportunity to achieve on merit and not be viewed through biased lenses. Without a reformation of power structures and serious antiracism work within academe, the race for inclusion is just another academic exercise.

Notes

1. Johnnella Butler, "Minority and Women's Studies: Do We Want to Kill A Dream?" *Womens' Studies International Forum* 7:3 (Winter 1984): 136.

2. Comprehensive Data on College Presidents Released," *Higher Education and National Affairs* 37:5, March 28, 1988: 1–5.

3. "Report on Women Presidents," *Higher Education and National Affairs* 37:5, March 28, 1988: 1–5.

4. "Typical College President: White, Male, and Married." *On Campus With Women* 18:4 (Spring, 1989): 8.

5. Reginald Wilson, "Women of Color in Academic Administration: Trends, Progress, and Barriers," *Sex Roles* 21:1/2 (1989): 92.

6. Reginald Wilson, "Women of Color in Academic Administration," 90–91.

7. *Ibid.*, 85.

8. *Ibid.*, 88.

9. Johnnetta Cole, "The Road to Higher Education: Realizing the Dream," *Higher Education and National Affairs* 39:1, January 15, 1990: 5.

10. Kellis Parker, "Ideas, Affirmative Action and the Ideal University," *Nova Law Journal* 10 (1986): 763.

11. *Ibid.*, 768.

12. *Ibid.*

13. Ruth Farmer, August 1989.

14. Yolanda T. Moses, "Black Women in Academe: Issues and Strategies." Baltimore: Project on the Status of Education of Women, Association of American Colleges, 1989. Moses' report is an excellent overview of campus life for Black women students, faculty and administrators at predominantly White and historically Black colleges and universities. In addition to pointing out problems, Moses offers strategies for improvement. Other works which discuss the conditions of women administrators on campus include Carter, et al. (1988), Howard-Vital (1989), Mercer (1990), Pearson, et al. (1989) and Sandler (1980).

15. See *Women's Review of Books* January 1992.

16. Gerda Lerner, "Reconceptualizing Differences Among Women," *Journal of Women's History* 1:3 (Winter 1990): 111.

17. See Moses, "Black Women in Academe," 17; and Wilson, "Women of Color in Academic Administration," 89. Moses and Wilson both acknowledge that sexism hinders the development of women of color at historically Black colleges and universities. Wilson comments on the fact that Black women fare better statistically in White colleges than in Black ones (that is, they hold more administrative positions).

18. See Peggy MacIntosh, "White Privilege and Male Privilege: A Personal Account of Coming to See Correspondence Through Work in Women's Studies." Wellesley: Wellesley Center for Research on Women, 1988. Working Paper No. 189.

19. "Growing Your Own: Women Faculty Members." *On Campus With Women* 19:2 (Fall 1989): 2.

20. Kirsten Fermaglich, "Kluge Money to be Used for Minority Faculty Fund," *Columbia Spectator* CXIX:25 (October 8, 1990): 1, 8.

21. Cherríe Moraga and Gloria Anzaldua, eds. *This Bridge Called My Back* (New York: Kitchen Table Press, 1983). This anthology includes writing by radical

women of color which touches on the harsh realities of racism and internalized oppression for African American women, Asian American women and Latinas.

22. *Initiatives* 52: 2 (1989) explores, in several articles, the hiring strategies within higher education, ways of creating equity on campus as well as the various stresses which affect the lives of women administrators.

Conclusion

Pedagogy and Politics

Our struggle for changes in academia mirror and remain shaped by the larger social, political, and economic environment. We have been in a time of retrenchment and political backlash, a time where imperialist invasions and financial bailouts of malfeasants are funded while humanist education, on all levels, remains not on the back burner but in deep freeze. As the self-appointed "education president," former president George Bush succeeded in continuing a manifest destiny legacy pursued in the Reagan years: "education" is the glorification of "America" in conquest and domination, that is, the glorification of war. The national commitment to making the U.S. a strong political-economic presence in the world has historically been militaristic. With policy-makers predominantly White, wealthy, and male, it is unlikely that decisions are being made to improve the conditions of majority people, that is, people of color.

The decision to rationalize White racism through the popularized propaganda of "reverse racism" is furthered by the latest governmental assault on civil rights which maintains that laws requiring equitable hiring practices lead to quotas. The "Q" word, the red flag for an irrational obscurantist concept—the "oppression" of Whites by Blacks within a socioeconomic order dominated by Whites—is familiar to and pervasive in academe. Yet quotas have always been enforced, both inside and outside academe. With varying levels of optimum numbers of "others" allowed to enter certain fields, most employers have overt or covert guidelines. Quotas result in a majority of European Americans (usually males) in certain fields (high-ranking and well-compensated) and African Americans and/or women in other fields (low-ranking and low-paying).

African American women faculty and administrators function in a world of contradictions within educational institutions. We simultane-

218

ously have power, and lack it, in paradoxical relationships in which power is sexualized and racialized. Our intellectual abilities are questioned. We are made into fetishes. While shut out of decision- and policy-making processes, we are held responsible for outcomes. Often we are lumped into categories which deny our individuality, and are considered monolithic types rather than human beings. The negation of our humanity is reflected in the positioning of African American women as Other, in relationship to White males and females, and often the Other of Others in relationship to African American males and majority males and females, that is, people of color. Creating ourselves in our own images is a difficult task in a world which renders us both invisible and on display. It requires a re-learning. The authors in this book seek to develop a pedagogy of transformation and empowerment, where students and teachers interchange roles, and where knowledge is the purview of all. This approach may be regarded with suspicion and may be deemed superfluous if not anarchist. Our work, if assertive, "different," and spirited, cannot be easily dismissed, nor can it be compartmentalized, for it is inherently interdisciplinary and holistic: African American women do not fit only into African American Studies or Women's Studies but all studies. Holistic and liberatory studies demand that we transform academe and ourselves. We must educate in ways which reflect nonsexist, nonracist, and nonheterosexist pedagogy, and we must demand support for these endeavors.

Transforming Academe

Incorporating rituals, art and stories from the cultures of African, Native American, Asian, Arab and Latin American peoples into curricula introduces students to ways of teaching and learning which go beyond the typical linear thinking of academe, and transcends the false dichotomy of unknowing student and all-knowing professor. However, it is important that these cultures and pedagogies are presented as more than electives or optional information or a multicultural requirement. We must provide a context for our studies. For example, African American women who write autobiographically do not set out to write "theory," yet theory is conveyed in their words. To read these stories with an understanding of the powerful context of African liberation and philosophy follows a prerequisite of acknowledgment that for centuries African scholars, philosophers, and scientists have laid the foundation for much of what is considered the exclusive domain of Eurocentric thought. Since this intellectual foundation includes African art, African artistic culture should have a prominent place in learning within academe. We need to establish a new context in which our very "otherness" and difference in academe can no longer render our art and culture faddishly palatable in ghettoized settings, or in the realm of carnival entertainment, with the stereotypes of the primitive culture of noble savages. To provide a new context means questioning and encouraging others to critique the academic control of information and the shaping of knowledge through grades, course requirements, and categories of "worthiness and rigor."

Multicultural requirements are not necessarily seen or presented as beneficial to the improvement of education; rather, their introduction is seen as politically or economically motivated. The level of intolerance toward learning about people of color, particularly women of color, results from the subliminal, covert, and overt messages students receive from faculty and administrators. The dearth of faculty and administrators of color on campuses in positions of authority contributes to the concept that majority people are electives and unimportant. The important educational value of learning about a majority of the cultures among which we live remains lost to many in academe, where knowledge of the world's indigenous cultures is absent or minimal. Many young people see multiculturalism as a fad, and their knowledge and acceptance level are limited to fashion. For this reason, some White students wear pulseras (cloth wrist bracelets), or African jewelry, or Native American garb, while loudly criticizing an instructor for "forcing" them to learn about the lives of African American and Native American women, or the poetry of Latinas.

African, Native, Latin, Arab or Asian American students may choose to wear certain hairstyles, jewelry, and clothing as statements of knowledge about and pride in their cultures. If fashion replaces the political and spiritual meanings of customs, they may not fully realize that they participate in rendering their own cultural identities "exotic." An extension of this exoticism is romanticizing political heroes. Young students may admire the historical Malcolm X during his years as spokesperson for the Nation of Islam under Elijah Muhammed, yet ignore Malcolm X's later spiritual growth and evolving sexual politics. Hero-worshipping and rhetorical "militancy," as responses to the frustration and isolation in White academe, allow students of color to struggle against racism and with identity issues, but sometimes obscure their nonprogressive class and gender politics. For example, African American men may question the relevance of learning from and about women even if these women are of their race. Such patriarchal politics may be intensified when our students find themselves objectified subjects, whose marginalization is exacerbated during discussions and scrutiny of their cultures in predominantly White classrooms and within Eurocentric curricula. The contradictions in education which African American students face are closely tied to issues of self-knowledge reflected in the larger African American culture. These issues of identity, aberration and self-esteem are the under currents of our struggles in education:

> Our children did not know us
> They were bought and sold.
>
> Our children did not know us
> For our stories were erased or twisted
> When the truth could not be hidden.
> A people with no history, no stories to tell,
> No rituals to pass along
> Will die unknown.
> But we have never forgotten. . . .[1]

Romanticism, appropriation and escapism need to be more closely examined in all students' academic encounters with African lives. This is particularly so when the students are of European descent. European American students too easily become tourists floating through unknown terrain, often with the fervid hope that they never return. Or, at the opposite end of the spectrum, they may feel left out or angry at being "forced" to study cultures with which they do not readily identify, perceive as insignificant or inferior, or for which they may harbor feelings of guilt based on their skin privilege within a culture and state built on White supremacy. In all these cases, defining themselves in relationship to the diversity of humanity is threatening to students whose fears may lead them to verbally attack professors or other students.

Supportive discussion groups can help bridge the gap created by blocks and backlash resulting in the classrooms where Eurocentrism and patriarchal White supremacy are critiqued and decentered. Introducing first-year students to information by and about people of color as part of their core requirement helps if it is done without the special-topics approach of "minority" cultures, which colonizes people and distorts information. Courses dealing with women of color, taught by women of color, must be made available on more than a one-time basis. Making initiatives with others for programmatic support for curriculum integration projects in critical thought and pedagogies is also essential.

Transforming Ourselves

Personal spirit and energy can help transform academe from a prison of conventions into a place of learning and knowledge if we adopt a spirit which is activist and questioning. There are consequences. The discomfort and hostility which attempt to punish our unapologetic assertion of "difference" is the backlash to our audacity to challenge. There is little support for difference marked as inferiority and ingratitude. Critically examining the politics of "difference" means that we must also question our own personal attitudes as administrators, faculty, and students. Since the validity of research is determined by its proximity to the legitimized work of accepted scholars, Eurocentric thought shapes the direction of "scholarly" research even when we try to break from it. Attempting to decentralize the dominant and dominating culture, we often end up replicating it in a feminized or Afrocentric fashion. We need greater standards than those of academe.

Developing new standards for excellence in education will help us identify allies. People of all sexualities and socioeconomic classes have been, are, and will remain integrally connected to the spiritual and political development of African American communities. While challenging the hypocrisy of this society's intellectual and moral pretensions, and its pervasive and insidious racism, we cannot ignore our need to change and prepare our communities for greater independence, autonomy, and development. Ridding ourselves of the homophobia, sexism, ethnic chauvinism and classism which plague and pit us against each other paves the way for effective coalitions. Bigotry only demonstrates our foolish complicity in oppression and intellectual parochialism. Working through our pain and anger to build communities and coalitions can produce political and economic bases to educate and confront mental, sexual, and physical violence. Community-building through coalitions among ourselves and with others, is one of our most pressing issues.

Since words alone cannot challenge domination, the question of how our intellectual work will materialize in activist work is critical. Rejecting the academic arrogance of studying people like specimens in a laboratory, activist educators are accountable to community members. We can then speak in ways respectful of and responsive to communal life, a sign of our belonging to a people. Audre Lorde reminds us: "We cannot live without our lives." We certainly cannot educate without them.

Speaking Through Silence

I have come to believe over and over again that what is most important to me must be spoken, made verbal and shared, even at the risk of having it bruised or misunderstood.

Audre Lorde[2]

Survival for African American women has always meant knowing our place. This does not mean that we have not challenged what that place is, or whose right it is to define it for us. Rather, we are constantly aware that many think we do not belong in certain settings. Academe—a place of privilege which paradoxically inspires awe and fosters intellectual violence—is one of those settings. We have chosen academe because of our commitment to education, to serving ourselves and our communities. Yet often it appears that the only way to survive is through silence. Silence is the absence of our words and the presence of our complicity. If silent, we lose our ability to challenge. African American women have an important stake in reworking academe so that silence is not a prerequisite for professional progress (or survival). This requires courageous speech.

Critically speaking about our disciplines, and ourselves, places us on a path to learning different from academically acceptable and more-often-travelled roads. Yet, with all its difficulties, work for liberating pedagogy and thought is not devoid of fulfillment. Being neither martyrs nor pathmakers, we follow in the footsteps of ancestors whose faces and names have been erased from documented sources—but not from our memories. Their spirits propel us along paths of growth and understanding. If we allow fear to silence us, we betray our and their vision. Voicing and writing our stories, taking our spaces and sharing our spirits, we build what we need for survival and liberation.

Notes

1. Ruth Farmer, "The Passage," (an excerpt) *Woman of Power Magazine*, Issue 16, (Spring, 1990): 28.
2. Audre Lorde, *Sister Outsider*. Freedom, CA: The Crossing Press, 1984, 40.

Syllabi
and
Proposals

Audiovisual Resources
Nagueyalti Warren

Films / Videotapes

A Colored Girl: Ntozake Shange. Dist.: King Features Entertainment, 1975.

The Afro-American Tradition in the Decorative Arts. Dist.: North State Public Video, (videotape), 1978.

The American Woman: Portraits of Courage. Dist.: University of California Extension Media Center, 1977.

Angela Davis: Like It Is. Dist.: Ames Documentary Films, 1970.

Angela Davis, Portrait of a Revolutionary. Dist.: Pyramid Films, 1971.

Aretha Franklin: Soul Singer. Dist.: McGraw-Hill Films and University of Michigan Media Resource Center, 1969.

Autobiography of Miss Jane Pitman. Dist.: McGraw-Hill Films and University of Michigan Media Resource Center, 1969.

Beauty in the Bricks. Dist.: New Day Films, 1981.

Bessie Smith. Dist.: Canyon Cinema Co-op and Film-Makers' Cooperative, 1968.

Black Art and Black Literature, from *Blacks, Blues, Blacks!* series. Dist.: PBS Video (videotape), 1975.

Black Modern Art. Dist.: Unifilm, 1976.

Black Music in America: From Then Till Now. Dist.: Florida State University Regional Film Library, 1971.

Black Music in America: The Seventies. Dist.: Learning Corporation of America, 1979.

Black Music in Passage, from *Blacks, Blues, Blacks!* series. Dist.: PBS Video (videotape), 1975.

Black Woman. Dist.: University of California Extension Media Center, 1970.

Black Women Artists. Contemporary Crafts, Inc. (slide set). 1970

Boran Women. Dist.: Wheelock Educational Resources, 1973.

Note: Unless otherwise stated, entries are 16 mm films, available for sale or rental from the distributor indicated.

Bush Mama. Dist.: Unifilm, 1975.

Colored Girls or Black Women? Dist.: WNET/13 Media Services (videotape).

Creativity with Bill Moyers: Maya Angelou, from 12-part series. Dist.: PBS Video (videotapes), 1982.

The Dick Cavett Show: Alberta Hunter. 3-part series. Dist.: WNET/13 Media Services (videotapes), 1979.

Divine Drumbeats: Katherine Dunham and her People. Dist.: WNET/13 Media Services (videotape).

Fannie Bell Chapman: Gospel Singer. Dist.: Center for Southern Folklore, 1975.

Fannie Lou Hamer: Portrait in Black. Dist.: Rediscovery Productions, Inc., 1972.

Fear Woman. Dist.: McGraw-Hill Films, 1971.

Four Women Artists. Dist.: Center for Southern Folklore, 1977.

"Fundi:" The Story of Ella Baker. Dist.: New Day Films, 1981.

Georgia Georgia. Swank Motion Pictures, 1971.

The Georgia Sea Island Singers. Dist.: University of California Extension Media Center, 1965.

Got To Tell It: A Tribute to Mahalia Jackson. Dist.: Phoenix Films and University of South Florida, Division of Educational Resources/Films, 1974.

Harriet Tubman and the Underground Railroad. Dist.: Pennsylvania State University and Florida State University Regional Fils Library. 1965

I Am Somebody. Dist.: McGraw-Hill Films and University of Michigan Media Resource Center, 1970.

Inner Visions: Beah Richards. Dist.: PBS Video (videotape).

In the Rapture. Dist.: Indiana University Audio-Visual Center. 1976

"It'll be Gone When I'm Gone:" Lucreaty Clark, White Oak Basketmaker. Dist.: Florida Folklife Program (slide-tape program).

The Jazz of Marian McPartland. Dist.: PBS Video (videotape).

Mable Godwin: Somebody on My Mind. Dist.: Lydia F. Benitez-Brown (videotape), 1980.

Mahalia Jackson. Dist.: Phoenix Films, 1974.

Malawi: The Women. Dist.: Churchill Films, 1972.

Mary Church Terrell. Dist.: Afro-Am Educational Materials (filmstrip, record and guide).

Mary McLeod Bethune. Dist.: Afro-Am Educational Materials (filmstrip, record and guide).

Mary McLeod Bethune-Courageous Educator. Dist.: BFA Educational Media (filmstrip), 1966.

Me and Stella. (Elizabeth Cotten) Dist.: Phoenix Films, 1977.

Nellie's Playhouse. Dist.: Center for Southern Folklore, 1983.

No Handouts for Mrs. Hedgepath. Dist.: Pennsylvania State University, 1968.

Pinky. Dist. Films, Inc., 1949.

Quilts in Women's Lives. Dist.: New Day Film Co-op, Inc., 1980.

Rainbow Black. Sarah Webster Fabio. Dist.: Black Filmmaker Cooperative Distribution Service 1977.

Rosa Parks: Rush Toward Freedom. Dist.: Warren Schloat Productions, Inc., 1970.

Southern Accents, Northern Ghettos. Dist.: University of Michigan Media Center, 1967.

Spirit-Catcher: The Art of Betye Saar. Dist.: Pennsylvania State University and Films, Inc., 1977.

St. Louis Blues. Bessie Smith. Dist.: TCB Releasing, Ltd., 1929.

Taking Care of Mother Baldwin. Dist.: Perspective Films, 1973.

Tales of Two Ladies. Dist.: Indiana University Audio-Visual Center, 1961.

This is the Home of Mrs. Levant Graham. Dist.: Pyramid Films, 1970.

Toni Morrison. Dist.: Coronet/Perspective/Centron, 1978.

Valerie (Maynard), a Woman, an Artist, a Philosophy of Life. Dist.: Black Filmmaker Foundation Cooperative Distribution Service, 1975.

Women of the Toubou. Dist.: Phoenix Films, 1974.

Your Children Come Back to You. Dist.: Alile Productions, 1979.

Audiotapes/Records

A Celebration of Black Women in Literature: Alice Walker. Angela Greene, producer. Dist.: National Public Radio (audiotape).

Angelou, Maya. *Performance of Maya Angelou.* Dist.: Women's Audio Exchange (audiotape).

Black Women in the Women's Movement. Susan Horowitz, producer. Dist.: National Public Radio (audiotape).

Caesar, Shirley. *The Best of Shirley Caesar with the Caravans.* Savoy. Dist.: Down Home Music.

Carson, Josephine. *The Emotional Attitudes of the Southern Negro Woman.* Dist.: Women's Audio Exchange (audiotape).

Cox, Ida. *Wild Women Don't Have the Blues: Foremother, Vol. 1.* Rosetta Records, Dist.: Women's Audio Exchange And Down Home Music.

Davis, Angela, *Angela Davis Answers Questions about her Political Ideas.* Dist.: Women's Audio Exchange, (audiotape).

———. *Soul and Soledad.* Atco Records. Dist.: Down Home Music.

Dee, Ruby. *"What if I am a Woman?" Black Women's Speeches (1833-1908).* Folkways. Dist.: Afro-Am Educational Materials and Women's Audio Exchange.

———. *"What if I am a Woman?" Black Women's Speeches (1909-1971).* Folkways. Dist.: Afro-Am Educational Materials and Women's Audio Exchange.

Exum, Pat Crutchfield. *Black Women Writers.* Dist.: Everett/Edwards, (audiotape).

Forty Years of Women in Jazz. Stash. Dist.: Oak Lawn.

Franklin, Aretha. *Amazing Grace*. Atlantic. Dist.: Down Home Music, 1974.

———. *The Gospel Soul of Aretha Franklin*. Checker. Dist.: Down Home Music.

Hunter, Alberta. *Classic Alberta Hunter*. Stash. Dist.: Oak Lawn

———. Lucille Hegamin, Victoria Spivey and others. *Songs We Taught Your Mother*. Prestige/Bluesville.

———. *How I Got Over*. Columbia. Dist.: Down Home Music and Rounder 1965.

———. *The Life I Sing About*. Dist.: Women's Audio Exchange (audiotape).

Jazz Women. Stash. Dist.: Oak Lawn.

Johnson, Bessie. *Bessie Johnson 1928-29 Country Sanctified Series, Vol. 1*. Dist.: Down Home Music and Rounder. 1989

Jones, Bessie. *So Glad I'm Here*. Rounder. Dist.: Rounder.

Jordan, June. *Things I Do in the Dark and Other Poems*. Dist.: Women's Audio Exchange, (audiotape).

King, Coretta Scott. *Free at Last, Free at Last*. Dist. Women's Audio Exchange (audiotape).

Ladies Sing the Blues. 2 vols. Savoy. Dist.: Down Home Music. 1990

Lest We Forget. 3 vols. Folkways.

The Nashville Sit-in Story. Folkways.

Odetta. *Sometimes I Feel Like Cryin'*. RCA. Dist.: Down Home Music and Rounder.

Rainey, Gertrude "Ma." *Oh My Babe Blues*. Biograph. Dist.: Ladyslipper.

———. *Queen of the Blues*. Biograph. Dist.: Ladyslipper.

———. *Blues the World Forgot*. Biograph. Dist.: Ladyslipper.

Reagon, Bernice. *Folk Songs: The South*. Folkways.

———. *Give Your Hands to Struggle*. Paredon. Dist.: Ladyslipper.

———, and Sweet Honey in the Rock. *Sweet Honey in the Rock*. Flying Fish. Dist.: Ladyslipper.

Sanchez, Sonia. *Reading Selected Poems*. Dist. Women's Audio Exchange, (audiotape).

———. *Sonia Sanchez Reads her Own Poetry*. Dist.: Women's Audio Exchange (audiotape).

Shange, Ntozake, *for colored girls who have considered suicide when the rainbow is enuf*. Buddah. Dist.: Women's Audio Exchange.

Smith Bessie. *Any Women's Blues*. Columbia. Dist.: Ladyslipper.

———, and Louis Armstrong. *"St. Louis Blues"* Soundtrack.

Smith, Trixie. *Trixie Smith*. Collectors Classics. Dist.: Oak Lawn

Spivey, Victoria, Chippie Hill, Georgia White, Memphis Minnie, Nobby Cadillac, and others. *When Women Sang the Blues*. Arhoolie. Dist.: Down Home Music.

The Staple Singers. *Will the Circle be Unbroken*. Music.

Walker, Alice. *"You can't keep a good woman down."* Dist.: Pacific Radio Tape Library (audiotape). 1981

Walker, Margaret Alexander. *Anthology of Negro Poets*. Folkways.

————. *For My People*. Dist.: Women's Audio Exchange (audiotape).

————. *Prophets for a New Day*. Dist.: Broadside Press (audiotape).

————. *The Poetry and Voice of Margaret Walker*. Dist.: Women's Audio Exchange (audiotape).

Washington, Dorothy, narrator. *Excerpts from the Lives of Famous 19th-Century Women*. Dist.: Women's Audio Exchange (audiotape).

Washington, Portia. *Booker T.'s Child Portia/Booker T. Washington Address*, narrated by Roy L. Hill. Dist.: Women's Audio Exchange.

Waters, Ethel, Hattie McDaniel, Clara Smith, Ida Cox, and others. *Big Mamas: Independent Women's Blues*, vol. 2. Rosetta Records. Dist.: Women's Audio Exchange and Down Home Music.

Williams, Mary Lou, Lovie Austin, Lil Armstrong, and others. *Jazz Women: A Feminist Retrospective*, vols. I & II. Stash. Dist.: Ladyslipper.

Women in Jazz. 3 vols. Stash. Dist.: Oak Lawn.

Record, Audiotape, and Film Distributors

Afro-Am Educational Materials
910 5. Michigan Avenue
Chicago, Illinois 60605

Alile Productions
c/o Sharon Larkin
4809 San Vincente Boulevard—Ste 1
Los Angeles, CA 90019

Ames Documentary Films
336 West 84th Street
New York, NY 10024

Lydia F. Benitez-Brown
64 Sagamore Road -#L-1
Bronxville, NY 10708

BFA Educational Media
22111 Michigan Avenue
Santa Monica, CA 90404

Black Filmmaker Foundation
Cooperative Distribution Service
c/o Transit Media
Box 315
Franklin Lakes, NJ 07417

Blue Sky Films
2 Gross Lane
South Lancaster, MA 01561

Brandon Films, Inc.
34 MacQuesten Parkway So.
Mount Vernon, NY 10550

Canyon Cinema Co-Op
Room 220
Industrial Center Building
Sausalito, CA 94965

Center for Southern Folklore
P.O. Box 40105
Memphis, TN 38104

Chamba Educational Film Services
P.O. Box #U
Brooklyn, NY 11202

Churchill Films
662 North Robertson Blvd
Los Angeles, Ca 90069

Cinema-5
595 Madison Avenue
Los Angeles, CA 10022

Contemporary Crafts, Inc.
5271 W. Pico Blvd.
Los Angeles, CA 90019

Coronet/Perspective/Centron
465 E. South Water St.
Chicago, IL 60601

Eleanor Dickinson
2125 Broderick St.
San Francisco, CA 94115

Down Home Music, Inc.
10341 San Pablo Ave.
El Cerrito, CA 94530

Electra/Asylum/Nonesuch
92 N. La Cienga
Los Angeles, CA 90069

Everett/Edwards, Inc.
Cassette Curriculm
P.O. Box 1060
Deland, FL 32720

Film Images
1034 Lake St.
Oak Park, IL 60301

Film-Makers' Cooperative
175 Lexington Avenue
New York, NY 10016

Films for the Humanities
Box 2053
Princeton, NJ 08540

Films, Inc.
1144 Wilmette Avenue
Wilmette, IL 60091

Florida Folklife Program
Regional Film Library
Instructional Support Center
Tallahassee, FL 32306

Maryland Center for Public Broad-
casting
Attn: Program Circulation Mgr
Owings Mills, MD 2117

Folkways Records
43 W. 61st St.
New York, NY 10023

Georgia Council for the Arts
225 Peachtree St. NE
Suite 1610
Atlanta, GA 30303

GPN Educational Media
Box 80669
Lincoln, NE 68501

GTN Productions
230 Park Avenue
Suite 640
New York, NY 10169

Indiana University
Audio-Visual Center
Bloomington, IN 47401

Richard Kaplan Productions
Manhattan Plaza
400 W. 43 St.—#6
New York, NY 10036

Oak Lawn Books and Records
Box 2663
Providence, RI 02907

King Features Entertainment
Educational Film Division
235 E. 45 St.
New York, NY 10017

Library of Congress
Recording Laboratory
Washington, D.C. 20540

Florida State University
Regional Film Library
Instructional Support Center
Tallahassee, FL 32306

McGraw Hill Films
110 15th Street
Del Mar, CA 92014

National Educational TV
2715 Packard Road
Ann Arbor, MI 48104

National Public Radio
2025 M Street NW
Washington, D.C. 20036

NETCHE
P.O. Box 83111
Lincoln, NE 68501

New Day Films
P.O. Box 315
Franklin Lakes, NJ 07417

New Yorker Films
43 W. 61st Street
New York, NY 10023

North State Public Video
P.O. Box 3398
Durham, NC 27702

Ohio State University
Motion Picture Division
Film Distribution
1885 Neil Avenue
Columbus, OH 43210

Pacific Radio Tape Library
5316 Venice Blvd.
Los Angeles, CA 90019

Learning Corporation of
America
1350 Ave of the Americas
New York, NY 10019

PBS Video
475 L'Enfant Plaza, SW
Washington, DC 20024

TCB Releasing, Ltd.
Stone House
Rudge, Frome
Somerset, England

Time-Life, Inc.
Time and Life Building
Rockefeller Center
New York, NY 10020

Unifilm
419 Park Ave. South
New York, NY 10016

Pyramid Films
Box 1048
Santa Monica, CA 90406

Rediscovery Productions, Inc.
2 Halfmile Common
Westport, CT 06880

Warren Schloat Productions,
Inc.
Palmer Lane West
Pleasantville, NY 10570

Rounder Distribution
1 Camp Street
Cambridge, MA 02140

Shelby State Community College
Continuing Educ. Comm.
Services
P.O. Box 40568
Memphis, TN 38104

Smithsonian Institution
Division of Performing Arts
Collection of Recordings
Washington, DC 20560

Ladyslipper Records/Tapes
P.O. Box 3124
Durham, NC 27705

Pennsylvania State Univ.
PCR/Audio Visual Services
University Park, PA 16802

Perspective Films
369 W. Erie St.
Chicago, IL 60610

Phoenix Films
470 Park Ave. South
New York, NY 10016

Ed Pincus
40 Granville Rd.
Cambridge, MA 01238

University of California
Extension Media Center
Lifelong Learning
Berkeley, CA 94720

University of South Florida
Div. of Ed. Resources
Tampa, FL 33620

University of Michigan
Media Resource Center
416 4th Street
Ann Arbor, MI 48109

Western Kentucky University
Division of Media Services
Bowling Green, KY 42101

Wheelock Education Resource
P.O. Box 451
Hanover, NH 03755

Lance A. Williams
1254 S. Hudson Avenue
Los Angeles, CA 90010

WNET/13 Media Services
356 W. 58 Street
New York, NY 10019

Women's Audio Exchange
49 West Main Street
Cambridge, NY 19131

Spivey Record Productions
65 Grand Avenue
Brooklyn, NY 11205

Swank Motion Pictures
201 S. Jefferson
St. Louis, MO 63103

Visitation Workshop

Kaylynn Sullivan TwoTrees

The first step of the workshop is to create a safe place for exploration. I clear the space and build a small altar in the center of the room. I use things connected to the workshop (for example, a goddess workshop altar would have things on it made by other women at other goddess workshops to extend the circle of sisterhood).

The workshop is divided into four parts, corresponding to the four concentric circles of self and the four directions, beginning in the East with the relationship of Self to Self. This is an examination of our past, our secrets, what brought us to this place, and what we would like to change or strengthen. After some initial breathing and visualization exercises everyone begins to make a medicine bundle. I discuss bundles from different cultures, their ingredients, purpose, and structure. Materials are provided and everyone begins to work. I move around the room talking with each person. The validity of each person's creative vision is reinforced by helping with small design or conceptual problems which could be stumbling blocks to completion. These bundles are meant to be kept by the participants.

When these are completed we move on to the South, the place of creation and innocence. This is the place of relationship of Self to Tribe or Community. Here the visualizations, sounds, and breath exercises deal with vision—the individuals' visions of the future, and their ability and willingness to share these visions with their community. The making of the South is the Shield, a public symbol. It can be a sign of who one really is or it can be a mask. So we are dealing with the idea of disclosure and vulnerability, honor and trust. In the visualization we begin to use animal helpers as guides to a sense of community, as in nature. The shields are made with materials found in the area around where the workshop is held. Some things are provided but these are minimal. This is the first exploration of themselves outside of themselves. These shields are placed in front of each person as they return to the circle and we talk about their symbolism and significance.

We then proceed to the West, the place of introspection—death and rebirth. This journey is the Self in relationship to the environment and our home, Mother Earth. The visualization and breathing exercises further explore the life/death cycle in nature and the animal helpers. We then move outside for what I call observation and discovery. There are a series of body exercises to explore the terrain around us. We use our feet to feel the ground with eyes closed. We use smell, touch, taste, hearing—all in observation. The conclusion of this part of the workshop is to sit on the land and remember what has been experienced, and then return to one site which remains firmly fixed in view. Our relationship with the environment is constant and experiential, and this is amplified by our realigning ourselves with our surroundings in this way.

In the North, the place of wisdom and overview, we are assimilating the lessons we have learned in the other directions, so that we can examine the Self in relationship to Spirit or the Unknown. Here, seated in the circle, gathering objects with which we will work, we create an altar. This is the place which allows us to be in the presence of a Mystery in safety. The participants identify their own unknown and bring back from outside or make from the objects available a sanctuary for their own fear.

The workshop ends here, but as each altar is made others walk around, encourage and discuss. Food is shared at this time. The circle is felt rather than seen.

Teaching Grant for Development of Women, Race, Class, and Community (WORCC)—Seminar

Joy James

Overview

Teaching Women's Studies (WOST) courses on theory and African American women at U Mass-Amherst, I have focused on increasing students' ability to: (1) work effectively in a multiracial, non-Eurocentric classroom environment; and (2) conceptualize women's studies as broader than the focus on middle-class European (American) women.

This semester, WOST has scheduled two forums for Women's Studies majors and minors, on dealing with the issues of Eurocentrism and racism in Women's Studies. Still, we have considerable work to do in providing and presenting a holistic and balanced approach to Women's Studies, and in helping students develop "critical" thinking skills. Such skills would include integrated analysis of sex/gender, race, and class, and the ability to work with people from different backgrounds in praxis (theory and action) on these issues.

I believe that a seminar on theorizing on the connections between women, race, and class with a "lab" or internship in urban or local communities, would fill a critical vacuum in pedagogy for students. Pursuing this concept, I have held a series of meetings with WOST, African American Studies, and Social Thought and Political Economy (STPEC), as well as faculty, community educators, and university students this semester. In those meetings we discussed a WORCC (Women, Race, Class, and Community) seminar which could be used as a pilot for a mini-program or educational forums, and how such a learning environment might stimulate students developing critical thinking and social skills.

Exploring the idea of an "internship lab" to the seminar, I have also met with: WOST support staff (WOST offers intern programs separate from classes); the Director of Public Service and Social Change Program at Hampshire College; and community educators in Springfield, Hartford and Roxbury. Our discussions assure me that connecting university internship programs to courses on womanist/feminist political theory and praxis is practical, and timely. The challenge of community work as a learning tool in students' theorizing is not a new concept. However, the combination of all four elements—analyses on women, race, class, and community work—would be an innovative asset to student learning.

This WORCC seminar (possible mini-program) would not appeal to all WOST students. Yet, based on meetings with students, I can say that WORCC does appeal to students desiring multi-cultural pedagogy, multiracial classes, and learning connected to community service. Both African American and European American students (and support faculty) have expressed commitment to the concept and are willing to work to help implement it.

The seminar would deal with these aspects/concerns in its four components:

Women: In their autobiographical sketches at least a quarter of my students in theory class identify themselves as survivors of rape and incest. As a teacher I feel that I need to develop a stronger analysis of sex and sexuality (including issues around heterosexism). Although my teaching reflects a strong emphasis on gender and race, and an adequate emphasis on gender and class, it is superficial in its analysis of sexual identity, sexuality, and women coping with sexual abuse.

Race: The most challenging learning environment for the study of racism and racial identity is within multiracial groups. Unfortunately, since Women's Studies classes are over 90 percent European American, students lose the opportunity for exchange and debate with peers from other racial/ethnic groups. WORCC, in appealing to African American Studies and STPEC, as well as WOST students, fosters diversity in the classroom, permitting students to learn from each other in collective theorizing and work in interracial groups.

Class and Community. Even in Women's Studies, which is perceived as a discipline about transforming social relations, theory is often alienated from practice. A practicum on praxis would give students the ability to explore and refine their social theories and commitments through work in the community. Since the community would be outside the university, students would have the opportunity to develop their analysis and understanding of issues of poverty and economic relations in relationship to poor/working class communities.

Discussions with faculty, students and community educators tell me that such a seminar would greatly support my own growth as a teacher struggling to connect complex and difficult issues.

Description

This project facilitates a pedagogy that integrates issues on women, race, class, and community by developing a WORCC (Women, Race, Class, and Community) seminar with an "internship lab." This seminar would be open to students majoring in Women's Studies, African American Studies and STPEC.

Outcome

The project supports student education through collective learning. Students will work in small collective groups throughout the semester, maximizing their performance through cooperation rather than competition. Through their involvement in community work, students will better understand the relevance and application of their academic education beyond the university. Internships will be monitored through on-site visits with support staff and students assessments. This seminar can function as a pilot project for future interdisciplinary programs (with for example Women's Studies, African American Studies and STPEC.

Evaluation

WORCC will be evaluated through a series of reports and meetings, including a final project report and a student-organized forum to critically review the project. I will also write a critique of the project for further discussion on pedagogy and Women's Studies.

Black Women in America

Elizabeth Hadley Freydberg

Course Objective

This course utilizes Gloria Naylor's *The Women of Brewster Place* as its pivotal point to delineate the diverse populace of Black women, with the objective of examining, through an interdisciplinary and multimedia approach, the history, literature, music, and films of selected African American Women from the nineteenth century to the present, with emphasis on Black women as a people with a distinct cultural heritage and set of strategies for survival; in an effort to reveal and dispel many stereotypes of the Black woman.

Required Reading List

Andrews, William L., ed., in *Sisters of the Spirit: Three Black Women's Autobiographies of the Nineteenth Century* (Bloomington: Indiana University Press, 1986); Cleage, Pearl. *Mad at Miles: A Blackwoman's Guide to Truth* (Southfield Michigan: The Cleage Group, Incorporated 1990); Giddings, Paula. *When and Where I Enter . . . The Impact of Black Women on Race and Sex in America* (New York: William Morrow and Company, Inc. 1984); Lourde, Audre. *Sister Outsider: Essays & Speeches* (New York: The Crossing Press, 1984); Naylor, Gloria. *The Women of Brewster Place* (New York: Penguin Books, 1984); Sterling, Dorothy. *We Are Your Sisters: Black Women in the Nineteenth Century* (New York: W.W. Norton & Company, 1984); Washington, Mary Helen, *Invented Lives: Narratives of Black Women 1860-1960* (New York: Doubleday and Company, Inc., 1987); White, Evelyn C. *The Black Women's Health Book: Speaking for Ourselves* (Washington: The Seal Press, 1990); Wilson, Harriet E.

Our Nig; or, Sketches from the Life of a Free Black, In a Two-Story White House, North. Showing That Slavery's Shadows Fall Even There. 1859. (New York: Random House, 1983)

Note: An "African-American Women Supplementary" Booklet comprised of current articles from periodicals is compiled by the instructor for each semester the course is taught. The following articles are illustrative of what has been included in the past.

Course Agenda

Week 1: Introduction

Reading Assignments: *When and Where I Enter* . . . pp. 5–131; *We Are Your Sisters: Black Women in the Nineteenth Century*, pp. 1–69. Film: *Four Women.*

Week 2: Enslavement

Reading Assignments: *When and Where I Enter* . . ., pp. 135–259; *Our Nig; or, Sketches from the Life of a Free Black, In a Two-Story White House, North. Showing That Slavery's Shadows Fall Even There.* DuBois, W. E. B. "Damnation of Women."

Week 3: Religion

Reading Assignments: "Etta Mae Johnson," in *The Women of Brewster Place*; and *Sisters of the Spirit: Three Black Women's Autobiographies of the Nineteenth Century.* "Black Women and the Church," Videotape: Sermon by Reverend Bernice King, Daughter of Dr. Martin Luther King.

Week 4: Origins and Fallacies of Stereotypes of Black Women

Reading Assignments: "Mattie Michael" in *The Women of Brewster Place*; "Epilogue: Four Women" in *We Are Your Sisters: Black Women in the Nineteenth Century:* and *Invented Lives: Narratives of Black Women 1860–1960.* "The Politics of Sexual Stereotypes;" and

"Debunking Sapphire: Toward a Non-Racist and Non-Sexist Social Science." Videotape: *Ethnic Notions*.

Week 5 and 6: The Family

Reading Assignments: "Kiswana Brown" in *The Women of Brewster Place*; "The Black Family: Socialization and Conflict"; "Use of Social Welfare Programs and the Disintegration of the Black Nuclear Family"; and "Black Family Agonistes." Mothers Struggling Alone. Videotape: *On Becoming a Woman: Mothers and Daughters Talking Together*, directed by Cheryl Chisholm.

Week 7: They Only Hit Until You Cry: Child Abuse and Battered Women

Reading Assignments: "Lucielia Louise Turner" in *The Women of Brewster Place*; and *Mad at Miles: A Blackwoman's Guide to Truth*. "Battered Black Women, A Challenge for the Black Community," "Black Macho and the Myth of the Superwoman (segment)." Films: Camille Hatch-Billops' *Suzanne Suzanne:* and Ayoka Chenzira's *Secret Sounds Screaming: The Sexual Abuse of Children*.

Weeks 8 and 9: Relationships Between Black Women

Reading Assignments: "The Two" in *The Women of Brewster Place*; "Eye to Eye: Black Women Hatred, and Anger," and "I am your sister—Black Women Organizing Across Sexualities" in *Sister Outsider: Essays & Speeches*. "Between Mothers and Daughters"; "What Life is Like Living with a 14-Year Old Son"; "Lesbian Motherhood"; "Single Parents Working Together"; "Until Death Do Us Part"; "A Knowing so Deep." Videotape: *Storme: The Lady of the Jewel Box*, by Michelle Parkerson.

Week 10: Babies Making Babies

Reading Assignments: "Cora Lee" in *The Women of Brewster Place*: "What Must Be Done About Children Having Children"; and "Teenage Pregnancy." Videotape: *Teenage and Black Single Mothers*.

Week 11: Black Women and Education

Reading Assignments: "Teachers and Pupils" in *We Are Your Sisters: Black Women in the Nineteenth Century*, "Three's a Crowd: The Dilemma of the Black Woman in Higher Education"; "Racism and Women's Studies"; "Black Studies and Women's Studies . . . "; "Black Studies Today . . ." and "Roots III: Souls on Ice"; "Between Two Worlds"; "Racism on Campus"; Black Women and Women as a Minority Group.

Week 12: Black Women's Health and Related Issues.

Reading Assignments: *The Black Women's Health Book: Speaking for Ourselves*, "How to Cope When You're at the End of Your Rope at Work"; "Black Women and Stress"; and "So You Think You Have Troubles? Your Kids May Be Under Too." Videotape: *Colour* (30 min.); *Hair Piece: A Film for Nappyheaded People*.

Caribbean Social Order:
The Evolution of Contemporary Gender, Race and Class Contradictions in the Western African Diaspora
Helán E. Page

Your attendance and participation is essential (40 percent of grade). Periodically, you will be asked to work in a small group of three or four that will prepare a discussion of readings for the class. You will get half a grade for your group presentation and half for your personal work. Your mid-term will be an out of class exam (30 percent of grade). For this exam, you will be assigned two or three articles to analyze in terms of what you have learned in class. Your final grade (40 percent) is based on a seven to ten page approved research paper that you will propose. It must apply, and may critique, some or all of the theoretical perspectives presented in this course.

Required Textbooks

Cliff, Michelle. *No Telephone To Heaven* New York: Vintage Books, 1987. Mintz, Sidney. *Sweetness and Power: The Place of Sugar in Modern History* New York: Penguin Books, 1985. Sunshine, Catherine A. *The Caribbean: Survival, Struggle and Sovereignty* Boston: South End Press, 1980. James, C. L. R. *The Black Jacobins: Toussaint L'Ouverture and the San Domingo Revolution* New York: Vintage Books, 1963. Whitten, Norman E. Jr. *Black Frontiersmen: Afro-Hispanic culture of Ecuador and Columbia* Prospect Heights, Illinois: Waveland Press, 1974.

Required for the Mid-Term Exam

Sistren Collective *Lionheart Gal.* New York: Sistren Vision. Kincaid, Jamaica *Annie John* New York: Penguin. Mannoni, O. *Prospero and Caliban* (1950) Ann Arbor: University of Michigan.

Course Outline

Topic I: The Social Construction and Psychology of Oppression

Topic II: De-Peopling and Peopling the Caribbean (Geographically, Historically, Linguistically, Politically, Religiously, "Ethnically")

Assigned Readings: Sunshine, pp. Introduction–34. Whitten, "Afro-Hispanic Adaptation," pp. 3–34. Whitten, "Blackness in Northern South America: Historical Dimensions," pp. 35–56. Whitten, "Sacred Rituals and Social Structure," pp. 124–145. Taussig, "Slave Religion and the Rise of the Free Peasantry," pp. 41–69. Mintz, "Slavery and Forced Labor in Puerto Rico," pp. 82–94. Mintz, "The History of a Puerto Rican Plantation," pp. 95–130.

Topic III: The Economic Development of the Caribbean, Freebooters, Buccaneers, Piracy, "King Sugar," Multinationals

Assigned Readings: Mintz, "Intro." and "Food Sociality and Sugar," in *Sweetness and Power*, pp. 1–18. Mintz, "Production," in *Sweetness and Power*, pp. 19–73. Mintz, "Consumption," pp. 74–150. Mintz, "Power," pp. 151–186. Mintz, "Eating and Being," pp. 187–214. Whitten, "Exploiting Nature and Man," pp. 57–96. Enloe, "Carmen Miranda On My Mind," pp. 124–150. Enloe, "Blue Jeans and Bankers," pp. 151–17.

Topic IV: The Political Development of the Caribbean ("Origin" to Date)

Assigned Readings: Sunshine, pp. 35–64. C. L. R. James, "Prologue," *The Black Jacobins*, pp. 3–5. C. L. R. James, "The Property," and "The Owners," pp. 6–61. C. L. R. James, "Parliament and Property," and "The San Domingo Masses Begin," pp. 62–117. C. L. R. James, "And the Paris Masses Complete," pp. 118–144. C. L. R. James, "The Rise of Toussaint," pp. 145–162. C. L. R. James, "The Mulattos Try and Fail," and "The White Slave Owners Again," pp. 163–198. C. L. R. James, "The Expulsion of the British," and "Toussaint Seizes the Power," pp. 199–223. C. L. R. James, "The Black Consul," pp. 241–268. C. L. R. James, "The Bourgeoise Prepares to Restore Slavery," and "The War of Independence," pp. 269–378. Whitten, "Blackness in Northern South American: Ethnic Dimensions," pp. 174–202.

Topic V: The Caribbean Family and Society

Assigned Reading: Sunshine, pp. 227–233. Whitten, "Secular Rituals," pp. 97–123. Whitten, "Adaptive Strategies," pp. 146–173. Roumain, (entire novel), *Masters of the Dew*. Cliff, *No Telephone to Heaven*, (novel, use glossary) pp. 1–106. Cliff, *No Telephone to Heaven*, (novel, use glossary) pp. 107–208. Miller, "Gender and Law-Income Household Expenditures in Jamaica," pp. 379–397. Harrison, "*Three Women, One Struggle*": *Anthropology, Performance, and Pedagogy*, pp. 1–9.

Topic VI: The Tri-racial "Roots" of Caribbean Religiosity

Assigned Reading: Sunshine, pp. 65–68, 222–226. Taussig, "The Devil and the Cosmogenesis of Capitalism," pp. 93–111. Taussig, "The Baptism of Money and the Secret of Capital," pp. 126–139.

Topic VII: Language, Socialization, and Education

Assigned Reading: Fisher, *Colonial Madness*, xerox of selected chapters. Williams, *War in my Veins; Stains on my Name*, xerox of selected chapters. Williams, "Humor, Linguistic ambiguity, and disputing in a Guyanese community," pp. 79–94, xeroxed. Ashcroft, Griffiths, and Tiffin, "Re-placing Language: textual strategies in post-colonial writing," pp. 38–77, xeroxed article. Ashcroft, et al., "Theory at the Crossroads: indigenous theory and post-colonial reading," pp. 116–154, xeroxed article.

Topic VIII: Labor Migration

Assigned Reading: Sunshine, pp. 70–88. du Toit, "People on the Move: rural migration with special reference to the Third World: Theoretical and Empirical Perspectives," pp. 305–319. Enloe, " 'Just like One of the Family: Domestic Servants in World Politics," pp. 177–194. Film: *Voyage of Dreams*. (Available from: Cinema Guild, 1697 Broadway, New York, NY 10019.) Music: H2 Werka, etc.

Topic XI: Caribbean Basin Initiative or Caribbean Basic Initiation: Are the Politics Dependent or Self-Reliant?

Assigned Reading: Sunshine, pp. 106–138. Film: *Manos a la Obra: The Story of Operation Bootstrap*. (Available from: Cinema Guild, 1697 Broadway, New York, NY 10019.)

Topic XII: Crisis as a Way of Life

Assigned Reading: Sunshine, pp. 140–214. Zalkin, National and International Determinants of Food Consumption in Revolutionary Nicaragua, *1979–1986*, pp. 101–120.

Topic XIII: Alternative Models of Development: Cuba and Grenada

Assigned Reading: Sunshine, pp. 90–104, Ellis, "Media Concepts for Human Development in the Caribbean with Special Reference to Women," pp. 115–118. Film: *Grenada: The Future Coming Toward Us*. (Available from: Cinema Guild, 1697 Broadway, New York, NY 10019.)

Topic IX: A Fresh Approach to International Politics?

Assigned Reading: Enloe, "Conclusion," pp. 195–201. Mintz, "Caribbean Nationhood: An Anthropological Perspective," pp. 302–328. Antrobus, "New Institutions and Programs for Caribbean Women," pp. 131–134. Rubino and Stoffle, "Who Will Control the Blue Revolution? Economic and Social Feasibility of Caribbean Crab Mariculture," pp. 386–394.

The Psychology of Women

Kim Marie Vaz

Course Description

The course will introduce you to the psychological study of women's lives from a multicultural feminist perspective. Theories of personality development and behavior are presented and explored in light of their ability to account for variations in women's and men's experiences given several background variables, such as ethnicity and class.

Course Format

Discussions, group exercises, films, guest speakers, and lectures.

Course Goals

1. To examine commonalities and differences in the psychological development of all women and to develop your appreciation for and sensitivity to diversity;
2. To familiarize you with the impact of oppression on all women and the special problems created by oppression for Third World women;
3. To incorporate an analysis of economic, social, political, historical, cultural, and racial forces into the psychological literature on women;
4. To develop your skills in taking multiple cultural perspectives on women's lives and experiences; and
5. To promote your empowerment by encouraging you to develop your own critical, independent thinking skills (Brown-Collins,

1988, In P. Bronstein & K. Quina (eds.), *Teaching a Psychology of People* (Washington, D.C.: American Psychological Association), 103.

Course Requirements

Three exams: noncumulative, each worth 100 points, covering material from the readings, class discussions, films and guest speakers. Tests will be multiple choice and short answer.

Required Texts

Williams, Juanita. *Psychology of Women: Behavior in a Bio-social Context.* (3rd. edition) and *Psychology of Women: Selected Readings* (2nd. edition), (NY: W.W. Norton).

1. Introduction: What is Feminist Psychology? Who is the Woman in Psychology of Women?

Readings: Fujitomi, I. & Wong, D. (1980). "The New Asian American Woman"; Green, R. (1990), "The Pocahontas Perplex: The Image of Indian Women in American Culture"; Giddings, P. (1984). "Strong Women and Strutting Men: The Moynihan Report"; Moraga, C. (1986). "From a Long Line of Vendidas: Chicanas and Feminism." Williams, Chap. 1. Guest Speaker: Meher Marker Noshirwani, a sociologist from Pakistan, will speak on the roles and images of women in Pakistan.

II. Feminism and Psychoanalysis

A. Freud, Deutsch, Erickson. Readings: Williams, Chap. 2; B. Innovative Views of Women: Adler, Horney, Thompson. Special focus: Margaret Mead and Zora Neale Hurston.
Readings: Hurston, Z. (1978). Selections from *Mules and Men* "Why the Sister in Black Works Hardest," "Why Women Always Take Advantage of Men"; and a passage from *Their Eyes Were Watching*

God; Thompson, C. (1942). "Cultural Pressures in the Psychology of Women" in *Readings*; Williams, Chapter 3.
C. Contemporary Perspectives: Johnson, Miller, Chodorow, etc.

III. Mental and Emotional Disorders in Women

A. Eating disorders: Readings: Root, M. (1990). "Disordered Eating in Women of Color," *Sex Roles*, 7, 52S 35. Williams, Chapter 12. B. Stress: "Stress, Anxiety and the Superwoman." C. Women as Victims: Violence and Intimidation; "Sexual abuse and women."

IV. Gender Differences and Similarities: The Social Construction of Gender Readings: Special focus: flexibility in gender classifications

Amadiume, I. (1987). *Women, Wealth, Titles and Power From Male Daughters. Female Husbands: Gender and sex in an African society*, (London: Zed Press). Blackwood, E. (1984). "Sexuality and Gender in Certain Native American Tribes: The Case of the Cross-Gender Females, *Signs*, 10:27–42. Williams, Chap. 5.

V. Growing Up Female

Readings: Filmore, L. W. & Cheong, J.L. (1980). "The Early Socialization of Asian American Children." In *National Institute of Education, Conference on the Educational and Occupational Needs of Asian-Pacific-American Women*. (Washington, D.C.: Government Printing Office). Shostag, M. "Memories of a Kung Girlhood"; Williams, Chapter 6.

VI. Menstruation, Birth Control, Pregnancy, Menopause

Readings: Davis, A. (1983). "Racism, Birth Control and Reproductive Rights," from *Women, Race and Class*. (New York: Random House): Special Topic: Creating rituals for women's life cycles. Guest Speakers: Representatives from Planned Parenthood, and Nurse Midwives.

VII. Aging Women

Guest Speaker: Aaron Smith, Ph.D. The lived experiences of black grandmothers whose children are addicted to cocaine Film: *Three Grandmothers: A glimpse into the lives of three grandmothers in different parts of the world—an African village in Nigeria, a hill city in Brazil and a rural community in Manitoba.* Reading: Williams, Chap. 13.

VIII. Growing Up Black and Male

Dorothy Carey, an elementary school teacher of twenty years and current doctoral student in special education at USF. Readings: Hyde, W. (1990). *Half the Human Experience*, (Lexington: D. C. Heath and Company), Chapter 5; "Psychology of Men." Selected articles from *Essence*.

IX. Sexuality

Readings: Santos-Or~ i~, M. & Vazquez, M. (1989). "An Exploratory Study of the Expression of Female Sexuality: The Experience of Two Groups of Puerto Rican Women From Different Social Backgrounds," In C. Coll & M. De Lourdes MatLei (eds) *The Psychosocial Development of Puerto Rican Women.* (New York: Praeger) Williams, Chap. 7. Guest Presentation: Safer Sex Workshop.

X. Bisexuality and Lesbian Identity

Readings: Williams, Chap. 11; Martin, D. and P. Lyon, "The Realities of Lesbianism" In *Readings*, Hidalgo, H. & Christensen, E. H. (1979). "The Puerto Rican Cultural Response to Female Homosexuality," In E. Acosta-Belen, (ed.), *The Puerto Rican Woman* (New York: Praeger). Discussants: Representatives of the Gay and Lesbian Coalition.

Surveying Black Women's Fiction

Nagueyalti Warren

Part I

Surveying Black women's fiction is a two semester course designed to introduce the student to the fictional works of Black women in Africa and the diaspora. Beginning with the oral traditions of Africa, the West Indies, and the southern United States, the student will examine the tales and lore that eventually find expression in the Black women's literary tradition. Extensive use will be made of handouts from the following texts:

Ruth Finnegan. *Oral Literature in Africa* (Nairobi: Oxford UP, 1970). *Limba Stories and Storytellin'* (Nairobi: Oxford UP, 1980). Daryl Dance. *Shuckin' and Jivin': Folklore From Contemporary Black Americans* (Bloomington: Indiana UP, 1978). E. E. Pritchard-Evans (ed.) *The Zande Trickster* (Nairobi: Oxford UP, 1979). Leonard Barrett. *The Sun and the Drum: African Roots in Jamaican Folk Tradition* (Kingston: Sangster, 1976). Daniel J. Crowley, *I Could Talk Old-Story Good: Creativity in Bahamian Folklore* (Berkeley: U of California P, 1966).

Moving from the oral traditions, students will begin to analyze the literary efforts of the Afro-American woman by reading *Our Nig, Iola Leroy, Jubilee, Dessa Rose, Beloved, Mama Day and Song of Solomon.* This concludes the first semester. The second phase of this survey course begins with Grace Ogot's *The Promised Land* (1966) and *Land Without Thunder* (1968). *The Promised Land* is a collection of short stories which draws on East African folklore. Flora Nwapa's *Idu* and Buchi Emecheta's *The Joys of Motherhood* will also be read. Other works for this semester include *Maru, Mihoti,* and *Muriel at Metropolitan* by the South African writers Bessie Head and Miriam Tlali, the only novelist to emerge from Soweto. *The Hills of Hebron* by Sylvia

Wynter and Maryse Conde's *Heremakhonon* represent samples of West Indian fiction. For extra credit students may choose to read: Simone Schwartz-Bart, *The Bridge Beyond* (London: Heinemann, 1985); Paule Marshal, *Reena and Other Stories* (New York: The Feminist Press, 1983); Rosa Guy, *My Love. My Love or the Peasant Girl* (New York: Holt, Rinehart & Winston, 1985).

The fiction of Black women writers examined from a world perspective provides a window for viewing the Black experience as something other than a minority phenomenon. By comparing and contrasting the creative efforts of Black women in the diaspora, one can perhaps see a pan-African sisterhood that has often been ignored. These selected works will undoubtedly invite other comparison as well and should result in interesting discourse. In order to derive the most benefit from this course both sections are required and should not be taken out of sequence.

Part II

Tistsi Dangaremba. *Nervous Condition*; Bessie Head. *Maru*; Buchi Emecheta. *The Joys of Motherhood*; Flora Nwapa. *Idu*; Merle Hodge. *Crick Crack Monkey*; Maryse Conde. *Heremakhonon*; Sylvia Wynter. *The Hills of Hebron.*

Other Requirements

Two Short Critical papers (5–8 pages) One Research Paper (12–15 pages) Oral Midterm, Comprehensive final examination. Grading: papers 50% midterm 20% Final exam 30% Suggested Readings: *The Promised Land*, Grace Ogot (reserved). *Reena*, Paule Marshall.

Month 1

A. Course Outline and Introduction; B. Lecture: African Women's fiction—Begin reading *Nervous Condition*; C. *Nervous Condition* (discussion); D. Lecture: South African & Southern African Literature; E. Begin reading—*Maru*.

Month 2

A. Complete *NC* discussion; B. Lecture—Bessie Head; C. Discussion *Maru*/Begin reading *The Joys* . . . ; D. Discussion *Maru*; E. First Critical Paper Due Lecture: East African Literature; F. Discussion *The Joys* . . .; Begin reading *Idu*; G. Discussion *The Joys* . . . ; H. Lecture: West African literature *Idu*.

Month 3

A. Oral Midterm; B. Discussion: *Idu*. Begin reading *Crick Crack Monkey*; C. Complete *Idu* summarize West African lit; E. Begin reading *Heremakhonon*; F. Lecture: African-West Indian Connection; G. Discussion *Crick, Crack Monkey*; H. Discussion *Heremakhonon*; I. Lecture *Heremakhonon*.

Month 4

A. 2nd Critical Paper Due—Complete *Heremakhonon*—Begin reading—*The Hills of Hebron*; B. Discussion: *Hills*; C. Lecture: Transitional figures; D. Paule Marshall (lecture); E. Handouts (discussion); F. Discussion; G. Overview & Review; H. Final Exam Review Research Paper Due.

Month 5

Final Examination (Comprehensive).

Black Social And Political Thought: Theory And Practice: Black Social Movement

Patricia Colemen-Burns

Texts

Vincent Harding, *There Is A River: The Black Struggle for Freedom in America* (River). Abdul Alkalimat and Associates, *Introduction to Afro-American Studies: A Peoples College Primer* (Peoples).

Supplemental Texts

Molefi Kete Asante, *Kemet, Afrocentricity and Knowledge* (Kemet); Maulana Karenga, *Reconstructing Kemetic Culture* (Karenga); Walker, David. *Appeal to the Colored People of the World and Expressly the U.S.* (Walker); Perry, Bruce. *Malcolm X: The Last Speeches.* (Perry).

Course Objectives

1. To examine basic social and political philosophies, ideologies, theories, paradigms, methodologies, and constructs appropriate to the discipline of Africana Studies. The course specifically examines the U.S., Carribean, and African experience.
2. To survey representative ideological and critical thinkers and scholars in Africana Studies from the classics to the present. The course utilizes a social and political liberation movement paradigm.

3. To develop basic analytical and critical thinking skills in examining the intellectual history and the classical and cultural antecedents, and influences of African American thought.

Requirements

1. Attendance and participation in class discussions (5% of grade).
2. Short Analytical Paper (3–5 pages) and an oral presentation on the ideological and intellectual views of one of the persons or organizations studied.
3. Four (4) quizzes.
4. Final Class Project.

Organize a panel of students. Choose a topic which reflects an example of African American social and political thought in theory and practice. The groups should explore such subjects as personal/social transformation, oppression, family, fe/male relationships, popular culture (music, literature, dance, "rap", art, etc.), diaspora, international affairs, economic policy, class struggle, grassroots organizing, spirituality, politics, social advancement, youth, education, racism, freedom, justice, Classical Egypt (Kemet), etc. Your grade for this final project will be the average between two (2) grades, i.e. an individual grade for this final project and an overall group grade. (This project is worth 25% of your final grade.)

Part I: Orientation and Introduction

Orientation to Course: A. Requirements. B. History and Development of Africana Studies. C. Discipline: Africana Studies Intro: Chp. 1 *River*. . . . pp. xi–xxvi
"WHO AM I? AM I REALLY WHO I THINK I AM? AM I ALL I OUGHT TO BE?"
(Frantz Fanon)
Theories of Afrocentricism, Concepts, Words and Ideas!!! Caution!!!

Part II: Theory and Methodology

Theory: Defining Social and Political Thought. A. The Classical Antecedents. B. Philosophy, Ideology and Politics: Theory and Practice. C. Epistemology, Ontology and Cosmology. D. The African Dialectic.

Methodology: A. Afrocentricism—Karenga (Kawaida) and Asante (Afrocentricity). B. Stages of Struggle in U.S.—Dodson/Harding C. Periods of Struggle—Peoples College Press. D. Social and Political Liberation Movement Paradigm—Coleman-Burns.
HANDOUTS

QUIZ #1

Part III: Intellectual and Ideological Development

A. Defining: The Intelligentsia. B. Political Tendencies: Revolutionary, Radicalism, Liberalism, Conservatism, Reactionary, and Counter-Revolutionary. C. Political Ideologies:
16th Century-19th Century Struggle for Black Liberation.
Reformism, Assimilation, Accommodation, Integration: Sojourner Truth, Harriet Tubman, Frederick Douglass, Ida B. Wells-Barnett, Booker T. Washington.
Nationalism, Pan-Africanism, Separatism: Revolutionary Nationalism, Martin Delany, Marcus Garvey.
Radicalism, Revolution, Marxism/Leninism, African Socialism: Toussaint L'Ouverture, Denmark Vesey, Gabriel Prosser, Nat Turner, Maria Stewart, David Walker, Anna Julia Cooper, W. E. B. DuBois.

QUIZ #2

The Modern Black Liberation Movement (1950s-1970s).
Civil Rights Period: Reformism, Assimilation, Accommodation, Integration: NAACP, CORE, SCLC, Martin Luther King, Jr.
Black Power Period: SNCC/Ella Baker
Black Nationalism: Nationalism, Pan-Africanism, Separatism: Kwame Toure (Stokely Carmichael), Malcolm X, RNA, Shrines of the Black Madonna.
Black Revolution: Radicalism, Revolution, Marxism/Leninism, Revolutionary Nationalism, African Socialism: C. L. R. James, Amilcar Cabral, Ella Baker, Black Panther Party, League of Revolutionary Black Workers, Angela Davis, James Boggs.

QUIZ #3

The Contemporary Struggle for African American Liberation (1970s-present).

Reformism, Assimilation, Accommodation, Integration: Electoral politics.

Nationalism, Pan-Africanism, Separatism: Afrocentrism, Louis Farakhan, Karenga, Asante.

Radicalism, Revolution, Marxism/Leninism, Revolutionary Nationalism, African Socialism: Angela Davis, James Boggs, Womanism/Feminism.

QUIZ #4

Final Class Projects.

Curriculum Study

Dianne Smith

Required Books

Curriculum and Instruction. Eds. H. Giroux, A. Penna and W. Pinar; *A Pedagogy for Liberation.* I. Shor and P. Freire; *Course Design.* G. Posner and A. Rudnitsky.

Course Objectives

(1) To enable students to identify and analyze different theoretical and philosophical approaches to curriculum theory and development.

(2) To understand the impact of these approaches on the development of curricular programs and policy in the public schools in the United States and abroad.

(3) To develop a theoretical discourse and method of inquiry that will enable students to interrogate and put into practice particular approaches to curriculum theory and development.

(4) To develop a coherent and creative course of study with a clear sense of purpose which can be utilized in an educational setting.

Course Content

This course will provide an in-depth study and contrast of major approaches in the field of curriculum theory. These approaches and their underlying assumptions will be examined from anthropological, sociological, and political perspectives. In addition, these approaches will be analyzed against a variety of specific topics relevant to the knowledge and social relations that characterize the everyday workings of public schools.

Course Requirements

Students will be required to plan and develop a course of study. One rough draft will be reviewed by the instructor and by other students. The final copy should be typed, double-spaced (no more than 25 pages). Students will participate in group presentations in class and other group activities assigned. This activity is not to be taken lightly. Students will write a book review of Paulo Freire's and Ira Shor's text. An explanation will be provided by the instructor.

Course Assignments

1. Introductory Class—Course syllabus, remarks, group assignments and film.
2. Rethinking The Discourse of Schooling: "The Emergency of Critical Pedagogy" and "Critical Pedagogy: A Look at the Major Concepts" McLaren (from *Life in Schools*); "Black-Eyed Blues Connections" Russell; Reading the World and Reading the Word and "Banking Education" Freire.
3. Curriculum Theory As A Field of Competing Discourses: Chs. 1, 2, 9, 10, and 12 from *Curriculum and Instruction*.
4. Rethinking The Role Of Teachers and Students As Transformative Intellectuals: "Teaching and the Role of the Transformative Intellectual" Giroux and Aronowitz; "Examining Closely What We Do" Kohl; and "The Other End of the Corridor: The Effect of Teaching on Teachers" The Boston Women's Teachers' Group.
5. Rethinking the Role of Teachers and Students (continued): "Gender Relations in Secondary Schooling" Kessler et al.; "Sexuality, Schooling and Adolescent Females: A Missing Discourse of Desire" Fine; "Peering Through the Well of Loneliness" Sears; and "Feminist Theories and Methods: How To Make Course Content and Pedagogy Less Alienating for Women" Rosser.

6. Curriculum Theory and The Hidden Curriculum: Chs. 15, 21 from *Curriculum and Instruction;* "Keeping Track, parts 1 & 2" Oakes; "Social Crisis and Curriculum Accords" Apple.

7. Curriculum and The Politics of Resistance: "Pupils as data-gatherers: Mucking and Sussing" Benyon and Atkinson; "Learning English and How to be Silent: Studies in Sioux and Cherokee Classrooms" Dumont; "Cultural Power and Multi-cultural Education" Quantz and O'Connor; "Nobody Mean More To Me Than You And the Future Life of Willie Jordan" Jordan. *Course Design Rough Draft Due (Optional).*

8. Curriculum and the Politics of Reproduction: "Education in Apalachia" Wood; "Sophie and Emile: A Case Study of Sex Bias in the History of Educational Thought" Martin; "Raceless-ness as a Factor in Black Students' School Success" Fordham; and "Toward a Sociological Perspective on Learning Disabili-ties" Christensen, Berber and Everhart.

9. Schooling and a Discourse of Democracy: *A Pedagogy For Liberation.* Freire and Shor (Chs. 1, 2, 3). *Book Review Due.*

10. Schooling and a Discourse of Democracy: Read Chs. 4, 5, 6, 7 in Freire and Shor.

11. Curriculum, School Reform and Social Change: "Empow-erment as a Pedagogy of Possibility" Simon; "Toward a Curric-ulum Relevant to Afro-Americans" Hale-Benson; "Critical The-ory as a Foundation for Methods Courses" Adler and Goodman; and "The Evolving Effort to Improve Schools: Pseudo-Reform, Incremental Reform, and Restructuring" Raywid.

12. Schooling and the Politics of Voice: "The Struggle for Voice" Sola and Bennett; "Asian-American Children: A Diverse Popu-lation" Pang; "Silencing in Public Schools" Fine; and "Child Abuse: A Demystification of Teacher Reporting" Smith.

13. Teacher Authority and the Politics of Teacher Education: "Au-thority, Ethics, and the Politics of Schooling"; "Teacher Educa-tion and Democratic Schooling"; "Schooling and the Politics of Ethics" from Giroux *Schooling and the Struggle for Public Life;* and "The Matter of Mystification: Teacher Education in Un-quiet Times," Greene. *Course Design Due.*

14. Each Group Is Required To Choose A Journal Article To Share With The Class—This Should Reflect A Critical Pedagogical Approach To Teaching and/or Research.

15. Wrap Up (Evaluation and Sharing Course Designs With Peers).

Book Review Guidelines

Underlying the idea of critical theory of education has been the pervasive influence and corpus of theoretical work done by Paulo Freire in the last twenty years. This is especially true of Freire's work in the field of critical literacy or emancipatory literacy. I want you to write a review of the book *A Pedagogy for Liberation*, Freire and Shor. The paper should be no longer than ten pages, typed and double-spaced. You should follow the outline below.

1. In describing the book, you should begin with a brief overview of the nature and scope of the author's subject, while at the same time providing a sense of the overall project of the book itself. Write this section as if you were the author of the book attempting to describe its major assumptions. Where possible, provide examples from the book that can be used in support of your claims.
2. In this section, you should point to those aspects of the book that offer, in your view, the most important contributions the book makes towards advancing and extending the discourse of a critical theory of education. Be specific in indicating what this book does to advance such a position.
3. Finally, include in this analysis a commentary on the specific limitations you think this book might have, and what issues it may have failed to address. Conclude by indicating how this book may have either strengthened or changed your own views regarding educational theory and practice.

Women of the African Diaspora

Adrianne Andrews

This course is a comparative study of the complex roles of women of African descent in cross-cultural perspective. The sociocultural contexts within which these roles will be examined include South Africa, the United States, Brazil, and the Caribbean. Among the topics to be explored are women's participation in these societies as workers in the public and private domains, gender relations, the impact of urbanization and industrialization, religious and political participation, health issues, class status, and Diasporan women as cultural workers.

Required Texts

Bernstein, H., *For Their Triumphs and Their Tears: Women in Apartheid South Africa*; Duley, M. and M. Edwards, *The Cross-Cultural Study of Women*; Fuentes, A. and B. Ehrenreich, *Women in the Global Factory*; Harley, S. and R. Terborg-Penn, (eds.) *The Afro-American Woman: Struggles and Images*; Holt-Seeland, I., *Women of Cuba*; Malson, M., et al., *Black Women in America*; Patai, D., *Brazilian Women Speak*; Simms, M. and J. Malveaux, (eds.) *Slipping Through the Cracks*; Steady, F., *The Black Woman Cross-Culturally*; Terborg-Penn, R., R. S. Harley and A. Rushing, (eds.) *Women in Africa and the African Diaspora*.

Course Requirements

Two Mid-Term Exams (each one is 30% of final grade). Final Research Paper and Oral Presentation on an approved topic of your choice related to issues confronting women of the African diaspora;

Ten to twelve double-spaced typewritten pages (30% of final grade). Discussion Questions (10% of final grade).

Introduction and Overview of the Course

Week 1: Readings: Steady—"Introduction," pp. 1–6; "The Black Woman Cross-Culturally: An Overview," pp. 7–42. Terborg-Penn— "African Feminism: A Worldwide Perspective," (Steady) pp. 3–24.

Women in Africa

Week 2: Readings; Steady—"The Black Woman in South Africa: An Azanian Profile," (Rivkin) pp. 215–230; "The Role of Women in the Struggle Against Apartheid in South Africa," (Lapchik) pp. 231– 262. Bernstein—*For Their Triumphs & For Their Tears,* appendix and pp. 5–128.

Week 3: Film: *Maids and Madams.* Readings: Steady—"Female Employment and Family Organization in West Africa," (Sudarkasa) pp. 49–63; "The African Woman as Entrepreneur: Problems and Per-spectives on Their Roles," pp. 141–168 (Simms); "The Second Sex in Town," (Gugler) pp. 169–184.

Week 4: Readings: Steady—"Black Women and Music: A Survey from Africa to the New World," (Jackson-Brown) pp. 383–402; "Im-ages of Black Women in Afro-American Poetry," (Rushing) pp. 403– 416.

African American Women

Week 5: Readings: Steady—"Racism and Tradition: Black Wo-manhood in Historical Perspective," (Ladner) pp. 277–284; "Female Slave Resistance: The Economics of Sex," (Hine and Wittenstein) pp. 289–300; "The Myth of the Black Matriarchy," (Staples) pp. 335– 348; "Sex Roles and Survival Strategies in the Urban Black Commu-nity," (Stack) pp. 349–368. Malson, et al.—"Family, Race, and Pov-erty in the Eighties," (Zinn) pp. 245–263.

Week 6: Readings: Malson, et al.—"A Response to Inequality: Black Women, Racism, and Sexism," (Lewis) pp.41–64; "The Dialec-tics of Black Womanhood," (Dill) pp. 65–78. First Mid-Term Exam.

Afro-Caribbean Women

Week 7: Readings: Fuentes and Ehrenreich—*Women in the Global Factory,* Chapter 1 (pp. 1–15) and Chapter 4 (pp. 34–47). Steady—"Household and Family in the Caribbean: Some Definitions and Concepts," (Gonzalez) pp. 421–430; "Women's Role in West Indian Society," (Justus) pp. 431–450; "Female Status, the Family, and Male Dominance in a West Indian Community," (Moses) pp. 499–514; "Black Women and Survival: A Maroon Case," (Bilby and Steady) pp. 451–468; "The Spread of Capitalism in Rural Columbia: Effects on Poor Women," (Rubbo) pp. 575–594. Film: *The Global Assembly Line.*

Diasporan Women

Week 8: Readings: Holt-Seeland—*Women of Cuba,* Chapter 4 "The Woman in Cuba: A Synthesis of History, Geography, and Contemporary Politics," pp. 79–107; Chapters 1, 2, 3, pp. 3–78. Film: *Portrait of Teresa.*

Week 9: Readings: Steady—"Images of the Woman of Color in Brazilian Literature, . . ." (Nunes) pp. 595–614 Patai—"Introduction: Constructing a Self," pp. 1–38; Chapter 3 "To Be a Mother Only to Your Own Children—That's Very Little," pp. 78–108; Chapter 4 "In Spiritualism There's Real Equality," pp. 109–125; Chapter 8 "Doing Laundry is Easier than Working in the Fields," pp. 175–178; Chapter 9 "In the Backlands We Work Hard and Marry Young," pp. 179–196; Chapter 13 "I Never Have Time to Sit Down," pp. 213–228; Chapter 15 "You're a Militant and Homosexual; Obviously There's a Problem," pp. 248–269; Chapter 19 "I'd Give Up Anything for Work," pp. 313–328.

Black Womanist Theory

Week 10: Readings; Malson, et al.—"Double Jeopardy, Multiple Consciousness," (King) pp. 265–296; "The Social Construction of Black Feminist Thought," (Collins) pp. 297–326; "Womanist Consciousness: Maggie Lena Walker and the Independent Order of Saint Luke," (Brown) pp. 173–196.

Week 11: Review and Discusssion, Second Mid-Term Exam.

Weeks 12 and 13: Oral Presentations, Research Papers Due.

Appendix

Bibliography
Nagueyalti Warren, Ruth Farmer, and Joy James

Autobiography and Biography

Albertson, Chris. *Bessie*. New York: Stein and Day, 1972.

Anderson, Marian. *My Lord, What A Morning*. New York: Viking, 1956.

———. *Gather Together in My Name*. New York: Bantam Books, 1974.

Angelou, Maya. *The Heart of a Woman*. New York: Random House, 1981.

———. *I Know Why the Caged Bird Sings*. New York: Random House, 1970.

———. *Oh Pray My Wings Are Gonna Fit Me Well*. New York: Random House, 1975.

———. *Singin' and Swingin' and Getting Merry Like Christmas*. New York: Bantam Books, 1976.

Bailey, Pearl. *Talking to Myself*. New York: Harcourt, Brace and Jovanovich, 1971.

———. *The Raw Pearl*. New York: Harcourt, Brace and World, 1968.

Bates, Daisy. *The Long Shadow of Little Rock: A Memoir*. New York: David McKay, 1962.

Billington, Ray Allen, ed. *The Journal of Charlotte Forten: A Free Negro in the Slave Era*. New York: Collier Books, 1953.

Brent, Linda. *Incidents in the Life of a Slave Girl*. New York: Harcourt, Brace, Jovanovich, 1973 [rpt].

Brooks, Gwendolyn. *Report From Part One: The Autobiography of Gwendolyn Brooks*. Detroit: Broadwide Press, 1972.

Cantarow, Ellen, and Susan Gushee O'Malley. "NAACP, SCLC, SNCC, Ella Baker, Got Them Moving," *Ms.* 8 (June 1980): 12.

Childress, Alice. *A Short Walk: The Extraordinary Road Travelled by a Black Woman in America*. New York: Coward, McCann & Geoghegan, 1979.

Chisholm, Shirley. *Unbought and Unbossed*. Boston: Houghton Mifflin (c), 1970.

Cliff, Michelle. *Claiming an Identity They Taught Me to Despise*. Watertown, MA: Persephone Press, 1982.

Clifton, Lucille. *Generations: A Memoir*. New York: Random House, 1976.

Cole, Johnetta B., ed. *All American Women: Ties That Bind, Lines That Divide*. New York: The Free Press, 1986.

Cooper, Anna Julia. *A Voice from the South by a Black Woman of the South*. Xenia, OH: Aldine Printing House, 1982.

Dannett, Sylvia G. L. *The Negro Heritage Library: Profiles of Negro Womanhood*, Vol. 1. Yonkers, NY: Educational Heritage, Inc., 1964.

Darden, Norma Jean, and Carole Darden. *Spoonbread and Strawberry Wine: Recipes and Reminiscences of a Family*. New York: Fawcett Crest, 1978; [rpt] 1980.

Davis, Angela. *Angela Davis: An Autobiography*. New York: Random House, 1974.

Dubois, Silvia. *A Bibliography of the Slave Who Whipped Her Mistress and Gained Her Freedom*. New Jersey: C. W. Larison, M.D. Ringoes, 1883.

Dunbar-Nelson, Alice. *Give Us Each Day: The Diary of Alice Dunbar-Nelson*, ed. Gloria T. Hull. New York: W. W. Norton & Company, 1984.

Dunham, Katherine. *A Touch of Innocence*. New York: Harcourt, Brace and Company, 1959.

Duster, Alfreda M., ed. *Crusade for Justice: The Autobiography of Ida B. Wells*. Chicago: University of Chicago Press, 1970.

Fauset, A. *Sojourner Truth: God's Faithful Pilgrim*. North Carolina: University of North Carolina Press, 1938.

Gaines, Ernest J. *The Autobiography of Miss Jane Pitman*. New York: Dial Press, 1971.

Gibson, Althea. *I Always Wanted To Be Somebody*. New York: Harper Brothers, 1958.

Giovanni, Nikki. *Gemini: An Extended Autobiographical Statement on My First Twenty-Five Years of Being a Black Poet*. Indianapolis: Bobbs-Merrill, 1972.

Golden, Marita. *Migration of the Heart: A Personal Odyssey*. Garden City, NY: Doubleday, 1983.

Gonzalez, Babbs. *I Paid My Dues*. East Orange, NJ: Expubidence Publishing Company, 1967.

Goreau, Laurraine. *Just Mahalia Baby*. Waco, TX: Work Book Publishers, 1974.

Graham, Shirley. *The Story of Phillis Wheatley*. New York: Messner, 1949.

Greenfield, Eloise. *Rosa Parks*. New York: Thomas Y. Crowell, 1973.

Griffiths, Mattie. *Autobiography of a Female Slave*. New York: New York Universities Press, 1857.

Grosvenor, Verta Mae. *Thursday and Every Other Sunday Off: A Domestic Rap*. Garden City, NY: Doubleday, 1972.

———. *Vibrations Cooking or The Travel Notes of a Greeche Girl*. Garden City, NY: Doubleday, 1970.

Harnan, Terry. *African Rhythm—American Dance: A Biography of Katherine Dunham*. New York: Alfred A. Knopf, 1974.

Hemenway, Robert. *Zora Neale Hurston: A Literary Biography*. Urbana: University of Illinois Press, 1977.

Holiday, Billie. *Lady Sings the Blues*. New York: Doubleday, 1956, 1984.

Holt, Rackham. *Mary McLeod Bethune*. New York: Doubleday, 1964.

Hurston, Zora Neale. *Dust Track on a Road: An Autobiography.* Philadelphia: J. B. Lippincott, 1942, [rpt] 1971.

Jackson, Jessee. *Make a Joyful Noise Unto the Lord: The Life of Mahalia Jackson, Queen of Gospel Singers.* New York: Thomas Y. Crowell, 1974.

Jackson, Mahalia. *Movin' Up.* New York: Avon, 1969.

Kellersberger, Julia Lake. *A Life for the Congo: The Story of Althea Brown Edminston.* New York: Fleming H. Revell, 1947.

Kennedy, Flo. *Color Me Flo: My Hard Life and Good Times.* New Jersey: Prentice-Hall, Inc., 1976.

King, Coretta Scott. *My Life with Martin Luther King, Jr.* New York: Holt, Rinehart and Winston, 1969.

Kitt, Eartha. *Thursday's Child.* New York: Duell, Sloan and Pearce, 1956.

———. *Alone With Me: A New Autobiography.* Chicago: Henry Regnery Company, 1976.

Leib, Sandra R. *Mother of the Blues: A Study of Ma Rainey.* Amherst: University of Massachusetts Press, 1981.

Lightfoot, Sara Lawrence. *Balm in Gilead: Journey of a Healer.* Reading, MA: Radcliffe Biography Series, 1988.

Lorde, Audre. *Zami: A New Spelling of My Name.* New York: Crossing Press, 1982.

Meriwether, Louise. *Don't Ride the Bus on Monday: The Rosa Parks Story.* Englewood Cliffs, NJ: Prentice-Hall, 1973.

Moody, Anne. *Coming of Age in Mississippi.* New York: Dial Press, 1968.

Moore, Carmen. *Somebody's Angel Child: The Story of Bessie Smith.* New York: Thomas Y. Crowell, 1969.

Murray, Pauli. *Proud Shoes, The Story of an American Family.* New York: Harper and Row, 1956, [rpt] 1978.

———. *Song In a Weary Throat: An American Pilgrimage.* New York: Harper & Row, 1987.

Nadelson, Regina. *Who is Angela Davis? The Biography of a Revolutionary.* New York: Peter H. Wyden Publisher, 1972.

Norton, Eleanor Holmes. "The Woman Who Changed the South: A Memory of Fannie Lou Hamer." *Ms.* 11 (July 1972).

Peare, Catherine Owens. *Mary McLeod Bethune.* New York: Vanguard Press, 1951.

Prince, Mary. *History of Mary Prince, A West Indian Slave. 1831.* In *The Classic Slave Narratives,* ed. Henry Louis Gates, Jr. New York: New American Library, 1983. pp. 183–238.

Shakur, Assata. *Assata: An Autobiography.* London: Zed Books, 1987.

Sterne, Emma Gelders. *Mary McLeod Bethune.* New York: Alfred A. Knopf, 1957.

Stewart, John. *Bessie Jones: For the Ancestors: Autobiographical Memories.* Urbana: University of Illinois Press, 1983.

Stewart, Maria W. *America's First Black Woman Political Writer: Essays and Speeches,* ed. Marilyn Richardson. Indiana: Indiana University Press, 1987.

Taylor, Susie King. *Reminiscences of My Life in Camp with the 33rd United States Colored Troops.* Boston: S. Taylor, 1902.

Terrell, Mary Church. *A Colored Woman in a White World.* Washington, D.C.: Ransdell, 1940.

Truth, Sojourner. *Narrative of Sojourner Truth: A Bondswoman of Olden Time.* Chicago: Thompson Publishing, 1970.

Vivian, Octavia B. *Coretta: The Story of Mrs. Martin Luther King, Jr.* New York: Fortress Press, 1970.

Waters, Ethel, and Charles Samuels. *His Eye is on the Sparrow.* Garden City, NY: Doubleday, 1950.

Webb, Sheyann, and Rachel West Nelson (as told to Frank Sikora). *Selma, Lord, Selma: Girlhood Memories of the Civil-Rights Days.* University, AL: University of Alabama Press, 1980.

Wells-Barnett, Ida B. *Crusade for Justice: The Autobiography of Ida B. Wells,* ed. Alfreda M. Duster. Chicago: University of Chicago Press, 1895, [rpt] 1970.

Wilson, Harriet E. *Our Nig; or, Sketches for the Life of a Free Black, In a Two-Story White House, North. Showing That Slavery's Shadows Fall Even There. 1859.* New York: Random House, 1983.

Wright, Sarah E. *This Child's Gonna Live.* New York: Dell, 1969.

Fiction and Poetry

Angelou, Maya. *And Still I Rise.* New York: Random House, 1978.

———. *Just Give Me a Cool Drink of Water. . . . 'for I Diiie.* New York: Random House, 1971.

Bambara, Toni Cade. *Gorilla, My Love.* New York: Random House, 1972.

———. *The Salt Eaters.* New York: Random House, 1972.

———. *The Seabirds Are Still Alive: Collected Stories.* New York: Random House, 1977.

Braxton, Jodi. *Sometimes I Think of Maryland: A Book of Poetry.* Bronx, NY: Sunbury Press, 1977.

Brooks, Gwendolyn. *Maud Martha.* 1951. New York: Harpers and Brothers, Publishers, 1953.

———. *Selected Poems.* New York: Harper & Row, Publishers, 1944; 1963.

Bulkin, Elly, and Joan Larkin, eds. *Lesbian Poetry: An Anthology.* Watertown, MA: Persephone Press, 1981.

Butler, Octavia E. *Kindred.* New York: Doubleday, 1979.

Cade, Toni. *The Black Woman: An Anthology.* New York: Signet, 1970.

Campbell, Marie. *Folks Do Get Born.* New York: Rinehart and Company, 1946.

Clarke, Cheryl. *Living as a Lesbian.* Ithaca: Firebrand Books, 1986.

————. *Narratives: Poems in the Tradition of Black Women,* 2nd ed. New York: Kitchen Table Press, 1983.

Clifton, Lucille. *Two Headed Woman.* Amherst: University of Massachusetts Press, 1980.

Cooper, J. *California Family.* New York: Doubleday, 1991.

Dunbar, Alice. *The Goodness of St. Rocque and Other Stories.* New York: Dodd, Mead & Company, 1899.

Giovanni, Nikki. *Black Feeling, Black Talk, Black Judgement.* New York: William Morrow, 1971.

————. *My House.* New York: William Marrow. 1972.

————. *Night Comes Softly: An Anthology of Black Female Voices.* New York: Nik-Tom Publications, 1970.

————. *The Women and the Men.* New York: William Marrow, 1975.

Guy, Rosa. *A Measure of Time.* New York: Holt, Rinehart and Winston, 1983.

————. *My Love, My Love, or The Peasant Girl.* New York: Holt, Rinehart and Winston, 1985.

Harper, Francis Ellen Watkins. *Iola Leroy.* 1893. Boston: Beacon Press, 1987.

Heidish, Marcy. *A Woman Called Moses. A novel based on the life of Harriet Tubman.* Boston: Houghton Mifflin, 1976.

Hull, Gloria T. *Color, Sex, and Poetry: Three Women Writers of the Harlem Renaissance.* Bloomington: Indiana University Press, 1987.

Hurston, Zora Neale. *I Love Myself When I Am Laughing . . . and Then Again When I Am Looking Mean and Impressive,* ed. Alice Walker. Old Westbury, NY: The Feminist Press, 1979.

————. *Jonah's Gourd Vine.* Philadelphia: J. B. Lippincott, 1934, [rpt] 1971.

————. *Moses, Man of the Mountain.* Chatham, NJ: Chatham Booksellers, 1939, [rpt] 1974.

————. *Mules and Men.* Bloomington: University of Indiana Press, 1935, [rpt]] 1970.

————. *Seraph on the Suwannee.* New York: AMS Press, 1948, [rpt] 1974.

————. *Tell My Horse.* Philadelphia: J. B. Lippincott, 1938.

————. *Their Eyes Were Watching God.* Urbana: University of Illinois Press, 1937, [rpt], 1978.

Jones, Gayle. *Corregidora.* New York: Random House, 1975.

————. *Eva's Man.* New York: Random House, 1976.

————. *Song for Anninho.* Detroit: Lotus Press, 1981.

————. *White Rat.* New York: Random House, 1977.

Jordan, June. *Naming Our Destiny: New and Selected Poems.* New York: Thunder's Mouth Press, 1989.

————. *Passion: New Poems, 1977–1980.* Boston: Beacon Press, 1980.

————. *Some Changes.* E. P. Dutton Inc., 1971.

————. *Soulscript: Afro-American Poetry.* Garden City, NY: Doubleday, 1970.

——. *Things That I Do in the Dark: Selected Poems, 1977*. Boston: Beacon Press, 1981.

Kincaid, Jamaica. *A Small Place*. New York: New American Library, 1988.

Larsen, Nella. *Passing*. New York: Alfred A. Knopf, 1929.

——. *Quicksand*. New York: Alfred A. Knopf, 1982.

Lorde, Audre. "Audre Lorde: A Special Section." *Callaloo: A Journal of African American and African Arts and Letters*, 14:1 (Winter 1991). Baltimore: Johns Hopkins University.

——. *The Black Unicorn*. New York: W. W. Norton, 1978.

——. *Need: A Chorale for Black Woman Voices*. Latham: Kitchen Table Press, 1990.

Marshall, Paule. *Brown Girl, Brownstones*. Old Westbury, NY: The Feminist Press, 1959, [rpt] 1981.

——. *Praisesong for the Widow*. New York: G. P. Putnam's Sons, 1983.

——. *Soul Clap Hands and Sing*. Chatham, NJ: Chatham Booksellers, 1961, [rpt] 1971.

Morrison, Toni. *Beloved*. New York: Alfred A. Knopf, 1987.

——. *The Bluest Eye*. New York: Holt, Rinehart and Winston, 1970.

——. *Song of Solomon*. New York: Alfred A. Knopf, 1977.

——. *Sula*. New York: Alfred A. Knopf, 1973.

——. *Tar Baby*. New York: Alfred A. Knopf, 1981.

Naylor, Gloria. *Linden Hills*. New York: Penguin, 1986.

——. *Mama Day*. New York: Ticknor & Fields, 1988.

——. *The Women of Brewster Place*. New York: Viking Press, 1982.

Parker, Pat. *Movement in Black: The Collected Poetry of Pat Parker, 1961–1978*. Ithaca: Firebrand Books, 1989.

Peterkinn, Julia. *Black April*. New York: Grosset and Dunlap, 1927.

Petry, Ann. *The Street*. 1946, 1976. Boston: Beacon Press, 1985.

Sanchez, Sonia. *A Blues Book for Blue Black Magical Women*. Highland Park, MI: Broadwide Press, 1973.

——. *Homecoming*. Highland Park, MI: Broadwide Press, 1968.

——. *I've Been a Woman*. Sausalito, CA: Black Scholar Press, 1979.

——. *Under a Soprano Sky*. Trenton, NJ: Africa World, 1987.

——. *We a Bad People*. Highland Park, MI: Broadwide Press, 1970.

Shange, Ntozake. *Betsey Brown*. New York: St. Martin's Press, 1985.

——. *A Daughter's Geography*. New York: St. Martin's Press, 1983.

——. *for colored girls who have considered suicide when the rainbow is enuf*. New York: Macmillan, 1977.

——. *Nappy Edges*. New York: St. Martin's Press, 1978.

Walker, Alice. *The Color Purple*. New York: Harcourt Brace Jovanovich, Publishers, 1982.

———. *In Love and Trouble: Stories for Black Women.* New York: Harcourt Brace Jovanovich, 1973.

———. *In Search of Our Mother's Gardens.* New York: Harcourt Brace Jovanovich, 1983.

———. *Meridian.* New York: Harcourt Brace Jovanovich, 1976.

———. *Revolutionary Petunias and Other Poems.* New York: Harcourt Brace Jovanovich, 1973.

———. *Temple of My Familiar.* New York: Harcourt Brace Jovanovich, 1989.

———. *The Third Life of Grange Copeland.* New York: Harcourt Brace Jovanovich, 1979.

———. *You Can't Keep a Good Woman Down.* New York: Harcourt Brace Jovanovich, 1981.

Walker, Margaret Alexander. *For My People.* New Haven: Yale University Press, 1942.

———. *Jubilee.* Boston: Houghton Mifflin, 1966.

———. *October Journey.* Highland Park, MI: Broadside Press, 1973.

———. *Prophets for a New Day.* Highland Park, MI: Broadside Press, 1970.

West, Dorothy. *The Living is Easy.* 1948. New York: The Feminist Press, 1982.

Wheatley, Phillis. *The Poems of Phillis Wheatley.* 1838. Revised Edition. Ed. Julian D. Mason, Jr. Chapel Hill: University of North Carolina Press, 1989.

Williams, Sherley Anne. *Dessa Rose.* New York: Berkeley Books, 1986.

———. *The Peacock Poems.* Middletown, CT: Wesleyan University Press, 1975.

Literary Criticism

Barthold, Bonnie J. "Women: Chaos and Redemption," in *Black Time: Fiction of Africa, the Caribbean, and the United States.* New Haven, CT: Yale University Press, 1981.

Bell, Roseann P., Bettye J. Parker, and Beverly Guy-Sheftall, eds. *Sturdy Bridges: Visions of Black Women in Literature.* New York: Doubleday, 1979.

Braxton, Joanne M. "Ancestral Presence: The Outraged Mother Figure in Contemporary Afra-American Writing," *The Barnard Occasional Papers on Women's Issues,* 3:2, 1988.

———, and Andrée Nicola McLaughlin, eds., *Wild Women in the Whirlwind: Afra-American Culture and the Contemporary Literary Renaissance.* New Jersey: Rutgers University Press, 1990.

Christian, Barbara. *Black Feminist Criticism.* Oxford: Pergamon, 1985.

———. *Black Women Novelists—The Development of a Tradition, 1892–1976.* Westport, CT: Greenwood, 1980.

———. "No More Buried Lives: The Theme of Lesbianism in Lorde, Naylor, Shange, Walker," *Feminist Issues,* 5:1, 1985.

———. "The Race for Theory," *Gender and Theory: Dialogues on Feminist Criticism,* ed. Linda Kauffman. Oxford: Basil Blackwell, 1989.

————. "Shadows Uplifted." *Feminist Criticism and Social Change: Sex, Class, and Race in Literature and Culture*, eds. Judith Newton and Deborah Rosenfelt. New York: Methuen Press, 1985.

————. "Somebody Forgot to Tell Somebody Something, African American Women's Historical Novels." *The Barnard Occasional Papers on Women's Issues*, 3:2, 1988.

Evans, Mari, ed. *Black Women Writers (1950–1980): A Critical Evaluation*. New York: Doubleday, 1984.

Exum, Pat Crutchfield. *Keeping the Faith: Writing by Contemporary Black American Women*. Greenwich, CT: Fawcett, 1980.

Fisher, Dexter. *The Third Woman: Minority Women Writers of the United States*. Boston: Houghton Mifflin, 1980.

Giddings, Paula. *A Poetic Equation: Conversations Between Nikki Giovanni and Margaret Walker*. Washington, D.C.: Howard University Press, 1974.

Gomez, Jewelle, "Imagine a Lesbian . . . a Black Lesbian . . . ," *Trivia*, 12 (Spring 1988).

Harris, Trudier. "Folklore in the Fiction of Alice Walker." *Black American Literature Forum* 2 (Spring 1977): 17–24.

Inge, Tonette Bond. *Southern Women Writers*. Montgomery: University of Alabama Press, 1990.

Melham, D. H. *Gwendolyn Brooks: Poetry and the Heroic Voice*. Lexington: University of Kentucky Press, 1987.

Morrison, Toni, "Rootedness: The Ancestor as Foundation," *Black Women Writers (1950–1980)*. New York: Anchor Press, 1984.

Pryse, Marjorie & Hortense Spillers, eds. *Conjuring: Black Women, Fiction, and Literary Tradition*. Bloomington: Indiana University Press, 1985.

Shockley, Ann Allen. *Afro-American Women Writers 1746–1933: An Anthology and Critical Guide*. New York: New American Library, 1988.

Stetson, Erlene. *Black Sisters: Poetry by Black American Women 1746–1980*. Bloomington: Indiana University Press, 1981.

Tate, Claudia, ed. *Black Women Writers at Work*. New York: Crossroad, 1983.

Walker, Margaret Alexander. *A Poetic Equation*. Washington, D.C.: Howard University Press, 1974.

————. *How I Wrote Jubilee*. Chicago: Third World Press, 1972.

Wall, Cheryl, ed. *Changing Our Own Words*. New Brunswick: Rutgers University Press, 1988.

Washington, Mary Helen, ed. *Black-Eyed Susans: Classic Stories by and About Black Women*. Garden City, NY: Doubleday, 1975.

————. *Invented Lives: Narratives of Black Women 1860–1960*. New York: Doubleday & Company, 1987.

———— ed. *Midnight Birds: Stories of Contemporary Black Writers*. Garden City, NY: Doubleday, 1980.

Arts and Culture

Brown, Marion. "Improvisation and the Aural Tradition in Afro-American Music." *Black World* 23. November, 1973.

Carawan, Guy, Candy Carawan, and Robert Yellin. *Ain't You Got a Right to the Tree of Life: The People of Johns Island, South Carolina—Their Faces, Their Words and Their Songs.* New York: Simon and Schuster, 1966.

———. *Freedom Is a Constant Struggle: Songs of Freedom Movement.* New York: Oak Publications, 1968.

Carter, Betty, and Akua L. Hope. "Bebop Womantones." *Heresies* 10: Women and Music 3 (1980): 2.

Cavin, Susan. "Missing Women: On the Voodoo Trail to Jazz," *Journal of Jazz Studies* 3 (Fall 1975): 1.

Childress, Alice. "Wedding Band," in *The Women's Theater: Ten Plays by Contemporary American Women,* ed. Honor Moore. New York: Vintage, 1977.

———. "Wine in the Wilderness," in *Plays By and About Women,* eds. Victoria Sullivan and James Hatch. New York: Vintage, 1973.

Chinax, Helen K., and Linda Walsh Jenkins, eds. *Women in American Theater.* New York: Crown Publishing, 1981.

Curtis, Natalie B. "Black Singers and Players" and "Negro Music at Birth," *The Musical Quarterly* 5 (October 1919): 7.

Dance, Daryl Cumber. *Shuckin' and Jivin': Folklore from Contemporary Black Americans.* Bloomington: University of Indiana Press, 1979.

Dewhurst, C. K., Betty McDowell, and Marsha MacDonald. *Artists in Aprons: Folk Art by American Women.* New York: E. P. Dutton, 1979.

DjeDje, Jacqueline Cogdell. *American Black Spiritual and Gospel Songs from Southeast Georgia: A Comparative Study.* Los Angeles: University of California, Center for Afro-American Studies, Monograph Series No. 7, 1978.

Drewal, Henry and Margaret, eds., *Gelede: Art and Female Power Among the Yoruba.* Bloomington: Indiana University Press.

Emery, Lynne F. *Black Dance in the United States from 1619 to 1970.* Los Angeles: National Press Books, 1972.

Epstein, Dean. *Sinful Tunes and Spirituals: Black Folk Music to the Civil War.* Urbana: University of Illinois Press, 1970.

Fine, Elsa Honig. *The Afro-American Artist.* New York: Holt, Rinehart and Winston, 1973.

Gay, Geneva, and Willie L. Baber. *Expressively Black: The Cultural Basis of Ethnic Identity.* New York: Prager, 1987.

Glaze, Anita J. "Woman Power and Art in a Senufo Village," *African Arts* 8 (Spring 1975).

Gossett, Hatti, and Carolyn Johnson. "Jazzwoman." *Heresies* 10: Women and Music 3 (1980): 2.

Handy, D. Antoinette. *Black Women in American Bands and Orchestras*. Metuchen, NJ: Scarecrow Press, 1981.

———. *The International Sweethearts of Rhythm*. Metuchen, NJ: Scarecrow Press, 1983.

Hawkins, Beverly. "Folklore of a Black Family." *Journal of the Ohio Folklore Society* 2 (1973).

Hurston, Zora Neale. "Hoodoo in America." *Journal of American Folklore* 44 (1931).

Jackson-Brown, Irene V. "Afro-American Women in Music: Focus on Roberta Martin 1907–1969." *Feeling the Spirit* 5 (1978).

Jones, Hettie. *Big Star Fallin' Mama: Five Women in Black Music*. New York: Harper and Row, 1974.

Journal of American Folklore: Women and Folklore. Special Issue 88 (January–March 1975).

Journal of Black Studies: Sea Island Culture. Special Issue 10. (1980).

Lippard, Lucy R. "Faith Ringgold Flying Her Own Flag." *Ms.* 5 (July 1976).

Mealy, Rosemari. "Some Reflections on Black Women in Film." *Heresies* 8: Third World Women—The Politics of Being Other 2 (1979).

Mertzer, Deena. "In Her Image: Women's Culture." *Heresies* 2: Patterns of Communication and Space Among Women 1 (May 1977).

Morgean, Beatrice, Harvey L. Smith, and Ann Money. "The 'Granny' Midwife: Changing Roles and Functions of a Folk Practitioner." *The Journal of Sociology* 66 (March 1971).

Nemser, Cindy. "Conversation—With Betye Saar." *The Feminist Art Journal* 4 (Winter 1975–76).

Placksin, Sally. *American Women in Jazz*. New York: Seaview Books, 1982.

Reitz, Rosetta. "Mean Mothers: Independent Women's Blues." *Heresies* 10: Women and Music 3 (1980).

Rushing, Andrea. "Images of Black Women in Afro-American Poetry." *Black World* 24 (September 1975).

Smith, Eleanor. "And Black Women Made Music." *Heresies* 8: Third World Women 2 (1979).

Southern, Eleen. *The Music of Black Americans: A History*. New York: W. W. Norton, 1971.

Twining, Mary A. "African-Afro-American Artistic Continuity." *Journal of African Studies* 2 (Winter 1975–1976).

Weems, Renita. "Artists Without Art Form[2]: A Look at One Black Woman's World of Unrevered Black Women." *Conditions: The Black Women's Issue* (1979).

History and Social Theory

Amin, Samir. *Eurocentrism*. New York: Monthly Review Press, 1989.

Baum, Willa K. *Oral History of the Local Historical Society*. Nashville: American Association for State and Local History, 1974.

———— et al. *Teaching Community History: Guides to Readings in Colonial Studies, Family History, Multimedia, and Oral History.* Chicago: Newberry Library, The Newberry Papers in Family and Community History, No. 77-1, 1977.

————. *Transcribing and Editing Oral History.* Nashville: American Association for State and Local History, 1977.

Bethel, Elizabeth Rauh. *Promiseland: A Century of Life in a Negro Community.* Philadelphia: Temple University Press, 1981.

Berry, Mary Frances and John Blassingame. "Africa, Slavery, and the Roots of Contemporary Black Culture." *The Massachusetts Review: Chants of Saints: A Gathering of Afro-American Literature Art and Scholarship, part 1.* 18(3) Autumn, 1977.

Cantarow, Ellen and Susan Gushee O'Malley. "Ella Baker: Organizing for Civil Rights," in *Moving the Mountain: Women Working for Social Change,* 1980.

Crawford, Vicki, et. al., eds. *Women in the Civil Rights Movement.* Brooklyn: Carson Publishing, 1990.

Daris, Elizabeth. *Lifting As They Climb: The National Association of Colored People.* Washington, D.C.: National Association of Colored People, 1933.

Davis, Angela. "Reflections on the Black Woman's Role in the Community of Slaves." *The Black Scholar* 3 (December 1982): 34.

Elaw, Zilpha. "Memoirs of the Life, Religious Experience, Ministerial Travels and Labours of Mrs. Zilpha Elaw, an American Female of Colour; Together With Some Account of the Great Religious Revivals in America, 1846," in *Sisters of the Spirit: Three Black Women's Autobiographies of the Nineteenth Century,* ed. William L. Andrews. Bloomington: Indiana University Press, 1986, pp. 49–160.

Foote, Julia A. J. "A Brand Plucked From the Fire: An Autobiographical Sketch." 1879, in *Sisters of the Spirit: Three Black Women's Autobiographies of the Nineteenth Century,* ed. William L. Andrews. Bloomington: Indiana University Press, 1986, pp. 161–234.

Frontiers: Women's Oral History. Special Issue 2 (Summer 1977).

Fry, Gladys-Marie. *Night Riders in Black Folk History.* Knoxville: University of Tennessee Press, 1975.

Fu-Kiau, K. Kia Bunseki, *The African Book Without Title.* Cambridge: Fu-Kiau, 1980.

Gollock, Georgina A. *Daughters of Africa.* Westport, CT: Negro University Press, 1932.

Grissom, Mary Ellen. *The Negro Sings a New Heaven.* New York: Dover Publications, 1930, [rpt] 1969.

Harris, Leonard, ed. *Philosophy Born of Struggle: An Anthology of Afro-American Philosophy from 1917.* Dubuque, Iowa: Kendall Hunt, 1983.

Harrison, Daphne Duval, *Black Pearls: Blues Queens of the 1920s.* New Brunswick: Rutgers University Press, 1988.

Haynes, Elizabeth Ross. "Negroes in Domestic Service in the United States." *Journal of Negro History* 8 (1923).

Henri, Floretti. *Black Migration: Movement North, 1900–1920.* Garden City, NY: Doubleday, 1975.

Hobson, E. C., and C. E. Hopkins. *Report Concerning the Colored Women of the South.* Baltimore: Slater Fund, 1896.

Humex, Jean McMahon, ed. *Gifts of Power: The Writings of Rebecca Jackson, Black Visionary, Shaker Eldress.* Amherst: University of Massachusetts Press, 1981.

Lee, Jarena. "The Life and Religious Experience of Jarena Lee, A Coloured Lady, Giving an Account of Her Call to Preach the Gospel," 1836, in *Sisters of the Spirit: Three Black Women's Autobiographies of the Nineteenth Century,* ed. William L. Andrews. Bloomington: Indiana University Press, 1986, pp. 25–48.

Loewenberg, Bert James, and Ruth Bogin, eds. *Black Women in Nineteenth Century American Life: Their Words, Their Thoughts, Their Feelings.* 1976. Pennsylvania: The Pennsylvania State University Press, 1981.

Merritt, Carole. "Slave Family History Records: An Abundance of Materials." *Georgia Archives* 6 (1978).

Noble, Jeanne. *Beautiful, Also, Are the Souls Of My Black Sisters: A History of the Black Woman in America.* Englewood Cliffs, NJ: Prentice-Hall, 1978.

Powdermaker, Hortense. *After Freedom: A Cultural Study of the Deep South.* New York: Russell and Russell, 1939.

Spruill, Julia Cherry. *Women's Life and Work in the Southern Colonies.* Chapel Hill: University of North Carolina Press, 1938.

Sterling, Dorothy. *Black Foremothers: Three Lives.* Old Westbury, NY: The Feminist Press, 1979.

———. *We Are Your Sisters: Black Women in the Nineteenth Century.* New York: W. W. Norton and Company, 1984.

Van Sertima, Ivan, ed. *Black Women in Antiquity.* New Brunswick: Transaction Books, 1990.

Wells-Barnett, Ida B. *On Lynching: Southern Horrors: A Red Record, Mob Rule in New Orleans.* New York: Arno Press, [rpt] 1969.

Williams, Fannie Barrier, "The Club Movement Among Colored Women of America." *A New Negro for a New Century: An Accurate and Up-To-Date Record of the Upward Struggles of the Negro Race,* eds. Booker T. Washington, N. B. Wood, and Fannie Barrier Williams. 1900. New York: Arno Press and *The New York Times,* 1969. 378–428.

Yellin, Jean Fagan. *Women and Sisters: The Antislavery Feminists in American Culture.* New Haven: Yale University Press, 1989.

Africana/Black, Feminist, and Womanist Studies

Abbott, Shirley. *Women Folks: Growing Up Down South.* New York: Tichner and Fields. 1983.

Abraham, Roger D. "Negotiating respect: patterns of presentation among Black women." *Journal of American Folklore: Women and Folklore,* 88 (January–March 1975).

Africa Report: Women and Africa: Special Issue, 26 (April) 1981.

Africa Report: Women in Southern Africa: Special Issue, 28 (March–April) 1983.

Albrecht, Lisa and Rose Brewer, eds. *Bridges of Power: Women's Multicultural Alliances.* Philadelphia: New Society Publishers, 1990.

Allen, Paula Gunn. *Sacred Hoop: Recovering the Feminine of American Indian Traditions.* Boston: Beacon Press, 1986.

Anzeldua, Gloria. "Haciendo caras, una entrada." *Making Face, Making Soul: Haciendo Caras.* San Francisco: Aunt Lute Foundation (1990).

Anzaldúa, Gloria, ed. *Making Face, Making Soul: Creative and Critical Perspectives by Women of Color.* San Francisco: Aunt Lute Foundation Books, 1990.

Aptheker, Bettina. *The Morning Breaks: The Trial of Angela Davis.* New York: International Publishers, 1975.

Arms, Suzanne. *Immaculate Deception: A New Look at Women and Childbirth in America.* New York: Bantam Books: 1977.

Bambara, Toni Cade, ed. *The Black Woman: An Anthology.* New York: New American Library, 1970.

Beal, Frances M. "Slave of a Slave No More: Black Women in Struggle." *The Black Scholar* 6 (6) March, 1975.

Bethel, Lorraine. "What Chou Mean 'We,' White Girl? Or, the Culled Lesbian Feminist Declaration of Independence." *Conditions Five: The Black Women's Issue,* Autumn, 1979.

The Black Collegian: Black Women. Special Issue. 9 (5) April–May, 1979.

The Black Scholar: The Black Woman. Special Issue 3 (4) December, 1971.

———. Black Women's Liberation. Special Issue 4 (6–7) March/April, 1973.

———. The Black Woman 1975. Special Issue (6) March, 1975.

———. Blacks and the Sexual Revolution. Special Issue 9 (7) April, 1978.

———. The Black Sexism Debate. Special Issue 10 (8–9) May/June, 1979.

———. *Court of Appeal: The Black Community Speaks Out on the Racial and Sexual Politics of Thomas vs Hill.* New York: Ballantine, 1992.

Black World: Black Women Image Makers. Special Issue 23 (10) August, 1974.

Burgen, Michele. "Rev. Dr. Pauli Murray." *Essence* 10. September 1979:5.

Burnim, Mellonnee. "Gospel Music Research." Special Issue. Black Issue. *Black Music Research Journal.* 1980–1981.

Callaloo 5: Women Poets. Special Issue 2 (February 1979).

Campbell, Bebe Moore. "Color Struck," *Essence* 9 (August 1978): 4.

Carson, Josephine. *Silent Voices: The Southern Negro Woman Today.* New York: Delacorte Press, 1969.

Chisolm, Shirley. "Race, Revolution and Women." *The Black Scholar* 3 (December 1971): 44.

Cliff, Michelle. "Object into Subject: Some Thoughts on the Work of Black Women Artists," *Heresis* 15: Racism is the Issue 4 (1982): 43.

Clifton, Lucille. "Turning," in *The Female Experience: An American Documentary,* ed. Gerda Lerner. Indianapolis: Bobbs-Merrill, 1977.

Collins, Patricia Hill, *Black Feminist Thought.* New York: Routledge, [rpt] 1991.

Conditions: Five: The Black Women's Issue. Vol II No. 2 (Autumn 1979).

Cornelisen, Ann. *Women of the Shadows.* Boston: Little, Brown & Company, 1976.

Cornwell, Anita. *Black Lesbian in White America.* Tallahassee: The Niad Press, 1983.

Crane, Louise. *Ms. Africa: Profiles of Modern African Women.* Philadelphia: J. B. Lippincott, 1973.

Davis, Angela. *Women, Culture, and Politics.* New York: Random House, 1989.

——. *Women, Race, and Class.* New York: Random House, 1981.

——, and Bettina Aptheker. *If They Come in the Morning: Voices of Resistance.* New York: The Third Press, 1971.

Davis, Marianna, ed. *Contributions of Black Women to America.* Vol. I. South Carolina: Kenday Press, Inc., 1982.

Dougherty, Molly C. *Becoming a Woman in Rural Black Culture.* New York: Holt, Rinehart and Winston, 1978.

duCille, Ann. " 'Othered' Matters: Reconceptualizing Dominance and Difference in the History of Sexuality in America." *Journal of the History of Sexuality,* 1:1 (July 1990), 102–127.

Eichelberger, Brenda. "Voices on Black Feminism." *Quest: a Feminist Quarterly* 3 (Spring 1977).

Ertel, Grace. "Quilting: A Heritage." *Essence* 9 (November 1978): 7.

Evans, Sara. *Personal Politics: The Root of Women's Liberation in the Civil Rights Movement and the New Left.* New York: Random House, 1980.

Farmer, Ruth. "Building International Coalitions Among Women of Color: Report From Zimbabwe." *Barnard Occasional Papers on Women's Issues* Vol. 5, No. 1, 1990.

Foley, Barbara. "History, Fiction, and the Ground Between: the Uses of the Documentary Mode in Black Literature." *PMLA* 93 (1980).

Gane, Gill. "Maya Angelou on Strength and Support." *Sojourner* 7 (December 1981): 4.

Giddings, Paula. *When and Where I Enter: The Impact of Black Women On Race and Sex in America.* New York: William and Company, Inc., 1984.

Gillespie, Marcia Ann. "The Rise and Fall of Janet Cooke." *Essence* 12 (August 1981): 5.

Gregory, Carole. "A Likely Possibility: Conversation Between Zora Neale Hurston and Carole Gregory." *The Black Collegian* 10 (April/May 1980): 5.

——. "On Becoming a Feminist Writer." *Heresies* 15: Racism is the Issue 4 (1982): 3.

——. "Black Activists." *Heresies* 9: Women/Organized/Divided. 3 (1980): 1.

Grewal, Shabnam, Jackie Kay, Liliane Landor, Gail Lewis and Pratibha Parmer, eds. Charting the Journey: Writings by Black and Third World Women. London: Sheba Feminist Publishers, 1988.

Hafkin, Nancy J., and Edna G. Bay, eds. *Women in Africa.* Stanford, CA: Stanford University Press, 1978.

Hageman, Alice, ed. *Sexist Religion and Women in the Church: No More Silence!* Associated Press, 1974.

Hammonds, Evelyn. "Toward a Black Feminist Aesthetic." *Sojourner* 7 (January 1982): 5.

———. "Development in Black Gospel Performance and Scholarship." *Black Music Research Newsletter* 4 (Spring 1981).

Harley, Sharon, and Rosalyn Terborg-Penn, eds. *The Afro-American Woman: Struggles and Images.* Port Washington, NY: Kennikat Press, 1978.

hooks, bell. *Ain't I a Woman: Black Women and Feminism.* Boston: South End Press, 1981.

———. *Feminist Theory: From Margin to Center.* Boston: South End Press, 1984.

———. *Talking Back, Thinking Feminist, Thinking Black,* Boston: South End Press, 1989.

———. *Yearning: Race, Gender, and Cultural Politics.* Boston: South End Press, 1990.

Johnson, Willa D., and Thomas L. Green, eds. *Perspectives on Afro-American Women.* Washington, D.C.: ECCA Publications, 1975.

Jordan, June. *Civil Wars.* Boston: Beacon Press, 1981.

Joseph, Gloria I., and Jill Lewis, eds. *Common Difference: Conflicts in Black and White Feminist Perspectives.* Garden City, NY: Doubleday, 1981.

Journal of Afro-American Issues: Black Women, Sexism, and Racism. Special Issue. 2 (Summer 1974).

King, Deborah K. "Multiple Jeopardy Multiple Consciousness: The Context of A Black Feminist Ideology." *Signs* 14:1 (Autumn 1988).

Ladner, Joyce A. *Tomorrow's Tomorrow: The Black Woman.* New York: Doubleday, 1971.

Leith, Ross. *African Women: A Study of the Ibo of Nigeria.* London: Faber and Faber, 1939.

Lerner, Gerna, ed. *Black Women in White America: A Documentary History.* New York: Random House, 1972.

———. "Reconceptualizing Differences Among Women." *Journal of Women's History* 1:3 (Winter 1990): p. 106–122.

Lewis, Diane K. "A Response to Inequality: Black Women, Racism and Sexism." *Signs* 3 (Winter 1977).

Lindsay, Beverly. *Comparative Perspective of Third World Women: The Impact of Race, Sex, and Class.* New York: Praeger, 1980.

———. "Afterimages." *Sinister Wisdom* 17 (Summer 1981).

Lorde, Audre. *A Burst of Light.* New York: Firebrand Books, 1988.

———. *Sister Outsider.* Freedom: Crossing Press, 1984.

Malveaux, Julianne. "Three Views of Black Women—The Myths, the Statistics, and a

Personal Statement." *Heresies* 8: Third World Women—The Politics of Being Other 2 (1979).

Maracle, Lee. *Oratory: Coming to Theory.* North Vancouver, B.C.: Gallerie Women Artists' Monographs, Issue 1, 1990.

MBilinyi, Majorie and Meena, Ruth. "Report form Four Women's Groups in Africa," *Signs* XVI, no. 4 (Summer 1991).

McIntosh, Peggy. "White Privilege and Male Privilege: A Personal Account of Coming to See Correspondence Through Work in Women's Studies." Wellesley Center for Research on Women, 1988. Working Paper No. 189.

Miller, Carolynne L. "Genealogical Research: A Basic Guide." *Technical History News* 24 (March 1969): Leaflet No. 14.

"Minority Women." *Women's Studies Review* 3 (September/October 1981): 5.

Moraga, Cherríe and Gloria Anzaldúa, eds. *This Bridge Called My Back: Writings by Radical Women of Color.* New York: Kitchen Table Press, 1983.

Morrison, Toni. *Race-ing Justice, En-gendering Power: Essays on Anita Hill, Clarence Thomas, and the Construction of Social Reality.* New York: Pantheon, 1992.

New Letters. The Black Woman in America. Special Issue 41 (1974).

Nichols, Patricia C. "Black Women in the Rural South: Conservative." *International Journal of the Sociology of Language* 17 (1978).

Omolade, Barbara. "ERA and Black Women." *The Black Collegian* 11 (April/May 1980).

Opitz, May, Katharina Oguntoye & Dagmar Schultz, *Showing Our Colors: Afro-German Women Speak Out,* trans. by Anne Adams. Amherst: Univ of Mass. Press, 1992.

Patton, Gwendolyn. "Going Home." *Essence* 8 (June 1977).

Reiter, Ryna R. *Towards an Anthropology of Women.* New York: Monthly Review Press, 1975.

Rodgers-Rose, LaFrances. *The Black Woman.* Beverly Hills: Sage Publications, 1980.

Rodriguez, Clara E. "On the Declining Interest in Race." Women's Studies Quarterly 16, no. 3/4 (Fall/Winter 1988).

Russell, Michele. "Black-eyed Blues Connection." *Women's Studies Newsletter* 4 and 5 (Fall and Winter/Spring 1976–1977).

Sandoval, Chela. "The Struggle Within: Women Respond to Racism," Center for Third World Organizing. *Changing our Power: An Introduction to Women's Studies.* Cochran, Jo Whitehorse, et al., eds. Dubuque: Kendall/Hunt Publishing Co. (1988).

"Scapegoating the Black Family, Black Women Speak." Special Issue of *The Nation,* 249:4. July 24/31 1989.

Shapiro, Linn. *Black People and Their Culture: Selected Writings from the African Diaspora.* Washington, D.C.: Smithsonian Institution, 1976.

Shockley, Ann Allen. "The New Black Feminists." *Northwest Journal of African and Black American Studies* 2 (Winter 1974).

Sloane, Margaret. "Black Feminism: a New Mandate." *Ms.* 2 (May 1974) 11.

Smith, Barbara. ed. *Home Girls: A Black Feminist Anthology.* Watertown, MA: Persephone Press, 1982.

———. "Toward a Black Feminist Criticism." *Feminist Criticism and Social Change,* eds. Judith Newton and Deborah Rosenfelt. New York: Methuen and Co., 1985.

———. "Notes for yet Another Paper on Black Feminism, or Will the Enemy Please Stand Up?" *Conditions: The Black Women's Issue* (1979).

———, and Beverly Smith. "The Varied Voices of Black Women." *Sojourner* 4 (October 1978).

Southern Exposure: Generations. Women in the South. Special Issue 4 (Winter 1977).

Stack, Carol B. *All Our Kin: Strategies for Survival in a Black Community.* New York: Harper and Row, 1974.

Steady, Filomina Chioma. *The Black Woman Cross-Culturally.* Cambridge, MA: Schenkman Publishing, 1981.

Stone, Pauline Terrelonge. "The Black Woman in Transition." *Newsletter* 1 (Summer 1978) Center for Continuing Education of Women. Ann Arbor: University of Michigan.

Strobel, Margaret. "African Women: Review Essay." *Signs* 8 (Autumn 1982).

Uttal, Lynet. "Inclusion Without Influence: The Continuing Tokenism of Women of Color," *Making Face, Making Soul: Haciendo Caras.* San Francisco: Aunt Lute Foundation (1990).

Wallace, Michele. *Black Macho and the Myth of the Superwoman.* New York: Dial Press, 1973.

———. "Daring to Do the Unpopular." *Ms.* 2 (September 1973).

———. *Invisibility Blues: From Pop to Theory.* New York: Verso, 1990.

Washington, Cynthia. "We Started At Opposite Ends of the Spectrum." *Southern Exposure: Generations* 4 (Winter 1977).

Washington, Mary Helen. "Black Women Image Makers." *Black World* 23 (August 1974).

———. "These Self-Invented Women: A Theoretical Framework for a Literary History of Black Women." *Spelman Messenger* 97 (Winter 1981).

Watriss, Wendy. "It's Something Inside You: Interview with Anna Mae Dickson." *Southern Exposure: Generations* 4 (Winter 1977).

White, Evelyn C., ed: *The Black Women's Health Book.* Seattle: The Seal Press, 1990.

Wilson, Emily Herring. *Hope and Dignity: Older Black Women of the South.* Philadelphia: Temple University Press, 1983.

Education

Allen, Carolyn, et al. *Feminist Pedagogy: Positions and Points of View.* Madison: University of Wisconsin, Women's Research Study Center, Working Paper Series, No. 3, 1980.

Allman, Joanna, et al. *The Black Female Experience in America/A Learning/Teaching Guide*. Newton, MA: WEEA Publishing Center.

Anderson, Margaret L. "Changing the Curriculum." Signs 12, no. 2, (Winter 1987).

Anthony-Perez, Bobbie M. "Institutional Racism and Sexism: Refusing the Legacy in Education." *For Alma Mater: Theory and Practice in Feminist Theory*. eds. Paula A. Treichler, Cheris Kramarae, Beth Stafford. Chicago: University of Illinois Press (1985).

Aptheker, Bettina. "How to do Meaningful Work in Women's Studies," Women's Studies 17 (1989).

Aptheker, Bettina. "Strong is What We Make Each Other: Unlearning Racism Within Women's Studies." *Women's Studies Quarterly* 9 (4) Winter, 1981.

Baca Zinn, Mazine, et al. "The Costs of Exclusionary Practices in Women's Studies." *Making Face, Making Soul,* ed. Anzaldua, Gloria. San Francisco: Aunt Lute Foundation Book (1990).

Bell-Scott, Patrica and Guy-Sheftal, Beverly. "Black Women's Studies on the Threshold of Phase Two," Sage VI, no. 1 (Summer 1989).

Black Women's Studies, Special Issue of *Sage: A Scholarly Journal on Black Women,* 6:1, Atlanta: Sage Women's Educational Press.

Blicksilver, Edith. *The Ethnic American Woman: Problems, Protests, Lifestyle*. Dubuque, IA: Kendall/Hunt, 1978.

Butcher, Vada, et al. *Development of Material for a One Year Course in African Music for the General Undergraduate Student*. Washington, D.C.: Howard University Project in African Music; Final Report to the DHEW, Office of Education, ERIC Document No. ED-045-042.

Butler, Johnnella E. "Different Voices: A Model Institute for Integrating Women of Color into the Undergraduate American Literature and History Courses," Radical Teacher, no. 37 (1989).

Butler, Johnella. "Minority Studies and Women's Studies: Do We Want to Kill a Dream?" *Women's Studies Internation Forum* 7:3, 1984.

Cannon, Lynn Weber. "All Our Ways of Being: Taking on the Challenge of Diversity in the College Classroom." Memphis State University Center for Research on Women Research Paper, n.d.

———— E. Higginbotham, and M. Leung, "Race and Class Bias in Research on Women: A Methodological Note." Memphis State University Center for Research on Women. Research Paper Number 5, 1987.

————. "Transforming the Curriculum: Teaching About Women of Color." *Multicultural Education: Issues and Perspectives,* eds. James A. and Cherry M. Banks. Boston: Allyn & Bacon, 1989.

————, and Betty Schmitz. "Different Voices: A Model Institute for Integrating Women of Color into Undergraduate American Literature and History Courses." *Radical Teachers,* 37, 1989.

Carter, Deborah, Carol Pearson, and Donna Shavlik. "Double Jeopardy: Women of Color in Higher Education." *Educational Record,* Fall 87–Winter 1988, 98–100.

Chase, Judith Wragg. *Afro-American Art*. New York: Van Nostrand Reinhold, 1971.

Chamberlain, Mariam K., ed. *Women in Academe: Progress and Reports.* New York: Russell Sage Foundation, 1988.

Christian, Barbara. "But Who do You Really Belong to—Black Studies or Women's Studies?" Women's Studies 17 (1989).

Chu, Judy. "Asian American Women's Studies Courses: A Look Back at Our Beginnings," Frontiers 8, no. 3 (1984).

Coleman-Burns, Patricia. "African American Women—Education For What?" *Sex Roles.* 21:1/2 (July 1989), 145–160.

Cruikschank, Margaret. *Lesbian Studies: Present and Future.* New York: The feminist Press, 1982.

Dopkin, Doris, ed. *Strategies for Equality: Multicultural Women's Studies, Vol. 3.* New Brunswick, NJ: Rutgers University, Division of Continuing Education, Training Institute for Sex Desegregation of the Public Schools, 1979.

Frankenberg, Ruth. "Teaching 'White Women, Racism and Anti-Racism' in a Women's Studies Program," *Transforming the Curriculum: Ethnic Studies and Women's Studies.* Albany: (1991).

Franklin, Sarah, Lury, Celia, an Stacey, Jackie. "Feminism and Cultural Studies: Pasts, Presents, and Futures," Media, Culture, and Society, volume 13, no. 2 (April 1991).

Frye, Marilyn. "Assignment: NWSA—Bloomington—1980: Speak on Lesbian Perspectives on Women's Studies," Sinister Wisdom 14, (1980).

Heath, Shirley. *Ways With Words: Language, Life, and Work in Communities and Classrooms.* New York: Cambridge University Press, 1983.

Higgenbotham, Elizabeth. "Designing an Inclusive Curriculum: Bringing all Women into the Core." Women Studies Quarterly 18, no. 1/2, (Spring/Summer 1990).

Hill, Leslie L. "The Ford Foundation Program on Mainstreaming Minority Women's Studies," Women's Studies Quarterly XVIII, no. 1&2 (Spring/Summer 1990).

Hoffman, Leonore, and Deborah Rosenfelt, eds. *Teaching Women's Literature from a Regional Perspective.* New York: The Modern Language Association, 1982.

Hoffman, Nancy. "Black Studies and Women's Studies: Some Reflections on Collaborative Projects," Women's Studies Quarterly XIV, no. 1&2 (Spring/Summer 1986).

hooks, bell. "Feminism and Black Women's Studies," Sage VI, no. 1 (Summer 1989).

Howard-Vital, Michelle R. "African-American Women in Higher Education: Struggling to Gain Identity." *Journal of Black Studies,* Volume 20 #2, Dec. 1989, 1980–191.

Hull, Gloria T., Patricia Scott, and Barbara Smith, eds. *All the Women are White, All the Blacks are Men, But Some of Us Are Brave.* Old Westbury, CN: The Feminist Press, 1982.

James, Joy. "Reflections on Teaching: Gender, Race and Class." *Feminist Teacher,* 5:3 (Winter 1991).

Jones, Lillian H. "Ethnic and Women's Studies: an Attempt at Educating in the Academy," Radical Teacher, no. 37 (1989).

Kumagai, Gloria L. *America's Women of Color: Integrating Cultural Diversity into Non-Sex-Biased Curricula.* Newtown, MA: WEEA Publishing Center, 1982.

Lee, Valerie. "Strategies for Teaching Black Women's Literature in a White Cultural Context," Sage VI, no. 1 (Summer 1989).

Liu, Tessie. "Teaching the Differences Among Women From a Historical Perspective: Rethinking Race and Gender as Social Categories" Women's Studies International Forum 14, no. 4 (1991).

McIntosh, Peggy. "Varieties of Women's Studies," Women's Studies International Forum 7, no. 3 (1984).

McKay, Nellie, Sandra F. Daniel, and Martha K. Cobb, eds. *Black Women in the Academy.* Madison: University of Wisconsin, Women's Studies Research Center, Working Paper Series, 6, 1981.

Mercer, Joyce. "Difficult Winds Ahead." *Black Issues in Higher Education,* September 1990, 10–15.

Moses, Yolanda, "Black Women in Academe: Issues and Strategies." Baltimore: Association of American Colleges Project on the Status and Education of Women, 1989.

Multicultural Student Union Committee. "Report of the Multicultural Student Union Committee University of Massachusetts-Amherst," (February 1991).

National Council for Research on Women. *Mainstreaming Minority Women's Studies.* New York (1991).

Newhall, Amy W. *Teaching Women's Studies from an International Perspective.* South West Institute for Research on Women (1990).

New England Journal of Black Studies: Black Women in Black and Women's Studies. Special issues (1981).

Nicola-McLaughlin, Andree, and Chandler, Zala. "Urbana Politics in the higher Education of Black Women: A Case Study" *Women and the Politics of Empowerment.* Philadelphia: Temple University Press (1988).

O'Malley, Susan. "Introduction to a CUNY Faculty Seminar on Balancing the Curriculum." Radical Teacher, no. 37 (1989).

Orozco, Cynthia E. "Getting Started in Chicana Studies," Women's Studies Quarterly XVIII, no. 1&2 (Spring/Summer 1990).

Pearson, Carol S., et al, eds. *Educating the Majority Women: Women Challenge Tradition in Higher Education.* New York: American Council on Education/Macmillan (1989).

Radical Teacher no. 27 (November 1987). Special Issue: "Multicultural Women's Studies."

Radical Teacher no. 37 (1989). Special Section: "A Cluster on Curriculum Transformation."

Response XVII, no. 2 (Spring 1991). Special Issue: "Multiculturalism, Jews and the Canon."

Riley, Glenda. *Don't Forget Her Story: Women in History Courses, Some Suggestions.* Chicago: Newberry Library, The Newberry Papers in Family and Community History, No. 79–3, 1979.

Romney, Patricia, Tatum, Beverly, and Jones. JoAnne. "Feminist Strategies for Teaching About Oppression: The Importance of Process," Women's Studies Quarterly, volume 20, no. 1&2 (June 1992).

Rosenfelt, Deborah S. "Integrating Cross-Cultural Perspectives into the Curriculum: Working for Change in the California State University," Radical Teacher, no. 37 (1989).

Rothenberg, Paula. "Integrating the Study of Race, Gender, and Class: Some Preliminary Observations." Feminist Teacher 3, no. 3 (Fall/Winter 1988).

Scott, Patricia Bell, et al. *Teaching Community History: Guides to Readings in Women's and Ethnics History, Regional and Country History.* Chicago: Newberry Library, The Newberry Papers in Family and Community History, No. 78–1, 1978.

Singleton, Carrie Jane. "Race and Gener in Feminist Theory," Sage VI, no. 1 (Summer 1989).

Weiler, Kathleen. "Gender, Race, and Class in the Feminist Classroom." *Women Teaching For Change: Gender, Class, and Power.* Boston: Bergin and Garvey Publishers (1988).

References

Bibliography-in-Progress of Materials by and about U.S. Women of Color, 3rd Edition. *The Barnard Occasional Papers on Women's Issues,* 6:1, (Spring 1991). New York: The Barnard Center for Research on Women.

Biblowitz, Iris. *Women and Literature: An Annotated Bibliography of Women Writers.* Cambridge, MA: The Women and Literature Collective, 1976.

Black Career Women, Inc. *Black Women's Directory: Organizations Local and National.* Cincinnati: Black Career Women, Inc., 1980.

Cole, Katherine W., ed. *Minority Organizations: A National Directory.* Garrett Park, MD: Garrett Park Press, 1978.

Davis, Lenwood G. *The Black Woman in American Society: An Annotated Bibliography.* Boston: G. K. Hall, 1975.

Enabulele, Arlene B., and Dionne Jones, comps. *A Resource Guide on Black Women in the United States.* Washington, D.C.: Howard University, Institute for Urban Affairs and Research, 1978.

Haber, Barbara, ed. *Women in America: A Guide to Books, 1963–75.* Boston: G. K. Hall, 1978.

Redfern, Bernice. *Women of Color in the United States: A Guide to the Literature.* New York: Garland Publishing, 1989.

Roberts, J. R. *Black Lesbians: An Annotated Bibliography.* Tallahassee, FL: The Naiad Press, 1981.

Sims, Janet L. *The Progress of Afro-American Women: A Selected Bibliography & Resource Guide.* Connecticut: Greenwood Press, 1980.

Timberlake, Andrea, et al., eds. *Women of Color and Southern Women: A Bibliography of Social Science Research, 1978–1988.* Memphis State University Center for Research on Women, 1988.

Williams, Ora. *American Black Women in the Arts and Social Sciences: A Bibliographic Survey.* Metuchen, NJ: The Scarecrow Press, 1979.

Notes On Contributors

Adrianne Andrews: *Always told, with great pride in the grandmother's voice, that I was "a smart little girl," I was firmly convinced from a very early age that my calling lay in the area of anything that had to do with books and school. That belief, reinforced by admonitions to "Go to school . . . be something," has enabled me to return to college as a married woman with young children and eventually earn a doctorate supporting myself and two sons on fellowships and student loans. None of this would have been possible, however, without the Creator's beneficence, and the love of family and dear friends. For these I am eternally grateful, and with these blessings in my life I know I am empowered to survive, surpass, and surmount life's challenges, and most certainly those of academe.* Andrews teaches in African American Studies at Smith College.

Patricia Coleman-Burns: *When any of America's structures, especially those of progressive thought and higher learning, fail to draw upon the strengths of all its women and all of its diverse racial, ethnic, and cultural groups, and expressly of African Americans, our civilization loses.* Patricia Coleman-Burns is an administrator in the Minority Affairs Office, University of Michigan Nursing School. She is also President of the Board of Directors of the Women's Justice Center—My Sister's Place—Women's Legal Services.

Elizabeth Hadley Freydberg: *I have decided that in order to survive in the academy, I must maintain "tunnel vision." I intend to dedicate the remainder of my lifetime to restructuring characterizations in play scripts, film scripts, and literature which have for centuries promulgated stereotypes that generate and sustain global dissension, hatred, and violence. I educate future generations for a more peaceful, ecological society of diverse peoples—racial, cultural, gender, sexual, and differently-abled—for a genuinely pluralistic, multicultural existence.* Freydberg teaches in African American Studies and the Department of Theatre at Northeastern University. She is working on two books, *Bessie Coleman: The Brownskin Lady Bird,* on the 1920s aviatrix who was the first American to earn an international aviation license, and *Ethel Waters: A Bio-Bibliography* (forthcoming Greenwood Press).

Ruth Farmer: *I would like academe to become a place where more women of color can thrive. To attain this goal—which includes reshaping our vision of what constitutes education and knowledge—requires courage, patience, and tenacity on the part of those of us who care about the future.* Ruth Farmer is a poet, essayist, lecturer and activist. Her writings appear in the journals *Woman of Power, Conditions, Sinister Wisdom, Azalea, Barnard Occasional Papers,* and *Catalyst;* and the anthologies *Chasing Rainbows, By Word of Mouth* (Ragweed Press), *The Dojo Art Jam,* and *The Agatha Christie Compendium* (Unger Publishing Co.) Farmer is the former Associate Director of the Barnard Center for Research on Women, Barnard College, New York City.

Joy James: *It has taken me a while to understand this space called "academe." What I have figured out is that despite its mirrors and smoke, it cannot hide the heart of learning, which is political and desperately in need of loving commitments to radicalism.* James teaches theory and courses on African American women in political movements in Women's Studies, University of Massachusetts-Amherst. She has contributed to: *Women of Power; Feminist Teacher; Race and Class; Z;* and *Court of Appeal: The Black Community Speaks Out on the Racial and Sexual Politics of Thomas vs. Hill* (Ballantine, 1992). She is currently completing a book, *"Ancestor Mothers in the Praxis of African American Women."*

Helán Page: *The purpose of education is to help students clarify what they already know and to liberate their head, heart, and hands from their current political-economic bondage.* Page teaches "Ethnohistory of Racism," "Survival Strategies of Third World Women," and "Magic, Religion and Science in the African Diaspora" in Anthropology at the University of Massachusetts-Amherst. Her publications include "Dialogical Principles of Interactive Learning in the Ethnographic Relationship" (*Journal of Anthropological Research*), "Lessons of the Jackson Campaign: Discursive Strategies of Symbolic Control and Cultural Capitalization," *The Social and Political Implications of the 1984 Jesse Jackson Presidential Campaign* (Praeger Press, 1990).

Joyce Scott: *I think that there is something strange about the idea that it's not as aesthetically profound for someone to make a cup as it is for someone to make a painting.* The daughter of artist-quilt-maker Elizabeth Scott, Joyce Scott has lectured and/or exhibited at the Baltimore Museum of Art, Maryland Institute College of Art, Banneker-Douglass Museum, Cocoran Gallery of Art, and numerous other universities and museums. A recipient of a NEA fellowship, she has been artist-in-residence at the University of Michigan, Williams College, and taught at the University of Delaware and Morgan State. Her work, highlighted in "The Silver Needle: The Legacy of Elizabeth and Joyce Scott" (Osiris Productions 1990) video, includes the 1991 Cocoran exhibit in Washington, D.C., "I Con Nobody/Iconography."

Dianne Smith: *Womanist praxes have enabled me to claim my power and redefine myself as a thinking, knowing, and speaking woman. I want all women to be able to experience such a richness in their lives.* Dianne Smith teaches graduate courses on curriculum theory, research, and development in the School of Education, University of Missouri-Kansas City. She is committed to radical womanist education and critical pedagogy with a multicultural-multiracial context addressing race, class, gender, sexual orientation, and child sexual abuse.

Kaylynn Sullivan TwoTrees: *"Making things—objects, performances, installations, jewelry, or the form of a class or workshop—is my way of processing life, of finding meaning in it. In the "doing" a healing occurs. . . . I have gone through many stages, and most of them beginning in confusion and pain, and moving through struggle towards resolution. It now occurs to me that there is a possibility of creating from another place—of finding the spark in the effortless motion of enjoying life. I begin my making now with that possibility in clearest view. I find that I'm having fun."* Two Trees is artist-in-residence at the School of Interdisciplinary Studies, Miami University-Ohio where she lectures and teaches courses on Ritual Traditions. Her performance works include "Leave No Footprints," a solo performance of movement, text, and song in homage to the earth.

Kim Vaz: *I have a doctorate in educational psychology from Indiana University, Bloomington with a minor in African Studies. My dissertation was a qualitative study of the coping strategies of foreign wives of Nigerian citizens. I am now analyzing the data and am discovering the varied ways in which foreign wives experience identity transformations or identity expansions as a result of their cross-cultural contact. Currently, I am writing a life history of Nike Davies, Nigeria's top batik artist, entitled: "The Woman with the Artistic Brush: A Personal Narrative of Nike Davies." With the support of my colleagues in the Women's Studies Program at the University of South Florida, we are laying a foundation for our students to systematically study aspects of the lives of women of color, through a specific concentration on the area of women of color.*

Nagueyelti Warren: *I am a poet, and credit my survival in academia and other aspects of life to my ability to return home, to the place where "my spirit is rekindled, my space is mine." My strong and loving family, and the preparation of a historically Black college (Fisk University) have also been vital to my success—I survived Boston University, Simmons College and the University of Mississippi.* Warren is Assistant Dean for Multicultural Programs and Services at Emory University, Atlanta. Her forthcoming book is entitled *Lodestar and Other Black Lights: Selected Poems.*